GOING WITH THE PITCH
Adjusting to Baseball, School, and Life as a Division I College Athlete

By Ken Jacobi
Edited by Frank Roessner

Published in the United States of America

Copyright © 2010 by Ken Jacobi.
All rights reserved.

Also under title name
"What I Learned from Not Being an All-American"

Back cover Quote by Diego Marchi

Back cover statistics provided by the National
Collegiate Athletic Association (NCAA)
http://www.ncaapublications.com/productdownloads/PR2011.pdf

http://www.ncaa.org/wps/portal/ncaahome?WCM_GLOBAL_CONTEXT=/
ncaa/NCAA/Academics+and+Athletes/Education+and+Research/
Probability+of+Competing/Probability+of+Competing

Library of Congress Control Number: 2011903976

Library of Congress Cataloging-in-Publication Data
"Going with the Pitch: Adjusting to Baseball, School, and Life as a Division I
College Athlete"

www.createspace.com/3564847

ISBN: 1460919890
ISBN-13: 9781460919897

First Printing: 2011, Printed in the United States of America

Without limiting the rights under copyright reserved above, no part of this publication may be reproduced, stored or introduced into a retrieval system, or transmitted in any form or by any means (electronic, mechanical, photocopying, recording or otherwise) without the prior written consent of the copyright owner.

The scanning, uploading and distribution of this book via the internet or any other means without the permission of the author is illegal and punishable by law. Please purchase only authorized electronic editions and do not participate in or encourage electronic piracy of copyrightable materials. Your support of the author's right is appreciated.

Front Cover by Chris Sidarweck
Back Cover by Chris Sidarweck

DEDICATION:

To my teammates, who helped make my experience at Binghamton what it was.

To my mom, Marilyn, and Bob Costanzo:
For both of your continued support throughout college both on and off the field.

To my step-mom Kathy:
Thank you for caring as much as you did. I am forever grateful.

And to my father, Paul:
This book could have never been written without you, in more ways than one. Thank you from the bottom of my heart for your time and support.

Visit GoingwiththePitch.com for further insight into the "college baseball experience". Respond and comment to blog posts by providing *your memories, opinions, and experiences* of NCAA baseball. Also, see bonus photos and hear extra stories that were left out of the book.

"The site that brings players, fans, parents, and recruits together."

INTRODUCTION

The words still reverberate in my mind as if I heard them just a few hours ago: "You will be a totally different person when you graduate in four years."

These were my step mom's final words as she and my dad said goodbye. They both hugged me, wished me good luck then turned and walked out of my dorm room as if they were just going into the kitchen for a quick snack. But this time they were leaving for good. The silence poured into the room as I watched from the window my dad's SUV pulling out of the parking lot. I was officially a college freshman. This was my new life. As I sat there alone on my bed, I tried to imagine what college would be like. I had no idea what I was about to experience. The baseball, the classes, the friends and the memories to come were all unpredictable at the beginning of the journey.

My extraordinary experience at Binghamton University, located in the rolling hills of upstate New York, was truly a life-changing voyage. On day one, though, the only thing I felt was complete loneliness and an even deeper feeling of homesickness. I had known for quite a while that college was coming soon, but after working for *years* to get into the right college it was hard to believe I was actually here. And after the hugs, just like that, I was all on my own. Now it was solely my responsibility to become the different, better person my step mom had prophesied.

Four years later, I could finally confirm her prediction was dead-on.

College was a great time. Being a college student-athlete made for an even better time. That is not to say there weren't low points, but my four years at Binghamton were amazing. To see the stark difference between an incoming freshman and a graduating senior, and to experience this transformation first hand was a full four year process. Freshmen could sometimes disguise themselves on the field as being older and more mature, but that illusion quickly disappeared when I was around my classmates for even a little while.

I came to learn that a freshman just hasn't had the life experiences of a senior, and no amount of home runs, touchdowns, or three pointers in one semester could change that. It was only when I was a senior looking back that I realized how far removed mentally (and physically) a senior is from a freshman.

It would take a full four years as a Division I athlete for me to understand this. On day one, I was totally oblivious. I was still living the life of the clueless.

This story is about how my years at college transformed me from the young freshman sitting naively on my bed on move in day into the confident adult of today. It describes my journey as a student, a baseball player, and as a person. It's a record of how I became that "totally different person" and how baseball, school, and life caused this transformation.

On that first day, I hadn't yet attended a single class, met one friend, played one inning of baseball, or recorded even one memory. Quickly, however, Binghamton University and upstate New York became my home. The snow-covered hills became a comfortable backdrop to which I awoke each morning. It was a life that became so normal, I never felt it would end. But as the days became months, and the months turned to years, I began to see that college would not last forever.

What I saw, when reflecting on my time at Binghamton was a collage, years of scattered memories that only when deciphered and properly organized represented my story of growth, heartache and love. For four years, I was fortunate enough to play Division I college baseball.

Though my story is not filled with All-American accolades and trophies named in my honor, it does convey the very real life lessons and experiences that many student athletes experience at school, on the field and in our personal lives.

Most of us aren't first-round draft picks, and it always seemed that the few who sign $2 million contracts were the ones telling their stories. This memoir plays out a much different scenario than that of the rich superstar. It reflects what happens to many thousands of students across time and space. It is the simple story of an 18-22 year old kid just trying to figure out life, while also having to worry about Corporate Finance exams and breaking pitches. It is my insight into college athletics, but more importantly, it is my insight into what is it like to be a college *athlete*.

From my freshman year in high school, my sole objective was to land a scholarship to play college baseball. I knew very little when I started out, but what I did know was that if some coach liked me enough, there might be an opportunity to get paid to play baseball.

Well, when I say "paid", I really mean reduce my tuition payments, but nevertheless, the possibility was out there. It was much more about the pride of getting a scholarship than the actual financial benefit, but I am sure my family was happy about both.

Like so many northerners, I had dreams of playing down south, where sunny skies and warm breezes would greet me each morning. I always knew that I was a southerner at heart who just happened to be born in Connecticut. I had always assumed I would right this wrong. I hate the cold. I hate everything about it. I knew there were a ton of good baseball colleges down south that also offered the high academic level I sought.

This was the subject of my first lesson: Plans have a way of changing.

As I woke so many mornings to see snow on my Binghamton windowsill, I was constantly reminded that I did not make it down south. Nor did I forget this turn of fate when, in the on-deck circle in a mid-April game, I could see and feel the snow gusting at my face.

Binghamton is about as far away from Florida as you can get, geographically and meteorologically. The Binghamton weather is some of the worst in the country. If we got three sunny days a month during the heart of the winter, it was considered a decent month. Waking up at 7:52 AM every morning for my first class and immediately seeing my breath as I exhaled became the norm. Dusting snow off of my car was a daily ritual. Skidding on the icy roads was common practice. But this was the place where I got to play D1 college baseball — where I got to fulfill my dream.

This *is* a baseball story, but it is also the story of my full experience as a student-athlete. Being a college athlete was so much more than just competing on a field. Our assistant athletic director used to joke that we could only juggle two balls at a time, sports and school, and that if we tried to juggle that third ball (social life) we would surely drop all of the balls. Well, we defied this little analogy and juggled 5 or 6 balls at a time. This story details my juggling expertise.

When I was in high school, I read a book about an all-star ballplayer who went to the University of Florida, and I read other books about players' experiences in the Minor Leagues. But where was all the material about college sports and the vast majority of the student-athlete population who weren't going to play in the fabled Southeastern Conference? Where was the story about the people who had to fight and struggle to succeed? I wanted to hear from someone who didn't necessarily hit .405 with 22 home runs in college.

I was a talented baseball player. I had a few shortcomings that held me back, all of which I will get into, but I was exceptionally good. As the years at Binghamton went by, I only got better. I had all of the tools and dedication to be a superstar. But that never happened. I went through some very rough times. I got shortchanged and thus too many times had to take the short end of the stick. But every hurdle strengthened me and allowed me to overcome the factors stacked against me.

I am extremely proud of my four years at BU and what I accomplished. Stats and GPAs can only tell half of the story. The friends I made and the difference I hope I made in people's lives will live forever.

This is my story of what I learned from "Going with the Pitch".

PART I
FRESHMAN YEAR

CHAPTER 1

If I had to pinpoint an exact date my path to Binghamton began, it would be the day I was admitted to Hopkins School in 9th grade. However, like any good journey there is always a good back-story. Mine actually started four years earlier, when my brother was admitted into Hopkins. If he hadn't gone there, I doubt I ever would have, and if I never made it to Hopkins, it's a safe bet that I would have never made it to Binghamton.

Hopkins is a private school atop a Connecticut hill overlooking Yale and New Haven. When the snow has fallen and the trees are bare you can actually see most of downtown New Haven from a perfect eagle's eye view. The school is home to some of the most talented students from across the state, where they go to be groomed for a future Ivy League education. It is small in every sense of the word. Entering Hopkins, I never could have imagined myself going to a large state university of 14,000 students. Words like budget cuts and deficits were still years away from my vocabulary.

Baseball for me and my close friends was all we cared about come springtime. Sure, there were academics and the stress of getting into a top college, but baseball gave us the fun and excitement we so desperately longed for while studying trigonometry formulas. As much fun as baseball was however, by the start of my junior year it was time to start thinking seriously about the recruiting process and where I wanted to go to college. I had no clue what to do, but thankfully I had my dad there so we both could go through the process equally clueless.

I knew I had to go to showcases and write e-mails to coaches, but besides that I was a novice to the process. The summer after my junior year I knew it was time to kick into high gear, but I really didn't even know what that meant. Like so many other pursuits, I figured that if I was a talented player and worked hard offers would just come my way and the process would be easy. How wrong I was.

I decided against playing for one team and instead decided to train and tour some showcase events across the east coast. With my parent's strong help, we decided which schools would be a good fit for me both academically and athletically. Then it was up to me to email the coaches a schedule of showcases I was attending. It was great to send them my statistics and a video, but I knew the coaches would need to see me in person before they would have any serious interest in me. Of course, as it worked out, I did not send any information to Binghamton University.

My first major showcase was in Florida. Even my path there was one of luck, or fate, however you look at it. During my freshman year of high school, I hit a home run off freshman pitching phenom Josh Zeid, who threw well over 90 MPH and was an eventual 10th-round pick by the Philadelphia Phillies. We talked that summer, and he persuaded me to play for a travel team he was on that was going to play down south. I decided it was a chance worth taking.

The trip sucked. I was a bench player and got zero exposure. I thought it was a complete waste of a weekend and it pained me to sit on the bench for an entire week while I had to watch other players of equal (or lesser) talent showcase their skills. The only good that came of the week was an automatic invitation to a top showcase in Florida the last weekend in May – my prom weekend.

I really wanted to go south to college, and figured the only way to get there was to be seen by southern teams. I knew I had to skip my prom and make the trip down south. There was no debate. Any serious athlete will attest that he or she must miss numerous social events, family BBQs, and parties for the sake of sport. Over the years I got used to the fact that I was a baseball player first, and it required an immeasurable amount of sacrifice. But missing prom felt different. It was something everyone at our school looked forward to, and I was definitely bummed about missing the dance, but I had to try to do everything I could to get a scholarship. I regrettably declined offers to go to the big prom.

My dad and I headed to sunny, warm Florida and the Sunshine East Showcase hoping that this trip would turn out a bit better. I didn't want to think about the sacrifices that were being made – the time, the effort, and the huge financial burden put on my entire family, but as the plane's wheels lifted up off the ground, I could not ignore the fact that the stakes were now a lot higher. Baseball was still fun but there was definitely much more on the table now. All of my long tosses, lifts, and batting lessons were in a way investments. I had to use everything I had acquired over the years to now showcase my abilities.

Thinking back to the player I was then and the player I became, I am surprised *anyone* recruited me. Ironically, even though my stats didn't necessarily show it, I became a much better and more confident player as the years rolled on. I have to laugh when I think back to high school days when I thought I was a great hitter. Still, I was a talented senior, and I knew I would find a home somewhere. As I took the field on a bright sunny morning under the Florida skies, I was confident as ever that by the weekend's conclusion I would be well on my way to being admitted to a southern college.

I am not a morning person, so a showcase starting at 8 a.m. didn't flatter me. The first thing was the 60-yard dash, which I despised. The dash did not measure my actual game speed, so I always resented how much weight was put on it. When running down the line for a base hit or tracking down a long fly ball in the gap, I did not have to think about running fast. I just did it. But in the 60-yard dash, I had too much time to think and inevitably I over-exerted my body. Perhaps I should have taken some running lessons because I never fully figured out how to tap into my full speed potential. It was the primary barrier I attempted to hurdle as a baseball player and the one that I was never fully able to conquer. My poor form and approach hurt my speed, and lifting weights probably slowed me down just a little as well. I am convinced that if I was able to run a quicker 60, I would have gone somewhere much different than Binghamton. Too many times I got "negative" email responses from coaches about my speed. It was my Achilles heel, and I know it impacted the evaluation of many coaches.

This was never more true than during that first humid morning at Sunshine East when the race seemed much closer to a 90-yard "dash." I still remember the feeling of running in slow motion. As I crossed the finish line, I knew I was in trouble. The board flashed a 7.5. Even for me that was bad, and I knew it was a death wish for an outfielder.

It was probably the worst 60-yard dash I had ever run, but we ran it only once and that was that – although there was a ray of hope when one of the coaches said we might get the chance to run again.

The rest of the weekend was fairly uneventful. It was excruciatingly hot, and after two days of games under the sun, I had no energy left. My body was one big cramp. As I was packing my bag and making my way out of the dugout on Sunday evening, I heard a loud voice announce: "Anyone who wants to re-run their 60 can do so now on field number two."

Great, I thought. It hurts to walk, my hamstring has contracted to the size of a walnut, and I haven't slept in three days. How am I possibly going to run 60 yards, and do it faster than the morning before?

Still, I couldn't leave the showcase with a 7.5 time. I knew I had to run the damn race again. And as I started to run, I actually loosened up. At the finish line I saw 6.9 on the screen. However, the delay from when I saw the 6.9 to when I actually finished the race caused the screen to flicker 7.03. I decided to run it again. This time I ran a 7.09. Again I ran it and again finished with a 7.03. I knew I had a sub 7 race in me so I trotted back to the start line to try again. There was no one else left running by this point so I had the whole track to myself. It was my goal to break the 7-second mark and I wasn't leaving Florida any other way. In my last attempt I trotted in at 7.27. I was mentally and physically done but at this point I had no interest in quitting. As I started to jog back towards the starting line, the coach running the dash called me back. He asked me what I was clocked throwing and after I gave him a satisfactory answer he told me about an "invite only" showcase later in the summer in Wareham, Massachusetts. Though I never did run a sub 7 second race at Sunshine East, I left the field thinking I had won a moral victory. I could not have imagined how much more it was than that.

The rest of the summer flew by as I started talking to a number of schools. They were not big DI names, but were still very good baseball programs and, more importantly, good academic schools. I believed I was definitely good enough to play Division I, but there were a lot of good D3 programs that I did not want to discount.

Then came the (last) showcase of the summer in Wareham, Massachusetts. I had one of those weekends where everything went right. I was simply in the zone. I put three balls out in batting practice and raked the ball throughout the scrimmages. I still sometimes think what would have had happened if I had just an average weekend there. But I didn't have an average weekend. I had a brilliant weekend, and the assistant coach from Binghamton University, Coach, Mike Collins, was impressed enough that even before I got home I had a phone call from him. When he told me what school he was from, it took me a minute or two to recognize the name.

Except for one tournament in Binghamton when I was a sophomore in high school, I had no knowledge of the school or the baseball program. I distinctly remembered seeing the city, the school, and the baseball field and being thoroughly unimpressed.

Binghamton is in the rust belt, and is one of those places that you're sure looked beautiful 50 years ago but has suffered hard times. Buildings with no tenants lined the streets, and the sun was a seasonal visitor at best. The biggest attraction was a small collection of bars in the downtown area.

Still, when I made my official visit to BU, I got to see the college town from a student's perspective, and my opinion shifted. It actually looked like a place that I might be able to survive without going crazy. The campus looked like a train wreck with buildings of all different architectural styles just thrown together, but as time passed I realized that the city and its surrounding areas actually had a lot to offer. And more important than any building were the people I was going to be spending the majority of my time with, the baseball guys.

There, during my recruiting trip, I got to see the famous Baseball House, known as the RE, and that experience helped sway me toward

Binghamton. I was glad I had decided to make a visit because if I hadn't, I would have never really considered Binghamton as an option.

I tossed and turned for many nights trying to figure out if Binghamton was the right place for me to play baseball. The town and climate clearly had issues, and I didn't think the baseball field was up to DI standards. Still, the guys on the team looked like good people, it was a reputable academic school, I had a scholarship offer, and I was assured on my trip that in the next few years there would be a brand new turf stadium. (I graduated with the stadium still at least two years away). The school also had an amazing modern Events Center for training and a great weight room. Our hitting cages were among the best in the northeast. It definitely looked like a place I could thrive in.

I was right. I wound up some days spending six straight hours in the athletic area lifting, hitting and then practicing. They were full days of talking, breathing and living baseball.

On a late November afternoon, just hours before the signing deadline, I went to my kitchen table and signed my National Letter of Intent with Binghamton University. I was looking at some Ivy League schools and some D3 schools, some of which were down south, but at the end of the day, passing up all that Binghamton had to offer just to avoid the cold weather was too much to give up. I had a very generous scholarship offer and had a guarantee that I would be admitted into the highly regarded School of Management.

It seemed surreal signing the form. The years of hard work and stress had paid off. I was excited to finish my senior year and get started at Binghamton. I had a coach waiting for me who really, really liked me, and I had the scholarship to back it up. I expected great things.

But plans and expectations have a way of working out much differently than anyone can anticipate. How could I have expected that my assistant coach who recruited me would leave Binghamton before I ever arrived on campus?

CHAPTER 2

I stood staring as my new computer screen loaded up. It became a joke as time went on that by senior year everyone's computer was broken down and deathly slow, but my computer was brand new at the time and able to load a web page in less than 30 seconds. As my computer booted up, I patiently waited for my suitemates to arrive. I knew that going to a brand new place where I didn't know anyone was a chance to start over, and I was excited to get going. I had no responsibilities, no friends, no worries, and no drama. I knew this could only last for about 5 minutes, but I enjoyed the calmness. Put 5 guys in my suite, 25 guys on the field, 4 classes on my schedule, and 3-4 free nights a week without my parents, and I knew that soon I would have a very full life.

I was consumed by nervousness and uncertainty. Everything was new and, because it was new, it was also uncomfortable. It seemed surreal those first few days walking around campus. No matter how many stereotypical college images were thrown at me, it still didn't seem like it was *my time* to be at college. Every so often I would just stop and look around at all of the buildings and struggle to believe I was there. This large state university was quite a different world from my tiny, secluded high school. There were definitely times that fall when I was on the brink of tears. During the day I was fine but at night, alone in my bed, I would think about my family and wrestle with the fact they were not in the next room. The loneliness went away quickly as the time, memories, and people filled in the empty space but the silence of my first few nights at school was deafening. I was actually having a great time being there, but during those rare moments of weakness I realized how new this life was.

Four years later it was hard to even relate to the kid who once wrote in his freshman year that he wanted to cry at times because he could not go home. Now I want to cry because I can't go back to college. But back then college was still intimidating. It was a tough adjustment, not even considering baseball.

I always had my parents to push me at home, and it took some extra discipline to get all of my work done without anyone making sure it was getting done. I was lucky that my high school training gave me the discipline to get my work finished, because by about the second week I was already seeing kids skip classes, fail quizzes and miss assignments. Having gone to such a challenging high school however, I found that the adjustments to the academic demands at college were nothing special. Getting used to college baseball, on the other hand, was a whole other battle.

The great thing about being on a team right away was that I got to live with all of the other freshman who were in my situation. From poor tests in the classroom (we obviously tried to sign up for the same classes as soon as we could), to break ups in the dorms, to slumps on the field, we were there to help each other out and pick each other up. My new friends soon became like family. I was thankful I did not have the pressure and stress of trying to find kids who shared my interests. They were found for me.

I honestly had no idea how non-athletes find their friends. It truly was an enigma. After about an hour of loneliness following my family's departure though, my room was invaded by 5 other freshman baseball players. After the first few transitional nights, that room was never quiet again, even at 3 a.m. when I was trying to sleep. It seemed someone was always awake, and I quickly learned that in college your sleeping pattern is much different than in the real world. In a flash, these 5 guys became my best friends.

Schoolwork was the easiest part of the transition. While other kids were struggling to write essays, including my suitemate's infamous essay about "Gladatorial Combat" (a fictitious word), it was life as usual for me. School really was fairly easy. I didn't mind going to classes, and I was still in the mode where I thought lecture halls were just the coolest thing of all time. I was living out a movie.

But socially it was a huge adjustment. I had some fun in high school but I always thought that I would really be free at college to go out, meet girls and drink. I somehow failed to consider little things like getting up early for classes and/or practice the next day, actually getting into bars as a minor, and spending money that I didn't have on beer. Still, we managed to have our fair share of fun, and then some.

I remember very vividly the first night all the freshman went downtown to the Baseball House to meet our teammates. All I wanted to do that night was remember their names and not throw up. I was only half successful.

Binghamton's version of downtown would be a cruel joke to someone from a real city. It was just one street with a few small bars, but as a freshman I could have sworn I was in Las Vegas. We eventually fell in love with one particular bar named Uncle Tony's. I spent many fall nights there my first semester listening to Journey's "Don't Stop Believing." It became the baseball team's go-to bar, and for that matter the BU athletics bar. On any given night you could expect to see at least 50 people you knew. Uncle Tony's made Binghamton feel very, very small.

The Baseball House was within walking distance to the bars. This really was the only redeeming quality of the "house" at 23 Henry St., known as the "RE." The place was a dump – every negative thing you think of in a college frat was there: Beer cans scattered everywhere, 3-day-old pizza petrifying on the kitchen table, and bathrooms which would repulse cockroaches. It was that awesome!

When the freshman visited that first fall, the beer was always flowing and people were always hanging out and having a good time. It was college partying 101.

I took note of how comfortable and confident the older guys seemed to be at both the house and at the bars. They mingled with everyone and just looked relaxed. All of the freshman would just chill in the corner. Soon, though, we too would make friends, and by the end of the fall it wasn't as easy to pick out the freshmen anymore.

Going downtown the *first* time, though, was an absolutely terrifying experience. I clearly was not 21 and had no clue how I was going to get into the bar. Little did I know that at these bars being 21 was encouraged but by no means necessary. The freshmen walked down with some of the older guys, and I was amazed at how many people they knew. It seemed impossible that I would meet anyone.

Looking back, I probably knew more people than most. I loved meeting new people at school, and any time I had the opportunity to add a friend on Facebook I did so. There were times when baseball was bringing me down and I needed a break from the routine. It was important to have other friends to meet for dinner or to work with on a homework assignment.

The six freshmen went out together that first night. Joining my soon-to-be best friend, Jeff Dennis, were Kyle Klee, Tom Carberry, Bobby Warner and Michael Quinn, my roommate and other soon-to-be best friend. The guys were class acts and we quickly bonded.

Quinn was a down to earth guy with a great passion for the game. He was a great roommate, and we shared many memories and late night talks. When he left the program two years later, I was absolutely crushed. By graduation four years late however, I was numb to it all. In fact, by my junior year only three of the freshman would remain in the baseball program.

Even before I took one step onto the campus, my fate had unbeknownst to me been altered. Coach Mike Collins, who recruited me and saw me play, had left during the summer to take a head coaching job at Bloomsburg University, a Division III college in Pennsylvania. This had unfortunate consequences for my baseball career. The person I had in my corner had simply gotten up and left. Worse, due to a small back injury which I sustained during the fall of my senior year, Coach Collins was the only one who had seen me play. By the time head coach Tim Sinicki saw me play, I had already signed.

The replacement for Coach Collins was Ryan Hurba. I may talk bad about my coaches here or there throughout this story, but I realize I have only one perspective. Some people liked our coaches and had no problems with them. For that matter I got along with them very well. I do feel though that at times I was seriously mistreated and too often I felt that this staff failed to get the most out of me.

It was never malicious. I was very cordial with my coaches and I think they liked and respected me, both as a person and a baseball player. Unfortunately, I had the misfortune of being in the wrong class at the wrong time.

As freshman year progressed, I started to feel that my class was in a "gap year." Sinicki had been at Binghamton University for the previous 13 years and helped the program become Division I.[1] I always sensed he had an unwavering loyalty to his remaining older players, guys who were with him during the transition process from a Division III team into a respectable Division I team.

Coach Hurba, on the other hand, was brand new and obviously put his faith in his new recruits. Thus, my class was too young to be among the veterans in Sinicki's corner *and* too old to be in Hurba's corner. It was a recipe for disaster.

I mistakenly thought I was in a unique situation. But the more players I met throughout the years, the more players I realized were in similar situations. It was being repeated all across the country. Whenever a new coach came in, he instinctively wanted to play his players, who were usually described as having god-like talent. He needed to prove quickly that *his* guys could get the job done, and it made him look good when *his* guys succeeded. There were always guys like me caught in the middle.

Being stuck in the middle would become a recurring theme. I was a talented ballplayer but like so many minor league lifers, I could just never get ahead. Even the great ballplayers need some breaks.

Being a college student-athlete for barely two months did not allow for me to understand or even recognize what was happening under the hood of the car. On top, everything looked nice and shiny. How was I supposed to know that there was a faulty engine?

I struggled that first fall. It was a huge learning curve, and to this day I think that my play as a freshman was used to judge my ability for the next three years. Perhaps if I had come out of the gates immediately primed to be the number three hitter I could have permanently broken into the lineup, but I took my standard lumps as a freshmen. I needed time to develop all the facets of my game, and by the time I did develop them it was too late for me. My role had already been carved into stone.

At the time I thought I would be fine because all of the recruits were Collins' guys. I would just have to prove myself in the fall and make a bid for playing time. I was told that my competition would be another Collins outfielder, freshman Tom Carberry, so I was a bit surprised when a junior college transfer joined the outfielders during tryouts. They left out this little detail during my recruitment.

Varsity Field is the home of the Binghamton Bearcats. It is not much too look at. I used to joke that it was called PCF, Prison Camp Field. The field had everything you need to play baseball but not much else. There was no color or flair anywhere. The fence was solid mesh black with no advertising signs, no team banners, and no distance markers. The wooden bleachers behind home plate, with green paint chipping, were outdated. The cinder block dugouts were spacious but had 2 poles supporting the roof that were about 2 feet thick and obstructed the view from the bench.

The best part of the field was the outfield, but due to a "construction mishap," the new outfield being installed over the summer would not be ready to play on in the fall. This meant that the first time I would ever be on my *home* field would be sometime in early April.

It would have been nice to get to play on the same field every day on a consistent schedule so we could get comfortable and into a routine. It was hard enough adjusting to college baseball without having so many other variables thrown in, including a new assistant coach. We were always practicing at a different field and at a different time. Our tryout, for example, was held at NYSEG stadium, home of the Minor League Binghamton Mets, Class AA affiliate of the New York Mets.

The tryouts began by running the 60-yard dash. I wasn't too nervous about running it. I figured even if I ran another 7.5 it wasn't like they were going to cut me, and I assumed that they already new my 60 yard dash time. I surprised myself though with a decent run, which gave me some confidence that I belonged. The entire day, and for that matter the entire first fall, I felt a constant need to prove to the coaches and older players that I belonged. Every freshmen felt the same way.

After running, we lined up in deep right center and made our throws to the infield. I will never forget the first throw by Tom Carberry. The instant the ball left his hand everyone knew that it wasn't going to be within 50 feet of third base, its intended destination. The ball ricocheted off the seats halfway up the stadium seating, bounced around, and finally came to rest somewhere down the third base line. I was nervous as hell for my first throw but I could not help but laugh. It helped me relax tremendously. It was one of the worst throws I have ever seen, but Tom took it very well and I respected him for it.

That day was also my first day facing Coach Sinicki's batting practice. I have never faced a major league fastball, but I imagine that it is similar to what I faced that day. All 8 pitches came hard and in. I was shocked at how fast his BP was. Over the years I got more used to it, but during that first session I think I barreled just one ball. I was determined to get the barrel on the last pitch, so I started my swing extremely early and was able to connect for a home run. It looked good and felt good, but it was a perfect example of how good batting practice does not automatically equate to good hitting in a game. Yes, I smoked a home run, but I had compromised my entire swing to do so. If this was a game and I only had 2 or 3 pitches (as opposed to 8) to time him, or if he had thrown me a curve ball, I would have looked like a fool walking back to the dugout.

Still, I felt good about getting day one out of the way. I always knew that day two would be just a bit easier and it made me feel calm to know that the hardest day was over. I knew things were only going to get more comfortable from here on out. Each and every day would be another day to prove myself to my coaches and teammates, and I relished the opportunity.

As the fall season pushed on, I started to get a bit more comfortable. Everything was still new but at least I developed a routine. Class, class, lunch, small nap, maybe a lift, and then practice.

It took me a long time to figure out what kind of baseball player, and for that matter what kind of person, I was. I was never the freshman who was ready to go out there and hit .400 his first year. I was not the type to make a seamless transition to college. Having gained the confidence by the end of my playing days, it now seems so stupid to have ever doubted myself. But in my freshman year, I did not have the same mindset.

Another issue I had at the plate was my immature approach. I just looked to hit any ball that was in the strike zone. One of the hitters I looked up to, Brendan Hitchcock, tried to teach me about having a plan at the plate, but I never really understood this as a freshman. He described basic mental strategies such as looking on one side of the plate if a pitcher keeps throwing you there, or taking (and not looking like an idiot by swinging at) 2-0 breaking balls on the corner of the plate.

In high school I did not need to care about any of that, but in college the pitchers were too good to just go up there and hit. Honestly, it probably took until my senior year to fully comprehend just how important one's approach and mental preparation are.

It wasn't just a mental barrier I had to overcome. There were physical parts of my game as well that needed tinkering. For one, my swing was a bit of a mess. My stride was way too long, and it left me exposed to even the worst breaking balls. In high school I got away with it but at college my huge stride made me a dead man walking. Also, I needed to put on some weight and muscle, and do it quick. Glenn Katz, a coach who I had worked out with before Binghamton, had been a big help with this in high school but now being at college it was time for me to kick it into another gear. Still, Glenn was able to teach me the importance of being stronger than your opponent both mentally and physically. Although I was still a work in progress when I graduated high school, Glenn had set the foundation for me. There were no redshirts in our program for players who needed a year to grow so the urgency to be physically ready to play was pushed hard. With the small roster size, redshirts were not a luxury our coaching staff had.

Baseball was tough that fall. I was raw and young and not used to failing. I would come home from practice and sit in my room, wondering if I would ever figure this out. Everyone knew I was a very talented athlete, but I was extremely skeptical about ever hitting well in college.

Though it was not my coaches' style, I really could have used a pep talk or two.

My dad came up for a weekend scrimmage, and it was the first time he had seen me since he dropped me off. I had a rough game, but his positive words about how I looked good out there made feel better. Even though it was obvious that breaking balls were killing me, my dad was able to help me understand that I needed patience. "Soon" he said, "You will be able to cream a breaking ball." He was right.

Everybody has a different timetable, and I definitely needed some time to adjust. My dad was smart enough to know this. I think my coaches failed to realize that some very good players don't look very good at the start. This is not to say that I didn't have some good moments in the fall. I had my days where I put 2 or 3 balls out in a batting practice and looked like the superstar within me. But most days were a grind.

Still, I managed to survive the fall and, as the snow arrived, I moved into my first off-season. I knew how much I had learned and was very satisfied with how much I had grown in just a few months. After fighting every day to simply keep up, it was nice to go inside and be able to work on my game with a little less pressure. I was eager to get my game ready for the approaching spring. It was less than 6 months until opening day.

CHAPTER 3

In high school most good athletes do not have an off-season. You are either playing your preferred sport in an "off season" league or playing another sport. I played football my first two falls in high school and played only baseball my last two. My winters were consumed with basketball. So it was weird when fall ball ended after the first semester and I was officially in my first real off-season. There were no foul shots to be taken, nor zone defenses to work on. All I had to focus on was baseball.

The weather turned bad in Binghamton around mid October, so by early October we had to shut down baseball. Southern schools were smack in the middle of their fall season but ours was long over by Halloween. Even after our sanctioned fall season, our training was rigorous. We still had a little thing called school, but now we had lifting, running, and individual hitting lessons with Assistant Coach Hurba twice a week. There was more down time, but it wasn't like we had all day to just lounge around and sip Coronas. There was still a lot of work to be done.

I hated the running aspect of our winter program, but I loved the team lifts. It was a ball in the weight room with 25 guys all juiced up on NO Explode, a (legal) energy-boosting drink, blasting music, talking baseball and lifting iron. It was 20 degrees outside, dark and snowing, but inside the weight room the temperature was pumped up to the maximum. There was no pressure, and I had a nice meal at the dining hall to look forward to afterward. Friday lifts were even better because afterward I would go home, nap, eat and then enjoy the rare off-weekends of the winter.

The off-season is huge in college sports. It is the only time to get big and strong, and fix any flaws in your game. Come the season, there is simply no time for drastic changes. I obviously had a lot of work to do and needed to get started right away. The fall season ended on a Saturday; I was in the weight room and batting cages on Tuesday. I knew that if I waited to really get going in January it would be too late.

While we were all working hard to chisel our bodies in the weight room, Coach Hurba was working hard with us in the cages to exterminate any bugs in our swings. Coach Hurba did a fantastic job fixing my stride so that I simply picked up and put down my foot in the exact same spot. In games I still tended to have a longer stride, but by making it second nature in practice to shorten up, it minimized the stride in the game.

When I left for Thanksgiving break, I felt like my swing was much more ready for college pitching. Unfortunately, due to NCAA rules, I only got two 45-minutes sessions per week with coach Hurba. I tried to go to the cages on my own time as much as possible, but obviously I would have liked more time than what the NCAA rationed out. With my schedule and the number of people vying for cage time, it was difficult to hit on a consistent basis. Finding a time slot, a hitting partner, and an empty cage was always an uphill battle.

Though I worked extremely hard during the week, I pretty much had the entire weekend off. It was nice to relax and hang out with my new best friends while drinking a few beers. We quickly bonded over ESPN and Keystone Light. Even without having played a season together, we instinctively knew how to enjoy our free weekends.

The new recruits started to flock in by October. It seemed like once or even twice a week a kid would visit the school. It was hard to believe that a year earlier I was the clueless recruit. The smart and/or lucky recruits came on the weekends after fall ball was done. They got to experience the full "social life" at Binghamton. We did our job showing them a good time. It was an unwritten rule that we were obligated to show our recruit a "good time" to ensure that he would show up for his morning meeting with the coach feeling less than 100%. We succeeded time after time. I can't imagine what the coaches thought when some of the recruits actually committed to the program the *next* morning.

Getting picked to host a recruit was a nice benefit because it meant a free meal with the coaching staff and the player at a local restaurant. I was more than pumped when it was my turn to host. A night out at a restaurant was a happy reprieve from dining hall food. It seemed that every few weeks we would hear of another player who had signed.

Most of the recruiting process was done behind closed doors. Current players were insulated from the bulk of the process, including the hundreds of phone calls and e-mails being sent and received by the coaches each week. The only time we were involved was when a recruit came to campus. We all very casually took the business side of the program for granted.

Coach did a brilliant job separating the two. All of the hotel booking, budgeting, and gear management was done in a way that the players assumed would be handled properly. Things were organized and, more importantly, were separated from the actual baseball. We took it for granted that all of our gear would show up on time and that the buses and hotels would be ready for us when we needed them.

We also took it for granted that every year we would have new talent coming in to help us try to win an America East Championship. According to Coach Hurba, every player who committed to BU was the steal of the century and was projected to start as a freshman. I quickly learned that, like every other recruiting class at every other school, some players panned out and some didn't. Still it was intimidating (and a bit condescending) to hear how great (and what I interpreted as how much better than us) these new players were going to be. Some players were terrific, but there was a general feeling that the new players were more often than not about two levels below their advertised sticker price. The players were very talented, but they were not the gods they were made out to be.

If every player played like he was described by our coaches, every year we would have five pitchers throwing 90-plus miles per hour and every hitter would be a .400 batter who ran a 6.7. Hurba was a great recruiter, but it got to be a joke after a while that none of the recruits would actually ever make it to Binghamton because they would all be scooped up in the Amateur Draft in the early summer. What wasn't a joke, though, was how passionate Coach Hurba was about his recruits. It should have been a telling red flag that my class was in trouble. I totally missed it.

CHAPTER 4

The "party season" ended with finals week and soon enough it was time to go home for the long five-week winter vacation. I was already 1/8 done with college.

Five weeks at home is a long time for a kid who just got used to living on his own. As tough a transition as it was to leave home, it was equally tough to transition back to "home life." I had a talk with both my mom and dad very early on in the break about my struggle transitioning back to my old life. I felt like I had been ripped out of my new world, and it was important to let him know how I was feeling. I felt incredibly confined after having so much freedom for the semester.

But as I always say, "I survived." When I returned to school, I was itching to get going. I was sick of having zero games under my belt. Even when I was enjoying myself in the fall, deep down it still weighed on me that I hadn't done a single thing yet for the program. In a way, I was envious of the fall sports that started playing games right at the beginning of the school year.

In 2006 there was no rule about when a college baseball team could start practicing, so we started on the second day of classes in January, even though our first game wasn't until March. Warm-weather teams were starting ridiculously early, scheduling games in early February. They got a huge head start on the poor northern teams still running around basketball courts in poorly lit gyms.

Several western and southern teams were starting *games* in late January! It was ludicrous. There was no way a northern team could compete with that. Not only did they start early, but later in the season they only needed to play their 3 conference games *a week*, while northern teams were fighting to get in 5 or 6 games a week in order to play a full schedule.

What the weather meant to us was over five tedious weeks of indoor practices. It is painful to spend a month playing baseball in a gym. The days drag on, and every night I would torture myself by looking at all of the scores of the games being played down south. There are only a certain amount of groundballs you can take on a gym floor. Even hitting, which I loved to do, became a chore.

The winter also brought the first of many major roster changes. Bobby Warner, one of the six original freshmen in my class, was released. Bobby struggled defensively throughout the fall, and it was decided he would never be a Division 1 player. Whether he was good enough is beside the point. The point is that after just one fall season and zero official games, he was cut. He was recruited by the "Collins administration" and Hurba, who understandably wanted to start getting his guys into the program, had no problem with Coach Sinicki releasing him. Perhaps Warner was never going to be good enough to play at Binghamton, but his release was a telling sign of the times that lay ahead.

As the season neared, we started to gear up for opening day. This included hitting live pitching. The single worst part of being indoors for preseason was hitting live against pitchers in the cages. It was dark, and I felt cramped in the batter's box with nets all around me. I hadn't seen a real pitch in months and my timing was completely off. Trying to see spin on the ball was a fruitless endeavor, and it was just way too easy to look dreadful at the plate. The worst part, however, was how many guys would get beaned. With the pitchers still rusty and the batters having delayed reactions in the artificial lighting, there were frequent hit by pitches.

After swinging through three straight fastballs my first at bat, I left the box scared to death that I was going to go into my first game in two weeks having swung and missed on every pitch in preseason. Thank

God those fears were diffused in my next at bat when I made contact. By the second weekend, live hitting indoors closely resembled hitting in a real game, and I was able to get comfortable enough to occasionally rope a line drive.

Sitting on my futon 3 years later, I had a chat with then top freshman pitcher Mike Augliera. We discussed facing each other during scrimmages. It was always a fun rivalry facing the pitchers in practice and talking smack afterwards. He told me how much he hated facing me, even in the cages, because I would always give him a challenge and hit him fairly well. I couldn't help but think that 3 years ago these same words could have been coming out of my mouth. Too many times as a younger collegiate player I became overly intimidated by a pitcher and, by doing so, had given the upper hand away before I ever entered the batters box. Here a great player was doing the same thing, practically admitting defeat to me *before he even threw a pitch*!

I understood this poor mental attitude because I used to think the same things when I faced some of our top pitchers. I almost gave in before the at bat started. I convinced myself that his slider was too sharp, his windup too whacky, or the lighting too dim. Staring into a pitcher's eyes in the cages my freshman year, I had all but laid down my bat on home plate. I was good enough to hit our pitchers, but I didn't have someone, like a senior, telling me the obvious. Even before I entered the cage, I was as good as done.

I wonder if the pitchers realized how vulnerable I was. Until I talked to Mike my senior year, I had no idea I had this mental advantage over him. Had I known, I sure would have utilized it.

I wasn't the only one who had issues with indoor workouts. Danny Salazar had a much worse experience than me. His struggles could be described as cataclysmic. Salazar, a spring semester junior college transfer, was coach Hurba's first recruit. Coach Hurba proved to be an excellent recruiter at times, but he definitely struck out in his first at bat.

Danny was an all around solid ballplayer brought in to replace Bobby Warner at catcher. The problem was that before coming to Binghamton in the middle of January, he had never been outside of Los Angeles. The weather, the culture, and the lifestyle of upstate New York proved all too much for him to acclimate to while also being asked to go to classes and play baseball.

First he decided to ease his burden by dropping the academic aspect of college. He quickly stopped going to classes (and focused hours each day building his MySpace page) and soon after that his baseball experience took a turn for the worst. Salazar had never thrown balls indoors before, and he struggled mightily with the low ceilings in the batting cage area. Whether the arm trouble came because of the low ceilings (causing him to alter his throwing mechanics) or whether the low ceilings just exacerbated his sore shoulder is unknown. What is known is that his physical pain became a mental one as he came down with "Chuck Knoblauch Syndrome." (Knoblauch was the Yankees second baseman who late in his career suddenly was unable to make an accurate throw to first base. It got so bad that he was on the verge of quitting before his manager Joe Torre convinced him not to.)

Salazar's problem started as an inability to throw the ball back to the pitcher indoors. Balls would carom off the walls, the benches and at times the other players. One ball actually skipped off the concrete floor and bounced right into the groin of one of the pitchers standing nearby. Once we all realized that he was not mortally wounded, we laughed hysterically as he dropped to the ground.

The throwing epidemic spread quickly for Salazar. Team defense, a part of practice that was necessary but dreaded, was the next crime scene. Simple throws to second and third bases landed 30 feet from the intended targets. One time it got so bad that Coach Sinicki lined everyone up with a partner 15 feet apart to play catch and said that if he heard one ball hit the ground we were running the entire rest of the practice. No more than a minute into the exercise we heard a large clank. Poor Danny Salazar had thrown a ball away. We ran for the next 45 minutes, without a break.

The last straw for Salazar came opening weekend against Delaware State. He was put in as a defensive replacement late in the game to give starting catcher Pat Haughie a break. In all of baseball, the return throw from the catcher to the pitcher after a pitch is one of the least thought about actions in a game. But when you have a catcher who is literally unable to make that throw, it changes the game. Balls landed everywhere around the pitcher except in his glove. It got so bad that poor Salazar would walk 10 feet out from home plate and try to lob the ball back to the pitcher. Nothing worked, and coach was sadly forced to take him out of the game. He never got an at bat as a Bearcat. It was like Moonlight Graham from the movie "Field of Dreams." One game, no at bats.

A few days after the Delaware State debacle, Salazar was mentally finished. He had legal issues in California which required him to go home, and it was more than obvious that even though he claimed he would be back, we all knew we would never see him again. Danny was a terrific kid who unfortunately ran into a tough stretch. Having no one to help him through it, he was forced to pack up and leave. Already now I had seen two players come and go. The list would only get bigger, much bigger.

CHAPTER 5

Eventually January turned to February and then to March, and it was finally time to begin my college career. We opened at Delaware State, not exactly the deep south, as the snow piles in the parking lot reminded me. Nonetheless, after a month of preseason I definitely felt as prepared as I was going to be, and excited to get started. A feeling of nervousness lasted the entire bus ride. Thankfully, as I got older, I was able to relax before a game, but as a freshman I constantly worried about the worst case scenario.

As the team drove to Delaware, I thought about all of the showcases, workouts, classes, and hours spent worrying about grades and the SATs that got me to this point. Unfortunately, I had to think in a cramped style because as a freshman I had to double up on the bus. The older you got the better chance you had of getting your own row, but more important the older you became, the farther back in the bus you got to sit. That first trip I was sitting two to a seat, and right behind the coaches.

I was also nominated to be on "bat duty." Our bat bag did not have wheels, so Tom Carberry and I had to lug around a 60-pound bag of bats to every road game. Many of them were either wood bats or weighted bats that, despite our strong protests, we still had to be brought along. I still occasionally feel the weight of the bag on my shoulder late at night.

We got to the hotel on Friday night. We had 4 games scheduled for the weekend so it was important to get a good night's sleep. The second I got off the bus I knew I was going to need it. Maybe it was the snow piles, or the wind gusting in my face, or maybe it was just the thermometer that read 43 degrees, but something told me it was going to be a long weekend. I went to bed (on the pullout couch) thinking I still had every college game and every college at bat still ahead of me. I would never be able to say that again.

When we got to the field early Saturday morning, I was nervous as all heck. It was cold and unbelievably windy. I had a huge knot in my stomach and kept thinking that the next time I was in my warm, cozy bed I would appreciate it so much more. There was no shelter, either physically or mentally. I was really here. I must have looked like just one of the guys out there during pregame, but I felt like everyone was staring at me and judging my every move. It was my first time experiencing the two-hour college pre-game, and it seemed like the game would never start.

The college pre-game was a marathon. Both teams had to take batting practice on the field, stretch, take infield/outfield, run sprints and incur a speech by the coaches. Then finally, after going over the ground rules and allowing time for the grounds crew to groom the field, the game would finally start. Even in the 30-degree weather, it was hard not to be loose.

My family made the 5-hour drive to root me on. They should have gotten an award for sitting through those games. The wind was swirling over 30 mph into their faces. It was painful.

The junior outfielder with whom I was competing for playing time, Mike Papili, got the start in left field in game one, but the coaches told me to be ready all day. It was something I would hear from them way too much during my career.

Sitting nervously on the bench, I tried to visualize as many at bats as possible where I would load my hands in a seamless and fluid movement. It kept me from being too anxious and also helped settle my stomach. I always felt that my few failures during high school ball came when my hands became still, so of course I wasted hours in front of a mirror and in my mind making sure that my load was perfect.

The problem with this approach, however, is that during a game there are hundreds of variables; it is impossible to be completely prepared. Still, I tried to focus in my mind on the perfect swing so at the very least I could feel good about myself and gain some confidence. I came to discover, however, that a huge flaw of visualization was that I controlled *all* of the moving parts. This gave me a false sense of confidence. It also gave me a false sense of uneasiness during the at bat when I realized that things were much different than what my mind had prepared me for. The pitcher looked different; the speed was different and even my heart rate was different.

As it turned out, being able to visualize and make a *tiny* adjustment within the at bat/game was a more important skill to master than making a *huge* adjustment in my mind or in a sterile, unchanging batting cage area before the game.

I could feel like Babe Ruth in my mind, but once I got up there at game speed it was no longer just in my mind. This is not to say that visualization is a bad thing. However, it is counterproductive to visualize a perfect, mistake-free swing just to feel good, when in reality an at bat is an imperfect, ever-changing activity. It was good that in my mind I made sure my hands were loaded properly, but at times I let this become a barrier rather than an asset. Visualization was a useful tool in practice, but only if I was able to completely stop thinking about it once I entered the box.

Some of my best at bats were not well-planned, modeled swings at all but were instead unorthodox mistakes where I made an in-flight adjustment. Conversely, some of my worst at bats were by-the-book swings where I had no aggressiveness and failed to hit the throttle when I needed to.

A perfect example of this visualization issue is hitting an outside pitch. Hitting a ball to the opposite field as opposed to pulling it is the difference of a split second. As a lefty, if I hit the ball too early I would pull the ball to the right side of the field. Thus, in my mind I would try to visualize hitting the ball on the bat at the exact right time and place in order to send a line drive to left field. In reality though, it all happens so fast that trying to replicate my visual image to a "T" actually became a barrier. It was impossible with so much going on in a game to actually worry about hitting the ball at the perfect time and location on the plate.

Having a textbook swing ingrained in my mind did not guarantee a good game. It simply made me feel that I was in more control of my swing. This acted like a Band-Aid and lulled me into a false sense of confidence. I tried to control more than was controllable. That is the beauty of baseball; the pitch and situation are never the same. Baseball happens at real speed.

Soon I discovered that having a perfect visual in my mind was not half as important as having a perfect feel at the plate. Incorporating my sub-conscious mind and finally letting my "feel" take over my "sight" elevated my game to another level.

Baseball is a game of reaction, so having the proper feel in the box was what mattered. Visualization was simply one piece of the puzzle in getting this ideal "feel" at the plate. In game 1 of over 200 games, however, all I could do was sit on the bench and try like heck to see myself hitting a home run.

We jumped out to an impressive early lead and by the 6th inning we were up 12-0 – well on our way to a perfect season. It was time to get the freshmen in the game.

From the bench, this college hitting thing looked pretty damn easy, so I relaxed just a little bit. The game looked fast from the sideline, but when I got up there late in game 1 it really did feel just like any other game. The intimidation I had felt all week vanished. It was just me vs. the pitcher.

I never took the bat off my shoulder. I took ball four low and away and trotted to first base. I still had not recorded an official AB. We hit so well that first game that I was able to get up one more time very late in the game. On a 2-0 pitch, I ripped a fastball toward the hole between the first and second basemen. The second baseman got moving a split second too late as the ball flicked off of his open-webbed mitt. The ball trickled into shallow right field for my first college hit. 1-for-1!

After the team thawed out on the bus, game 2 got underway, this time with me starting in left field. Except for the icy wind howling at my face, I was having a great time out there. It turned out to be the first of many crazy games I played at Binghamton. After beating Delaware

St. 14-0 in game 1, we found ourselves down 6-0 after the first inning in game 2! We battled back to make it 6-5 going into the top of the 9th.

I was having a great game, having all three hard-hit groundballs sneak through the infield for hits. Ironically, it was the most "luck" I had in terms of balls finding holes in my entire career. Before I knew it, I was 4-4 on the season.

In the top of the 9th things got interesting. Our leadoff hitter, Aaron Davis, hit a skyrocketing ball down the right field line. He was a senior, and had not hit a home run in his career. This was it as the ball, clearly fair, hit the foul poll and came back into play. From nowhere though the umpire came running out into the middle of the diamond, ruling that the ball hit the fence and scored it a ground rule double. Davis was stranded on second base as the umpires gathered around the pitcher's mound and then ruled that it was too dark to finish the game. The umpire had all but admitted that it was too dark for him to see whether the ball was fair or foul! We lost by 1.

That night I experienced my first meal money. Every player on the team was given $20 per day for meal money on the road. However, when my parents were around to take me out to eat dinner, not only did I get a free meal with them, but I got to pocket the $20. I thought this was a great business arrangement. A big bowl of pasta and a warm pullout couch greeted me after the long day at the park. Before I even hit the pillow I was out. When we showed back up for the next day's doubleheader, it had felt like we had never left the park.

Game 3 of the series turned out to be a nightmare. Delaware St. exploded for 21 runs on 23 hits. Our 11 runs were no match. I went 2-for-5, but the memory of the game was definitely us giving up 3 touchdowns. By the time game 4 started, it was very late in the day and it was obvious to everyone we weren't going to be able to finish the game.

By the 6th inning the sun had almost set, and it was too dark to play. This time the game ended in a *tie*. I had no idea a college contest could end in a tie, but after one weekend the team was 1-2-1. I was hitting .600.

It was a good first weekend, but there was no time to reflect on it because on the bus ride home I had to study for my business law midterm. I spent 5 hours thawing out in a cramped bus studying torts and laws. Studying on the bus was hard any time, but trying to do it on the moving bus with dim lighting while sitting next to another sweaty guy took things to a new level. This was not what I dreamed about in high school!

Week 1 was over in a flash. The next week we were going on our big trip – to Fresno State in California, and I all could do was pray that I would survive the week of lifting, practice, and two midterms.

CHAPTER 6

I was excited to go to California for a number of reasons, the obvious one being that Binghamton was still blanketed with a foot of snow. The trip was fully funded and nothing was asked of us except to play baseball and do everything we could to win. I was still not used to Division I athletics and expected to be asked for dues at any moment.

I also was excited to play out west because it was the first time I would play against well known schools. Fresno State, Washington State, Gonzaga, Lafayette, and Bucknell were all in the same tournament.

I got through my tough week of mid terms and essays and was relieved when spring break finally came. For baseball players there really is no such thing as spring break, but that is what we called it. It was more like Spring Baseball trip. A small part of me wished I could go to Cancun and drink my break away with thousands of other college kids, but that feeling quickly went away when our team bus departed from the Events Center parking lot. It was tough to look on Facebook and see all of my friends on the beach having the times of their lives but I knew that I was the lucky one. Deep down I knew that 99 percent of the partiers would have given their (non-throwing) arm to be able to go to California to play baseball for a week in front of thousands of fans. I was the lucky one, not them.

The 15-hour trip to our hotel in Fresno was a long day of travel. It seemed like we would never reach the west coast. By far the coolest part of the trip was getting to wear my BU gear around the airport. By senior year it was common to do so, but as a freshman I still thought it was great wearing our green Bearcat gear in public. I had worked hard in high school to get here, and I was going to make sure I looked the part of a Division I athlete.

Our first game in Fresno was against Lafayette. Basically, we traveled 3000 miles to play a school 100 miles away. Still, to play at Fresno State's field made the experience totally worth it. Beiden Field was a baseball palace that sat 5,757 people.[2] The red seats wrapped around home plate and formed a perfect half circle, encompassing the entire infield. From the outfield, the place looked like a totally closed off stadium. The early spring grass was cut short with a pristine green shade showing through the now almost nonexistent brownish winter grass. The empty field looked as if it was begging to be played on. After competing for years on crappy, poorly maintained northeast fields, this palace was a breath of fresh air.

The millions of dollars the school spent on the facility were certainly not wasted. We were told that for Friday night conference games you couldn't find an empty seat. It was the first truly great stadium I got to play in at college, and playing in an atmosphere like that *does* change the playing experience. I cannot imagine what it would have been like to play an entire career at a place like Fresno, with loyal, die-hard fans. They had the legit stadium and the real fans that you dream of playing in front of.

I always wondered when we went to a place like Fresno St. if those players appreciated what they had. However, knowing some of those guys through summer ball, most of them surprisingly attested to how envious they were of the teams *above them*, like the Georgia and Florida St. caliber-type teams. They envied the 5 hats that Oklahoma St got or the leather couches in the locker rooms of Miami. Whenever I brought up to these guys the size of our locker room (it was very small for 25+ guys) or our stadium seating (an old wooden bench) they looked at me as if I had 4 eyes. Their baseball world was a stark contrast to ours. I always used to joke that our entire fan base consisted of our parents and this one crazy fan who wore a green wig to all of our home games. But Fresno State had real fans who didn't have any affiliation with the players. They were just fans who followed their team religiously.

The weather for the week was, as the locals said, "The worst they had seen for this time of year in 30 years." It was wet and cold. It was not Delaware State cold, but it was still long sleeve cold. This would be the first of many trips where we brought the bad weather with us.

I started vs. Lafayette and within three innings I was 0-for-2. Twice I had barreled balls up but had nothing to show for it. First I missed a fastball down the middle and grounded out to second base, and my next at bat I hit a hanging 2-strike slider to shallow left field. I was missing my pitches.

Though I was struggling at the plate, I did get to make my first diving catch in college. It was a low liner to shallow left, and I did a little slide catch and scooped the ball out of the air just inches from the ground. I popped up and showed the crowd the ball. It was a beautiful catch and one of the last nice ones I ever made. Soon my days in the outfield would be over. No one could have ever predicted that soon I would be a full-time designated hitter.

I led off the bottom of the 8th with us up 2-1. I used to love starting an inning because the pitcher always wanted to get ahead of the first batter, and I always thought that the leadoff guy got more pitches over the plate. I crowded the plate a little bit because they had been peppering me away, and I looked for a good outside fastball to hit. The pitcher left one right out over the plate, and I ripped it right down the third base line for a clean double. It led to a huge insurance run.

The game was on Gametracker, an online tool that tracks every pitch of the game live, so my dad and mom in Connecticut, sister in Florida and brother in Virginia could all "watch" my double pop up on the screen. It was very cool. It was another good game, and I was thrilled with my collegiate start. I knew it would be a fight to stay in the lineup, but I knew if things went the right away the potential was there.

After a washout against Washington State, we were matched against the host school. It was a Friday night game and the entire Fresno State fan base seemed to be in attendance. I was praying I would get the start, and my coaches answered my prayers.

The game was one of the most memorable of my life, and not for a good reason. We lost an absolute heartbreaker against the number 21-ranked team in the country, and my 5 strikeouts didn't help the cause.

We had Fresno State on the ropes up 6-3 in the bottom of the 8th when things quickly unraveled. The win was within our grasp until a ground ball that deflected off of our pitcher and bounced to our second basemen was botched. Our starting second baseman, Matt Simek, had been ejected the inning before for arguing a strikeout call, so backup Ryan James was in his place. "RJ" was an excellent ballplayer but for whatever reason this one time his glove came up too early, and the little dribbler snuck under it. That triggered a rally that could not be stopped.

We managed to send the game to extra innings, but the wind had been knocked out of our sail. After fighting for 12 innings, Fresno delivered the knockout punch, a walk-off base hit to the outfield. Binghamton had blown its biggest game in program history. Our lack of ability to close out games was an ugly omen for the season.

My five-strikeout showing was one of the worst games I ever played. Their pitchers had good stuff, but even when facing a Major Leaguer five strikeouts would have been excessive. I struck out in every conceivable way – swinging, looking, and missing bunts. I did it all. My swing was wildly aggressive and uncontrolled. I would overswing on a lot of pitches and expose my weaknesses, especially on breaking balls.

I think it's safe to say that the pitchers were able to find this vulnerability. On a good note, though, I ended the game 1-for-6. Somehow I managed to hit a line drive base hit in the midst of all the mess.

The next day we played Miami of Ohio. A lefty was throwing, so I was given the day off. It would sadly be the first of many "days off" against lefties.

We seemed deflated after the Fresno game, and dropped our two next games to Miami and Gonzaga badly. We did end the trip on a high note, beating Bucknell. I scattered a few more hits over the week and was moved up to the No. 2 spot. It was a great honor hitting in the middle of a lineup stacked with upperclassmen I had a ton of respect for, but it was probably a premature move. I still needed the extra protection of hitting in the 7 or 8 slot.

Leaving California, I was thrilled with how I had started my Binghamton career. Then again, at that moment I was just happy to be healthy. The day before I had survived a violent crash against the left field wall, and my body still ached. I arrived at the wall at the same time as the ball and all three simultaneously crashed. The ball caromed off the wall, deflected off my temple and ricocheted into no man's land. I went down hard and quick. I was totally discombobulated when the centerfielder came over and threw the ball in. I am sure it looked hilarious from the stands, but it sure hurt at the time. My head wouldn't stop ringing the entire trip home.

We landed in New York to a depressing scene. Snow had blanketed the ground with a fresh coat. Literally within hours, we went from California's green pastures and rolling hills to a barren, snow-covered landscape. It was below freezing when our bus arrived at the Events Center. Returning from a road trip on a late Sunday night was always the worst part of any trip, regardless of the weather, as 25 guys would jam into our tiny locker room all at the same time, throwing their dirty uniforms everywhere in an effort to get home as soon as possible. The icicles hanging from the Event Center only made a fairly disheartening scene an extremely depressing one. It was a harsh fact: The northeast winter still had weeks before its fury would end.

Once back at school, it was time to start another week of classes, lifting, practice, dinner, and then homework/chill out time. The school week dragged on as there were no weekday games because temperatures in March made it impossible to play them. To cope, the team went downtown at least one night each week. We were always exhausted the next day, but we always managed to have a good time and survive. It kept our sanity in a life of repetition and stress.

For our next weekend we traveled to Lehigh in Bethlehem, Pennsylvania for a 4-game series. This was the first trip that I realized that Binghamton and most other northeast schools were always struggling to stay within very tight budgets. That meant we would be leaving for Lehigh at 7:30 a.m. Saturday morning to avoid the expense of a hotel Friday night.

Lehigh was the most "brown" place I had ever seen. It was not just the team's brown uniforms. Pennsylvania in March meant that all of the trees were still a grayish brown. The grass had not yet turned green, and it looked more like a hay field than a green pasture. The dark clouds that hovered over the field all weekend supplied the finishing touch.

This is not a criticism of Lehigh's field. It is simply a fact that just because the "spring" baseball season started, it did not mean that spring in the northeast had begun. We were still weeks away. College baseball literally ignores the seasons. School is over by early May, so we were forced to play before the fields were at all ready.

Only baseball could get away with this structure. I always used to think how "ridiculous" it would be to play hockey on semi-frozen ice because it was still too warm outside for the rink to completely freeze. They would never allow it. This is an extreme example, but we were playing on fields that were too cold, too hard, and too dry, but we had no choice but to play in those elements.

The weekend was a marathon, but after 34 hard-fought innings we had won 4 straight games. My hot streak ended as I went 1-for-6 on the weekend, but I was thrilled that we had swept Lehigh. It gave us some credibility as a good northeast team. Unlike my previous two weekends though, this weekend my hard-hit balls seemed to consistently land in a fielder's glove. The baseball tides were changing.

So after 13 games we were 7-5-1. I could not believe that in a flash, we had already played this many games. Things were going so fast that other interests like partying and girls seemed to take a back seat. I was unattached at the time and even though I wanted to try to continue to meet people, I knew it was a hopeless cause. There were priorities in life, and baseball and school took up most of that.

I had heard so many stories about freshmen getting a 1.6 GPA that I was on a mission to do well. This sometimes meant putting in a lot of extra work. I quickly got the reputation as being "that kid" who was always studying. It was the only way I knew, so I did my best to block out the many distractions that faced an 18-year-old living on his own. I always found time though for Fox's "24" and "American Idol." I still had some of my earlier priorities in tact.

CHAPTER 7

On March 28th we finally had our first home game, a twin bill against Niagara. It was not warm. In fact, it was miserably cold and with dark clouds hovering low in the sky. Still, it was great being on my home field. March 28th had felt so far away during the fall when we were informed of the unavailability of our field, but now I had finally made it home. It wasn't Yankee Stadium, but playing on our own field made me feel good. We were no longer nomads.

We split the doubleheader in a very uneventful day of baseball as I went 1-for-4 with 2 RBIs. I was hitting very average, but a sense that I was not playing well started to creep into my head. Whether my negative play started my negative thinking or vice versa is hard to tell, but I definitely started to press just a little. The waterfall had started.

I did not start game 2, but got into the game as a pinch runner. It is ironic because as my career progressed I was taken out of more and more games for a pinch runner. I don't know what changed in the coaches' minds that converted me from a pinch runner to the guy who needs a pinch runner, but there was definitely a change in opinion. I probably didn't get too much faster over that time, but I certainly did not get slower. As time went on though, the myth that I could not run well on the bases became a legend and the legend soon became a "fact."

It was just like my "inability" to hit lefties. It was repeated enough times that not only did the coaches become convinced it was true, but some of the players started to believe it as well. To fit the new reality, my base hits against lefties were considered flukes. I never tricked myself into thinking I was a Ricky Henderson on the base paths or Don Mattingly against a lefty pitcher, but the constant clawing at my game slowly ate away at me. At some point deep into my college career, I looked into the mirror and realized how much of my game I had *learned* to doubt. Reality and fiction seamlessly blurred together. Nonetheless, the transformation did not happen over night, and early on during my freshman year I was still one of the guys who was asked to enter the game as a pinch runner.

Our next weekend was my version of a homecoming. We were playing a 3-game series at Central Connecticut State. Having played multiple times at CCSU's field in years past, I felt that the weekend was a home series. My entire family was able to make the easy drive and caught a full weekend of early spring college baseball. It was a bit damp in the air, but being on the field that day gave me the feeling that the weather was finally breaking.

My swing felt good all weekend. After struggling to find the right position of my hands for a few weeks, they magically found a comfortable position right behind my left ear. The swing was sound, but baseball is much more complicated than just having a good swing. I couldn't seem to evade my very freshman attitude at the plate; I lacked confidence. The only way I knew to counter it was to try to convince myself that I was comfortable by actually saying words aloud such as "belief, talent, and ability." These were mere Band-Aids.

I was very unsure at the plate. There were so many new variables being thrown at me that I was constantly worried that that any deviation in any part of the swing would cause the entire equation to be wrong. Thinking positive was only going to get me so far. At the end of the day, I needed to have some failures at the plate and learn from them. I needed to process and understand all of the variables and learn how to deal with all of the external cues firing in my mind. This took time.

These growing pains were the only way I was ever going to become the hitter I knew deep down I could be. As a freshman though, it felt like I would never gain the confidence I needed at the plate. My coaches didn't seem to understand that it took me time to be able to slow the game down and properly assess the signals all around me. Saying and believing were two very different things, and only time and more at bats could fuse the two.

Nonetheless, I managed to have a solid weekend at CCSU, gathering 3 hits, including a nice line drive down the right field line. On the surface I was doing well, but my strikeouts were starting to climb. To me, striking out was the worst possible thing a hitter could do. If you can't put the ball in play, you have zero chance of getting a hit. There are no cheap hits on strike outs. It is not an accident that fast runners who put the ball in play have a lot of "luck". Worse than physically striking out, I started to worry too much about what the coaches were thinking every time I fanned. Statistically I was still doing well, but it felt like I was suddenly pressing to not fail.

Looking back, my pitch selection and my inability to slow the game down, relax, and have fun hitting caused my strikeouts to start to spike. This eventually led to a full-fledged slump that lasted almost a month. There was nothing worse than getting into the box, blinking, and all of a sudden being down 0-1 on a pitch right over the middle of the plate because everything was happening too fast for me to process. Then I would hurry back into the box without preparing for the next pitch, and I would chase a curveball in the dirt. I started some at bats basically down 0-2. There are only so many times one can dig himself out of an 0-2 jam. My batting average was good on the surface, but there were flaws that needed serious attention.

As a team we were starting to get the reputation of being very up and down as well. We went from losing game one of the CCSU series 8-2 to winning game two 10-1, to losing game three 11-2. It seemed through the first 18 games that we were either really good or really bad – and had the potential to be both on the same day. The lack of consistency was killing us, and as the season played out, it would be our eventual demise.

CHAPTER 8

"If you think you can, you will. If you think you can't, you're right."

I think I got a pretty fair deal my freshman year. I was competing with a junior college transfer and, for the most part, we were playing when we were doing well. The competition was honest and the coaches had no bias. I started out hot so I played a lot. When I began to struggle a little during April, I did not complain when Mike Papili started to play a little more. It was the fairest competition I ever had. It was not an accident that both Mike and I were recruited by the old regime.

I was still playing a good deal, getting at bats and doing everything that was asked of me as conference play began to approach. The little frustration I did have stemmed from the fact that in batting practice I was ripping the ball, but in the games I was having trouble barreling balls up. It did not fully click at the time, although now it is obvious, that the problem lay in my approach and mental state.

Athletes who treat every snap, shot, or at bat as life or death usually end up buried in a hole in the middle of the desert. The ability to relax and trust the game is a learned art that doesn't come naturally to very many people. My scholarship, batting average, and playing time would instantly flash into my brain whenever I faced adversity, instead of focusing on the actual task at hand. Allowing negative thoughts to creep into my head was like suffering from a contagious disease. In a game that as Yogi Berra says "is 90% mental, the other half is physical", *one* simple negative thought alone is enough to bring down a ballplayer. I had multiple unhelpful thoughts racing around in my head as my bad streak slowly morphed into a full fledged slump.

It is ironic that I viewed each at bat as a life or death struggle my freshman year since that was probably the only year where each at bat wasn't a make-or-break situation for me. That year however, the "what ifs" constantly played in my head. What if I missed my pitch? I only get four at bats a game; what if I swung at a bad pitch? Would that set me up for a disastrous weekend? What would I do if I got cut? Where else would I want to go to school? The questions turned what would have been a great stretch of hitting into an average one at best. I had a lot to learn.

The nicest part of the Connecticut series had nothing to do with baseball. For a few hours after the game, I got to go home and see my own room and my dog. It was only a tease, but just to be home for even a little while was big for me emotionally. Soon though, my mom dropped me off at the hotel, and I was back to being a college baseball player. At the hotel, the team watched the Yankees opening night. My eyes shut to the thought that the Yankees season would still be going on even when next year's fall season was over. Now that is a long season.

April finally came and with it came midweek games. April also brought showers – snow showers, that is. A doubleheader against Cornell was turned into just one nine inning game because even the coaches who would do anything to get every game in had to admit that the weather was simply too cold and miserable for two games. It was up to that point in my career the coldest game I ever played in. The cold felt like 1,000 daggers piercing the skin. The snow gusted in my face as I was trying to pick up the spin on a curveball. I was forced to sacrifice flexibility for warmth as I had on about 5 layers. The only way to mentally survive was to think about hot chocolate after the game and to *never, ever, ever* think about the teams playing down south in 80-degree weather.

During pregame, I kept thinking that when hitting, I had better get my hands loaded early and get the barrel out because the last thing I wanted was to get jammed in. On a 1-2 pitch in my first at bat, with a runner on third and less than two outs, the Cornell pitcher delivered a fastball up and in near my hands. I threw the bat at the ball doing anything to just tip it and stay alive to see another pitch. The ball clipped the handle of the bat and rolled towards second. Shockwaves of pain rolled up my arms and throughout the rest of my body as I became paralyzed, unable to begin the 90-foot journey to first base. It was a big RBI, but my hands were still vibrating 3 innings later. I took off my batting gloves and looked down at my shaking, fire red hands in disbelief.

My day finished 1-for-5 with a single up the middle. We won 8-3 and happily went inside disbelieving that we actually survived the game. The only good thing about the weather was that there was no need to take the usual half hour to rake, water, and drag the field. The entire field was frozen under about a half inch of white snow.

CHAPTER 9

Our coaches had said since day one that the fall season, the winter workouts, the preseason, and the first part of the regular season were all in preparation for conference play. Being in the America East meant that winning the conference tournament was the only way to get into the NCAA championships. We were never going to get an at-large bid into the tourney, so the only way to reach our ultimate goal was to win the America East Tournament. Everything that had happened up to our opening conference weekend vs. Stony Brook was just preparation.

Conference games had a new intensity. Whether we were playing the first-place team or the last-place club, every game was important in the final standings. We had only 24 conference games, so it was almost like an NFL schedule where every win and loss had a potentially huge impact on the standings. One stupid pitch could change everything, as I would soon learn.

Stony Brook, our first conference foe, was also in the State University of New York school system, and our schools were very similar. Throughout my time at BU we seemed to be very equal teams, each year exchanging the upper hand. It wasn't as big a rivalry as Michigan-Ohio State, but when the teams were shoving each other near second base in an "almost brawl," you couldn't tell us that the rivalry was any different.

We left for Long Island on Thursday afternoon. These conference weekends would become infamous for their long and stressful days. The year before I got to BU, Northeastern played its last America East Game, shrinking the field to seven teams. This resulted in a scheduling change in which conference weekends went from three games to four. While much of the country was playing three nine inning conference games on Friday, Saturday, and Sunday, the America East would be playing a nine inning game on Friday, a seven-inning doubleheader on Saturday and another nine inning game on Sunday. The new format made the whole weekend different. The entire strategy of the weekend changed with this. It became quite the feat to defeat a team four straight times.

We dropped the first game against Stony Brook on Friday by a score of 8-3. Their bats came out strong and buried us before we really had a chance to strike. The middle of our order, on which we depended for the bulk of our offense, went 2-for-15. The depth wasn't as strong as it would be in my next few seasons, so when the heart of our order floundered, so did the team.

I again had some hard-hit balls but had nothing to show for it except an ugly "0-for-4." I had hit 6 line drives in my last 5 games and had only one hit. I could sense my frustration mounting, even though I was back to hitting the ball hard and limiting my strikeouts. In the scorebook though, it looked like a slump.

Saturday was a total washout, so two games were scheduled for Sunday. A rainout on the road was the epitome of a wasted day. All we had was our hotel room and cable TV to pass the time. Our coach would usually take us out to eat just to break up the day. If we were really lucky, we would go to a nearby batting cage. The rainout days were so lazy that by the evening I would be begging for a game. All I could hope for was that the next day would be better.

Sunday was chilly and cold as well, but just nice enough to have playable field conditions. The day was an all out blitz of high intensity games. I had played some big high school games, but to stay locked in from noon until almost six p.m. was a difficult task for a freshman. Luckily, we won both games, 3-1 and 4-3, and moved ahead of the Seawolves.

The two wins were huge for our confidence as we treated every loss in conference as a huge burden.

I do not think other teams in the conference treated losses quite the same way we did. Our coaching staff made sure that we took every loss as a crisis, so losing the first game of the series probably seemed much worse than it really was. After the rain-shortened weekend, though, we were happy as could be with a 2-1 conference record. Bus rides home were always better when we won, and as an added plus we always got more time to eat when we stopped!

What took getting used to, however, was having only two minutes with my family before hopping on the bus. I was used to high school baseball where I would see my mom or dad at home and talk about the game. We would discuss where I went wrong and what the team and I needed to do differently next time. Now all I had time to say was "hi" and "bye." Maybe if I was lucky, I would get a goody bag of food, but then I would have to get on the bus. It was a little bit of a lonely feeling, but I got used to it.

Freshman year was quickly becoming a season of highs and lows both as a player and as a team. Things would look grim and dire, but soon thereafter things would pick up and I would find a hit or our team would sweep a doubleheader. It was exhausting to be living in a world of such swings. The only stability was my grades. I was managing my time very well and getting my work done before the deadlines, even if it meant having to write a paper in a hotel room. Ironically, the easiest part of college by far was academics. Everything else seemed to be in a state of uncertainty.

This pendulum of our season was never more aptly reflected than during our mid-week contest against St. Bonaventure. When we made the short trip to Olean, New York none of us thought of drunk, heckling fans lining the stands. We thought we were going to a very conservative, religious campus. We thought wrong.

The St. Bonaventure fans were relentless in their heckling. They were as good a group as I have ever heard. They especially liked our undersized third basemen, Ryan James, who had the unfortunate luck of playing just feet away from the hecklers' main circle.

Coach Sinicki always treated the mid-week games between conference weekends as something of a simulated game. Obviously he always wanted a win, but he definitely had a different strategy in mind. It was really the only time in our schedule to develop players and to take chances. We didn't get a long spring training to experiment.

We never played a mid-week game without the intention of winning, but we tended to use our younger pitchers more and experiment with the lineup. At times I felt like our coaching staff was caught in between the countervailing objectives of winning and player development. The net result of this predicament was what I called the "Gambling Paradox."

In it, our coach would start the game by putting money on the table he knew he would lose. The chance of winning was very low. With this play, the bench players would get some time in the game and our entire pitching staff, which needed work, would get to throw. However, as the game went on and coach realized that he might actually win, he would quickly switch strategies. He would begin to make substitutions and pitching moves in order to "steal the pot."

Trying to be patient and treat the game as an elevated scrimmage, coach would make a strong effort to stay calm when balls were booted. Whenever it became apparent though that our team had a real shot at winning the game, he quickly changed his stance and started to press on any mistake. There were countless times when a young bench player would be subbed out after two poor at bats for a regular player (like me) in a big situation. I could never tell his true position on these games. For every late-inning pinch-hit appearance for a sub, there would be a handful of times when we would be up one or two runs late in a game and he would refuse to put in our closer because he thought he needed rest for the weekend.

The St. Bonaventure doubleheader underscored this point of opposing strategies. Game 1 was ours. We were up 6-5 going into the final inning of a seven inning game. In the bottom half of the inning, though, St. Bonaventure hit two doubles and with our help (two errors), won in walk off fashion. It was an awful loss.

Initially the game was just another mid-week game, only important because our "second string" pitchers were getting their work in. However, once coach knew that the game was ours, he went into "win mode." As the winning run crossed the plate for St. Bonaventure, Coach Sinicki went from being calm and relaxed to infuriated and enraged, literally within a moment's time.

He reamed us out and threw a chair across the dugout to get his point across. It was another win that we let squander away, and I think coach was unsure of how best to handle this team. I understood my coach's frustration, but it seemed so odd to show this much emotion for a game that was deemed "less important." To his credit, it must have been difficult because every win on our schedule impacted the program and his reputation. However, he also needed to get everyone into the game in case we would need them down the road. When we gave away a win in one of these games that he was willing to lose, it must have really hit a nerve for him. A win in a "developmental game" was a bonus.

His anger stemmed not only from losing the game but also from *how* we lost. We had already blown multiple games, and he had already tried the calm, peaceful approach as a response. As I saw the bent chair leg lying on the dirt in front of our dugout, I got the idea that he was going for the "bad cop" approach this time. That, or he just got really frustrated. Coach did though apologize to us a few days later for the incident, and I respected him for it.

The only high note from game one was my first college home run. It was a fastball that caught too much of the plate, and I drove it deep into the right field gap, clearing the fence by 10 feet. My parents missed the game, but I was sure to get the ball for them. I was not about to let my first home run ball end up in some batting practice bucket.

As bad as game one was, game two was the complete opposite. This time we had the late inning heroics and won in extra innings 3-1. Our team had the potential to play as great as the 1927 Yankees or as bad as the 2003 Detroit Tigers, who in case you were wondering, were 43-119.

CHAPTER 10

The school year was flying by when the University of Maryland Baltimore County, better known as UMBC, came to town in mid-April. Slowly our huge mounds of snow were melting and small patches of greenish, grayish brown were starting to show. The trees began to bud, if ever just slightly. The winter jackets were put away. It seemed we might have escaped winter, at least for the weekend.

The series started on Thursday because of rain in the forecast. It was a good idea because Friday was a total washout. After suffering through months of sub-freezing temperatures and week-long snow storms, getting to springtime was literally a breath of fresh air. I spent many dark and cold nights in the winter waiting for a weekend of baseball with no hint or sight of snow. Even with rain looming in the forecast, Thursday's game was played under sunny skies and in warm temperatures. Finally!

UMBC was known for being one of the weaker teams year in and year out in the America East. It seems at every level of every sport some teams are consistently weak. Nonetheless, the games against UMBC were big because you had to win the "gimmies." Losses against them were devastating because most likely the other teams in the conference were going to beat them. If the top teams were all beating each other up, then games against teams like UMBC were the difference makers at the end of the season.

Our team took care of business in game 1, even if I did not contribute to any of our 14 runs on 13 hits. I was still hitting in the 2-hole, but my struggles were obvious. I was in a slump. My swing and approach still needed maturing, so a short, weekend slump took a lot longer to work out than it would have had I been a little bit older and wiser.

It was clear around the league that I could mash a fastball, but it was also clear that I struggled against breaking balls. Now that we were in conference play the other teams had scouting reports on us. Even on a 2-0 count, I was getting breaking balls. I had neither the time nor the capability to make the necessary adjustment during the season, so it was full steam ahead with what I had.

Ironically, as I became more experienced at hitting at the college level, I actually looked to hit curveballs in certain situations. The first thing that eventually made me a better breaking ball hitter was simply seeing a ton of them. Every practice, Coach Hurba would hook up the dreaded curveball machine and force the team to hit curveballs. Soon I got comfortable with them. Also, I eventually began to understand the pitchers' tendencies and strategies better and thus was able to start guessing that a breaking ball was coming much more accurately.

I never saw opposing teams' scouting reports, but I feel like I got a lot of hits my senior year because their outdated reports said to throw me off-speed pitches. The hanging curveballs literally fell into my barrel. As a freshman, though, I would simply sit on "dead red" fastballs and hope that I got that pitch. Usually it wasn't. I had no backup plan.

My last two at bats against UMBC in game one were both strikeouts against a lefty. At some point in each at bat I chased a breaking ball out of the strike zone. I was mired in a small slump where I wouldn't have hit a ball well off a tee, but my few at bats against lefties in the early part of the season seemed to be used in coaches' calculations as proof that I was an ineffective hitter against *any* lefty.

Perhaps they were correct that I was not *as good* a hitter against lefties, but it got to the point that they *never* let me hit against them. In fact, there would be less and less of a chance to prove myself against them as the season(s) went on. It got to the point that facing a lefty felt so foreign that a sort of self-fulfilling prophecy began to come true. It just pained me that their basis was a handful of at bats. They simply ignored the possibility that I was the type of hitter who needed a lot of at bats vs. lefties in order to feel comfortable. Without anyone in my corner, I was never given an opportunity to consistently face lefty pitching even if I was successful against them.

Not being able to get at bats against lefties affected me negatively in a number of ways. First, it destroyed my consistency at the plate because no matter how hot I was hitting, I would be benched for a game in which a southpaw was on the mound. Second, it helped prolong my slumps because it spread out my at bats over a longer period of time. If we were facing 2 or 3 lefties in a weekend, it only allowed me to have 5 or so at bats in the entire weekend. Getting so few at bats in a series didn't give me a chance to figure out what I was doing wrong and to hit my way out of a slump. Third, it took hits away from me. Most lefties were not dominant number one pitchers and even from the bench they looked very hittable. Fourth, even when I wasn't hitting lefties very well, it was still good to see the lefty arm slot once in a while. It forced me to keep my front shoulder in a lot longer. It assured that I didn't bail out too soon. Thus, seeing lefties had the tendency to "clean up my swing." It also made righties seem a lot easier to hit after. Last, it took playing time away from me both offensively and defensively. The coaches always wanted to have the option to pinch-hit someone for me in case a lefty came in. This meant that I couldn't play the field because then there would be no one to replace me defensively. It limited both my at bats and my ability to play the field.

The shame of it is that by senior year not only was I a good enough hitter to beat lefties, but I had gotten so many at bats vs. lefties in my summer ball leagues that there were days when I would have rather faced a lefty than a righty.

Game 2 was rained out, so that night I got a nice dinner with Jeff Dennis and my dad. Going back to the dorms that night for whatever reason felt right. I didn't want to leave my dad, but it actually felt comfortable leaving him and going back to my room. It was the first night I felt this way. It was the first time my dorm felt like a home. My friends and my bed were there. I was undergoing a big change in maturity, and my sense of comfort with my independence was a big step forward for me.

Before the start of the game on Saturday, Coach Hurba told me how thrilled he was with how I was playing. He revealed that the junior college transfer was originally the intended person to start in left field, but that I had really been holding my own. He said that there was no reason I could not continue to succeed and possibly play at the next level. I was down on myself from the game before, but his speech made me realize that I was doing a little bit better than I thought. Possibly I was being too hard on myself and that was adding to my recent struggles.

It was the last time in my four years that in a one-on-one talk with Hurba or Coach Sinicki I came out feeling better than I had when I went in.

Because we had an excellent senior centerfielder, I was spending most of my time in left field. I had never played left field before college, and it took a while to learn the subtleties of the position. The outfield is more complicated than it looks. Balls come off the bats with different spins and at different angles depending on where you are positioned. A slow first step could be costly. Misreading the flight or direction of the ball by a small amount was enough to throw off the entire play. Further, the throws to the various bases were all different from left field. It wasn't hard to learn any of this, but it certainly took some time. I was still very much learning the position when I was given the start there in game 2 of the series. I wouldn't have many games to start there after this one.

Going into the top of 5th inning we had a 3-0 lead. We were rolling as team, having won 4 of our last 5 games. Then things quickly changed. Errors and free passes are the usual culprits that start most big innings, and with one out the dreaded hit by pitch put the first runner on base. An error by our very reliable second basemen, Matt Simek, made it first and second with no one out. The next batter walked. The bases were loaded without a single ball being put in play. A force out at home still left the bases loaded, now with 2 outs.

The next play was one that changed the course of my season (and for that matter my career). It was a high fly ball that softly glided up into the sky like there was a small sail attached to it. On first glance, the ball appeared destined for a long flight time. I was new to left field, though, and didn't read the ball's trajectory as well as I needed to in order to make the catch. The ball wasn't struck as well as the loud ping from the bat made it appear, and half way down the left field line the ball gave out and headed straight down. I had to readjust my path once I knew the ball was not going to reach me. I decided on a last-ditch rescue effort and charged directly toward the line in the hope of making a diving catch.

I was taught from a very young age to be an aggressive outfielder and to leave my feet if I thought I could catch the ball. I hated it when I saw a catchable ball fall at the feet of outfielders so I instinctively dove full out. The ball hit the moist ground just inches away from my glove and skipped past me toward the fence in foul territory. In hindsight, I should have pulled up and blocked the ball. Two runs would have scored as opposed to the three that did.

This play always seemed to stick in my coaches minds when later in my career I became a de facto designated hitter. Perhaps a more experienced left fielder would have realized that the ball was not hit very hard, or perhaps he would have decided to play it safe and keep the third runner from scoring, but I took a chance and dove for the ball.

Nonetheless, we were still able to increase our lead in the bottom of the 5th with an insurance run. Going into the 7th inning up 5-3, we felt that the win was in our grasp. The only problem was that we did not have a Mariano Rivera ready to close. Zach Groh, our workhorse and number one pitcher, had thrown a lot of pitches and was showing signs of fatigue. His 24 consecutive scoreless inning streak was snapped earlier in the game and, knowing that a game 4 would not be played (due to rain), we went with our game 4 starter out of the pen, senior Jarrod Rampey.

With 2 outs and 2 on, UMBC's number 3 hitter, Joe Fowler, came to the plate. Rampey left the pitch out and over the plate, and Fowler punished the fastball for an opposite field home run. Our lead had been lost in the blink of an eye.

A 1-2-3 bottom of the seventh gave UMBC the win. It was another devastating loss. Even with a 5-1 victory in game 2, we had the feeling that we had let something slip out of our hands. We would only feel the full effects of the loss a month later when our playoff lives hung in the balance of a single game.

CHAPTER II

I knew going into my freshman year that there were going to be some growing pains, but I thought these would be pivotal for my success down the road. With that in mind, I thought I was somewhat prepared for the lows. However, I was nowhere near prepared enough for the most painful weekend of my young career. I was optimistic that this was an important learning experience, but as I hit rock bottom all I saw above me were walls caving in.

Until the Vermont series I was doing more than my fair share for the team. I was sleeping well at night, knowing that even though I had cooled off, I was still providing a spark with my bat. But that spark went out in a flash at Vermont.

Again, looking back, I o feel that in some small way my coaches used this single April slump as their basis for evaluating me as a player. Years down the road, my coaches seemed to use my shortcomings during this slide as evidence that I was not good enough in certain areas.

This ranged from my fielding skills, to my ability to hit lefties, to my mental toughness. Even into my senior year, I felt I was being judged by a rough stretch from three years before. The slump laid the foundation my coaches used when building my player profile. As I got older, a lot of the mistakes I had made as a freshman – like trying to be "too comfortable" at the plate or pressing to hit every pitch perfectly – were long past. Unfortunately, these traits had been labeled as permanent.

To get warmed up for the Vermont series, I went 0-for-3 with two strikeouts against Canisius in a mid-week non-conference game. After a bad game in high school, I was used to having my dad's input about what had gone wrong. If nothing else, it made me feel better to have him watching and taking mental notes. After the Canisius doubleheader, however, I had no one to express my frustration to so I went to my dorm room alone to listen to music. I stared at the screen for an hour, trying to sort out my at bats. I didn't get much school work done that night.

I should have put the day behind me and moved on. I didn't. The 0-fer put me in a sullen mood that carried into the weekend. Coach must have noticed the turmoil I was feeling because he pulled me aside during the Canisius games and sarcastically asked if I wanted to bunt. I felt like I was standing on an island as coach reamed me out. I looked at him in a curious way, responding, "Did I miss a sign?"

He said no and then asked if I wanted to be the type of player who bunts to get someone over or if I wanted to be the type of player who drove people in. I got his point. He must have seen my aggressiveness dwindling as I tried to be extra perfect at the plate.

After our horrific loss to UMBC, we needed to face a team like Canisius for two easy wins. Canisius ended its 2006 campaign at 18-36, next to last in the Metro Atlantic Athletic Conference (MAAC). However, Canisius would be proof that with the proper coach, the proper funding and the proper backing of athletics from the university, a program could quickly go from bad to good. By my senior year, Canisius had turned its program around and was an impressive 36-22, second in the MAAC.

In just a couple of years, Coach Mike McRae was able to take a team that won only four games in 2004 to a team that won 41 games in 2008 and 36 games in 2009.[3] In 2006, though, the team was just beginning to rebuild. It was still a very weak ballclub. The two wins padded our record to 17-11-1.

As we headed to Vermont, I realized for the first time all season how school was in direct conflict with baseball. First were the numerous classes I was missing for midweek games. Every time I got caught up in with classwork, I would miss a quiz or project and have to return to scramble mode.

Weekend road trips put me even farther behind. Any road series meant that Thursday and Friday classes were a wash. The week before Vermont was an absolute headache for me. I had a huge microeconomics test scheduled for Thursday afternoon, just a few hours before we were to leave. I spent the entire week trying to study for this test, get my homework done for my other classes, play a mid-week game (and miss more classes), get two lifts in, and also try to not get too down about my slump. I was treading water and fighting to stay afloat.

I had five hours on the bus to Vermont to stew over the first portion of the season. I had started hot and then cooled off quickly. Now I had to find a way to get back on track. The frustration only mounted when I began to think of some of the other players out-hitting me. I knew I was better than them.

It was maddening, but I thought soon enough I would bloop one in for a hit and that would start the chain reaction of multi-hit games. Unfortunately, Vermont was not the end of my struggles.

The last time I had been at the University of Vermont was three years earlier when I went with my dad to pick up my brother from school. The wind that day, coupled with the two feet of snow, made me vow I would never ever go back there again.

I should have stayed away. Once I knew Vermont was on our schedule, I looked to see when we would travel there. I figured that late April would be decent weather, but it was not late enough in the spring. The weekend was blanketed in clouds, cold temperatures, and a constant stream of rain.

The rain changed the schedule to a doubleheader Friday and a doubleheader Saturday. After three conference weekends, we had yet to play the intended format dictated by the America East. The rain would just not stop.

UVM's top pitcher, a lefty named Joe Serafin, started the first game. There are some players who for whatever reason simply dominate a team. Pitcher Frank Lary was a very average pitcher for the Detroit Tigers in the 1950s. He was 128-116 for his career. However, against the Yankees he was a remarkable 28-13.[4]

Serafin was our "Bearcat Killer." He didn't beat us in every one of his starts, but every time he went out there he shut us down. It was a guarantee that he would throw a gem, and the only way to beat him was to win a close, low-scoring game. He wound up getting drafted in the 37th round by the Chicago White Sox, so I guess we weren't the only team to struggle against him.

According to script, he blanked us in game one, 8-0. I was 0-for-1 before I got lifted for a pinch-hitter. It should have been 0-for-2 but Serafin pegged with me a 0-2 curve ball. I was in trouble in that at bat and thought God had sent me a gift packaged up as a large bruise on my thigh. It never felt so good to get hit by an 84 mph object. I gladly accepted the gift and limped to first base.

We won the second game, however, on Zach Groh's back. Vermont had their stud, be we certainly had ours as well. After another dominating performance, Zach lowered his ERA to an NCAA best 0.44. His slider was simply unhittable.

We took control of the series in game three by blowing UVM out 13-0. It took a slaughter for me to finally record an RBI, but a single passed the second baseman never felt so good.

Game four was a replica of our season. As good as we looked in games two and three, we looked that bad in the fourth game, losing 11-9. To be fair, it took a horrible call from the first base umpire for us to blow the game, but the record doesn't mention a bad call. All it says is that we lost.

What happened was Aaron Davis, our centerfielder, was on second base when the pitcher threw the ball to the backstop. Vermont played in a very old Minor League stadium and the backstop was over 60 feet away from home plate. Davis was able to score all the way from second on the passed ball, but the first base umpire claimed Davis missed third base. Somehow the umpire saw Davis miss the bag from across the infield. It was clearly not his call, but he punched Davis out and the home plate umpire, who didn't see the play at all, did not overturn it. The call killed us.

Still, that game was the first in a long time in which I felt good at the plate. I went 0-for-2 but put two balls hard in play. Regardless, a 1-for-8 weekend with three strikeouts did not sit well in my mind.

My worst at bat was my final one of the weekend. Even on a good weekend it always seemed that the last big play I was involved in left a lasting impression in my mind. Although I made huge improvements throughout the weekend, the last at bat took away any positive feelings I had. It was an immature approach stacked upon an already weak foundation at the plate.

A lefty was on the mound, but my coach decided to stick with me. I saw three pitches. I took two fastballs down the middle and swung at strike three, a ball that barely made it 55 feet. It was a classic awful at bat. I never felt so alone on a field in my life.

I was feeling low when we boarded the bus. We were going to shower in the visitors' locker room before heading out of town, so the bus took us to the athletic center. We almost never showered on get away day, but for some reason this weekend we decided to take the time to wash up. As the bus backed up to park, we heard a loud screech. The driver had inadvertently driven right into a lamp post. It was the finishing touch to a miserable weekend.

Due to the rain, we had all of Sunday to do nothing. It was my first day off in over two months. I was young and energetic, but needed a day of nothing. And that is just what I did. My big brother called and did his best to offer words of wisdom. Everything he said about relaxing and not fearing failure was correct. I was just too young and inexperienced to absorb it.

Our mid-week game against Le Moyne college would be a telling sign of things to come: First, I did not know if I was going to be in the lineup until minutes before the game. Second, I didn't start in left field because a lefty was throwing (not that I deserved to start, the way I was hitting). Last, I pinch-hit with just a moments notice to get ready, an approach my coaches unfortunately used on me more than once. It was a meaningless game in the record book that we lost 10-6, but the coaches really wanted to win the game because we competed with Le Moyne for recruits.

Le Moyne was located only an hour away in Syracuse, so the schools competed for a lot of the same players. As time went on, however, Le Moyne became much less of a threat to Binghamton. Soon Le Moyne would lose its membership in the MAAC, and a dispute with our athletic director assured that we never played each other again.

CHAPTER 12

Our next series was against first-place Maine, which had been a powerhouse in the 70s and 80s, making six college World Series appearances in those two decades. Though the Bears had lost some talent over the years, they were always a favorite in the America East. Their players seemed to look bigger and stronger than those in the rest of the league, almost as if they belonged in the SEC.

Maine looked like the Maine of old against us in the first two games and beat us soundly. We were 6-6 in conference play and smack in the middle of the pack. With two games left against Maine, we were in danger of falling out of contention.

Slumps are lonely places. It feels like you will never get out of them. All of the hard-hit balls seem to be caught and the ones that are not caught seem to be marked as errors. Still, I was getting at bats because Mike Papili, my main competitor, was struggling himself. During this stretch I had no beef about sitting on the bench because I knew I wasn't hitting very well and yet still I was getting a ton of at bats. It is ironic because over the next three years it would be the total opposite situation. I would be feeling great and hitting well, but could not get into the game.

Game two saw Zach Groh's shutout streak end at 42 innings. Even with Zach's streak over, we pulled out games three and four to "salvage the series." Coach Sinicki would always say let's "salvage the series" after we lost a game or two. It became an inside joke that whenever something initially went wrong, we had to salvage it. If someone spilled beer at the beginning of the night, he had to "salvage the night" or if someone bombed an early semester exam, he had to "salvage the semester." We had just salvaged our series vs. Maine, which I came to discover was one of the worst teams in our league at closing out series.

When we headed to Siena, the calendar had finally turned to May. Finals were a week away, and I really had to crack down on studying. After 14 weeks of work, I was not about to let finals get the better of me. This meant studying in my room after a full day of school, lifting, and a three-hour practice. I was very anti-library and refused to study there, so I put on some music, locked my dorm room door and got to work.

In my dorm room I felt much more in control of the material I was studying. I knew it was mental, but I enjoyed having some music on and being able to walk around every few minutes. The library made an already bad experience that much more excruciating. Everyone there seemed way too serious and stressed out. The very idea of doing work in a library bored me to death. Still, no matter where I studied, it took a lot out of me. When I hit my pillow at night I was instantly out.

Siena was an away game, so I was able to take a nap on the way, and I wasn't completely exhausted from my exam the day before. I loved road games because it meant I got a nap before the game and a nice meal afterward. Playing Siena was a great experience because it was the first school from which I had received a recruiting letter. I later learned that schools send out tons of these letters, but it was still humbling to play there knowing that they had some prior interest in me.

My first at bat was a disaster. With the bases loaded and one out, I popped up to the catcher. I slammed my bat down on home plate and jogged toward first base. It was the only time Coach Sinicki *ever* yelled at me in a game. He talked to me in a loud voice before, but it was the only time he really snapped at me.

I was one at bat away from being benched. Thankfully, I followed that at bat with a single and then I followed that up with double. Leaving Siena on a high note was a welcome feeling. It was the first time in a long time that I left the field happy.

Our next series matched us up against the Hartford Hawks. Like UMBC, Hartford always found itself towards the bottom of the standings, despite the addition of a new turf stadium. I was excited to play there not just for the seemingly easy wins but because it also meant going home to Connecticut again. Two trips in one year was a gift.

The weekend proved to be an extreme disappointment for the team, but getting to play in front of the locals was a special privilege for me. Once again we ran hot and cold. We put up 14 runs on day one and embarrassed the Hawks. Guys were joking in the dugout and poking fun at the other side. Day two didn't go as well.

In two games spread over 14 innings of play, we did not score a single run. Baseball is a crazy sport like that. Change the day, change the pitcher, change the venue, or for that matter change the weather and everything else can change.

In those two games we had only nine hits. The losses were devastating to our place in the standings. Hartford was 5-12 in conference play before that fateful Saturday. We had blown yet another opportunity.

My woes continued as I got myself into more two-strike counts. My best at bat, a 10-pitch at bat, still resulted in a strikeout. Our coach screamed at us after the game, but oddly enough it had nothing to do with the game. I think he was so frustrated about the entire day that he did not even want to talk about the game. Instead we were yelled at for not running out to our field for practices and also for calling Coach Hurba, "Hurbs" and "Herbie."

I thought it was an odd time to bring up such complaints. We should have been talking about our total lack of execution on the day, but instead we were getting yelled at about running out to *practice*. I could only think of Allen Iverson's famous speech where he denounced practice as *not* being the same as a game.

Thankfully, I got a chance to get away from everything Friday night. I went with my family to my old high school to see my sister in her improv performance. It was odd to see my school and some of my high school friends in the middle of a college road trip. The experience felt very similar to when I returned to my elementary school only to realize how small the hallways looked. I had only seen high school from a high school student's point of view. Going back changed my focus completely. I knew then that I could never go back to high school. That time was over.

Returning home Saturday night was doubly great because not only did I get to see my dog, Obie but I also had someone to share my misery with. It was a bad day for the Jacobis. I was 0-for-4 in the two losses. My sister was dreadful on the mound in her high school game. The two of us were almost comedic. It was a perfect lesson on how not to deal with adversity. We should have both gotten into each other's face and said, "Suck it up and move on."

Instead, I took a minute and went into my backyard to feel bad for myself. It was so warm that I pretended I was home in the summer for good. I noticed for the first time that the trees were in full bloom. I had my family and my dog beside me. Maybe things were not so bad.

When I got back to school after the weekend in Connecticut, I had to recheck our schedule online to make sure I was looking at it correctly. The season was flying by. We had only seven games left. I had finals week to go and then my freshman year would be over. Twenty eight weeks of school and practice were coming down to these last two weeks. It was time to put up or shut up.

Our mid-week games had ended, so instead of being smart and staying in each night in order to catch up on my sleep and work, I decided to pack my schedule tight. After a full day of school and practice, the guys and I went out Tuesday night and Wednesday night. How was I supposed to say no to 10-cent Tuesdays and 75-cent mug night on Wednesdays when I didn't have a game to worry about? I know it made us tired, but we really did need an occasional breather from baseball. Listening to some good music in a packed bar was the perfect recipe.

It was a full week before my exams. I studied for my finals, went to all of my classes, lifted twice, went to five practices, took extra batting practice twice, went out twice, and still found some time to watch the Yankees and to play NCAA Baseball on my Playstation 2. I was exhausted when I got to bed at 3:30 a.m. on Thursday the 11th. I had to wake up a few hours later to head to New Orleans.

CHAPTER 13

With Northeastern out of our conference, there was a bye week in the schedule that had never existed before. The University of New Orleans shared a similar free weekend, so it was scheduled that the two of us would play in New Orleans the weekend of May 12. When Coach Sinicki talked to me during the recruiting process, the trip to New Orleans was one of the highlights that interested me. None of us knew at that time, however, that a hurricane was on its way.

Tuesday, August 29, 2005, changed America forever. Hurricane Katrina made its second landfall over Louisiana. The hurricane took over 1,800 lives and displaced thousands more. Towns were destroyed and communities literally wiped off the face of the Earth. The damage topped $80 billion.

New Orleans was caught smack in the middle of the storm. The Superdome became world famous; images of its torn-off roof were shown on every major news network. Tulane University canceled classes for the semester and many other schools around the area were thinking about doing the same thing. The entire year of college athletics in the southeast was thrown into disarray.[5]

The University of New Orleans suffered its fair share of damage, but because the main campus/ baseball field was located on a hill most of the damage came from the high winds and heavy rain as opposed to the flooding. However, one levee breach on the London Avenue Canal did put the baseball field under feet of water for a prolonged amount of time. As the aftermath of the storm played out on CNN, it was unclear if there would be any baseball played in New Orleans that spring.

By December, however, UNO had reopened its doors and the baseball season was a go. We had no idea of what to expect when we flew into "The Big Easy." We had seen the pictures on TV, but those images could not possibly do justice to what we would see in person.

Our hotel was no more than 10 minutes from the airport, but in those 10 minutes we saw a ravaged world. Boats were "parked" by the sides of roads. Trees were left just as they had fallen, some of them still piercing houses. There was an endless stack of abandoned cars under the freeway. It looked as if the storm had hit eight days ago rather than eight months ago. The sight that really caught our eyes though was the Superdome. The roof was clearly torn off in places, just as the television had shown. Most of New Orleans looked like a ghost town.

We arrived at our hotel in the late afternoon, so we were on our own for dinner. There was a mall within walking distance, so most of the guys went there together. It was a scary walk. The line between black and white was never so clear in my life.

We walked passed a restaurant, a laundromat and a gas station. All were abandoned and wrecked to the point where it was hard to imagine that any business ever functioned there. Glass was cracked, weeds were abundant, and the huge business signs were lying on the broken pavement. It was clear from the people in the street that we were in an African-American neighborhood. Sadly, just down the street, where the white community resided, was the mall that looked like it had just won ABC's Home Makeover competition.

It was obvious to me after just two hours in New Orleans that President Bush and FEMA were failing.

The University of New Orleans did not look to be in much better shape. The basketball arena had parts of its roof missing, and FEMA trailers dotted the campus. Thankfully, the field was in decent shape.

We took one of three games from New Orleans but the games were overshadowed by my experiences down there. I was seeing fewer at bats each weekend, but I didn't have a problem with it. I just was not hitting very well. In my only game, I went 0-for-4 and felt a little overmatched.

New Orleans was also where Zach Groh's dominance took a vacation. Zach was still in pain from a line drive off his ankle the weekend before at Hartford, and it affected his pitching. He was knocked around for 6 earned runs over only 2 2/3 innings.

Before leaving for home, coach did let us go to Bourbon Street for a night. We were on a tight leash and obviously no alcohol was allowed, but I had never seen a street quite like Bourbon Street. Bars and strip clubs numbered in the dozens, but Jeff Dennis, Michael Quinn and I were much more concerned with finding somewhere to eat. We found a small restaurant on a side street and had one of the best meals of our lives, a true New Orleans meal of Gumbo, Creole, and Cajun. It was a meal for the ages, *and* it was on the university's bill!

Getting back from New Orleans meant finals week. Having done absolutely no work on the trip, I was flung into panic mode come Monday morning. I had a final on Tuesday and another on Wednesday and at first had no clue how I was going to cram a semester's worth of material into 24 hours of studying. I managed to pull it off though as it became very apparent that I was learning how to beat the academic component of college much more quickly than I was adapting to the baseball piece of the puzzle. Come Wednesday night, I happily threw my notebooks into the trash.

I was done with freshman year! Now all that lay ahead was baseball.

CHAPTER 14

Going into the last weekend of the regular season, we were tied with Albany at 10-8 in conference play. It just so happened that we were playing the Great Danes in a four-game series, so everything was coming down to one final series. I prepared for a little disappointment because I did not think I was going to be in the lineup. Nonetheless, I still took my swings and tried to get ready, but in my heart I didn't think I had a prayer of playing Friday.

Throughout the years I took a lot of punches to my psyche, but I never stopped taking extra swings or working out. There may have been a number of factors contributing to my problems on the field, but there was no way that failure would result from a lack of hard work. Now, without having to attend classes, I knew that baseball was my fulltime job. I spent my time either training or playing. Game days were full day events: Get up at 8 a.m., eat breakfast, get to the field, pull the tarp, warm up, play two games, take care of the field, shower, eat, and then finally around 8 p.m. I would get home. I always said that baseball didn't have to be your favorite thing to do in the world, but if you didn't really enjoy the game you had no chance of surviving a full year. There was simply so much you needed to invest into the sport to be successful.

From this I created the "96 rule," which simply stated that 96% of the time things sucked. We had to run, or clean up the field, or study for a test on a bus while everyone else was experiencing typical college life. The other 4% of the time, however, made this entirely well worth it.

Hitting a big home run or striking out a guy with the bases loaded and two outs made the 4% outweigh all of the tough times.

Now realistically, it was more like the "25 rule but I felt 96 flowed off the tongue better." In any event, I always used to joke whenever we had to clean up the cages that this was part of the "96 rule" and that the other 4% better damn well be worth it. It always was.

My family had to miss the Albany weekend, which was pretty rare, because my brother was graduating from the University of Virginia. Ironically, my parents would once again have to miss my last home series of my senior year in order to go to my brother's law school graduation. With graduations and the end of school buzzing around, one would think that the weather would cooperate. Instead, the weekend was cloudy, rainy and only in the low 50s.

The first game was played in horrid conditions, which at this point we were fairly acclimated to. I was only an innocent bystander as the 7-0 defeat put us in a very bad situation. I loved big games, and it hurt a little not being able to help my team out. It was the 14th time that season that we had been part of a shutout. We had been on the losing side only five of those times, but this was a playoff-like series, and everyone knows that stats and probability get thrown out the window in a single series.

With our back to the wall, our ace Zach Groh gave us the big pitching performance that number ones are supposed to give in big games. A win tied the series at 1-1.

Game three brought about my first chance to make an impact. I was pumped and ready to be the difference-maker. Thus it goes without saying I took a hack at the first pitch I saw, producing a line drive to the first baseman. Before I could put my bat down, I was out. As much as I wanted to help my team, Albany's 11 runs could not be matched. Going into the final game of the season, we were trailing Albany by a game.

It poured all day Sunday. We pulled the tarp twice, waited in the dorms for a few hours, waited in the locker room for a few hours, and were informed of multiple target game times over the course of the day. Finally the news came that the game was moved to NYSEG stadium for a late afternoon start.

With the wind howling and the mist coming down, our pitcher Mike Van Gorder pitched lights out. In the top of the 6th we held a one run lead with Albany threatening. The Danes had loaded the bases with two outs.

Albany's shortstop Sean Donavon, who would later become a very good friend during summer ball, hit a fly ball to left field. The ball was crushed, so my initial reaction was to take a small step back. However, in mid-flight the ball hit a wall of wind and dropped out of the heavens. Unlike earlier in the year when I dove and missed, this time I laid out and made the diving catch.

I got up and let out a small grunt. It was about as much emotion as I was ever willing to show on the field. It was one of the biggest catches of my life, but sadly it was also one of the last I ever made as a Bearcat. The catch saved three runs and helped lead us to a 4-2 victory. It was the program's record 27th win.

Everything seemed great. Unfortunately, there were two small glitches concerning our playoff bid. First, we were still even with Albany. The other problem was a league rule that stated that each team had to play a minimum of 21 conference games. We were 12-10 in the America East. Albany also had played 22 games. Stony Brook, however, had only played 20 games and needed to make up one game. We were their first rain-out, so it meant we had to travel to Stony Brook to play the next day.

Considering that Albany had the same record as us, it certainly didn't seem fair to make us play an extra game and not Albany. We had to drive four hours to play our fifth game in four days. Albany got to sit and watch as we scraped together a makeshift pitching staff.

The Albany game ended Sunday evening. We showered, ate a quick dinner and then headed to the bus for a 10 p.m. departure to Stony Brook. We got into the hotel around 2 a.m., 13 hours before first pitch.

Stony Brook had nothing to play for. It had already clinched the No. 2 seed. It was simple; we needed to win to join the playoffs. If we lost Albany was in. Our fate was completely in our tired, worn down, "pitcherless" hands.

My family had the hopeless plan of trying to make it to the game from Virginia following the graduation, but they had to give up on their fruitless journey when they hit traffic in New Jersey. It was better that they did not see the game.

By the time they reached New Jersey, we were down big. Our team was built around our conference starters. There was no reliable fifth starter. We were forced to pitch a sophomore with a poor track record who would be gone from the team within a year.

We never really had a chance. Around the 6th inning we were trailing 7-0. I could sense the pain and disappointment in our dugout.

I started the game but was not of much help. My second at bat was my last of the season. I fought off a number of fastballs to get to a 3-2 count, but an unexpected outside curve ball caught me off guard. (I just couldn't believe that a pitcher would throw me a 3-2 breaking ball!) I was a third of the way to first base when the umpire punched me out.

I was taken out when a lefty came in. Stony Brook, with nothing to play for, trounced us 12-3.

Seeing the seniors' faces gave me a horrible feeling. I knew my day would come, but to see these guys, who devoted so much time to baseball, be forced to call it quits hurt to watch. I could not help but tear up.

The season was over. It had just flown by and 51 games had passed. All of the studying, the fall workouts, the tests, the lifts, the snow, the essays, and the indoor practices – it was all over and we came up short.

Next year there would be no excuses. Next year.

The bus ride home was four hours of complete quiet time. As we neared Binghamton, a little chatter started. It was as if the loss had finally settled in our stomachs. I am not sure any of us thought we were going to miss the playoffs, and I think toward the end of the ride we kind of accepted the season as best as we could. Before everyone parted ways, we enjoyed one last night together.

After eating, sleeping and living with my teammates for nine months, the last night was a strange one. On the first day of fall ball there was no possible way to really comprehend that there would ever be a last day. It seemed so far away, and the climb seemed so steep and burdensome that it was hard to imagine ever saying goodbye. Once the season kicked into high gear and I got into a routine, it became even harder to believe that this life wouldn't last forever. After our loss to Stony Brook, everyone had to face the stark realization that the season was over. It was now just a small blurb in the media guide.

Everyone was excited to leave Binghamton and either report to summer ball or start post-college lives, but first we drank and drank until the wee hours one more time. I just had to make sure that I was up by 10 a.m. for my end-of-year meeting with the coaching staff. The meeting was tough considering the loss the day before, but the coaches promised it wouldn't happen again next year.

Of course at that point no one in the room could imagine the disappointment next year would bring. On this late May morning, next year seemed so far away. Feet of snow, months of coldness, and hours of studying and working out were all still ahead of me, *before the season would even start*.

In my meeting the coaches said they knew I had struggled the second half of the year, but they thought I was right where I should be after freshman year. I was offered a renewal of my scholarship, and I gladly accepted it. I shook their hands and departed. I thought I was in a great spot to succeed next season.

I went to my room and started packing. It was there I saw Tom Carberry in tears. His meeting with the coaches was right before mine, and I had to sit outside the office and listen to them say they were not renewing his scholarship.

This sucked. He didn't do very well in his *8 at bats*, but why not keep him for a while and see if he could regain his high school form? Injuries had hampered his play all year. Cutting players after just one season was something that was new and shocking to me. It truly was a business.

In hindsight, Tom probably wasn't going to be an All-Conference player and there were probably better outfielders out there, but it could not be ignored that another Collins' guy was phased out.

At times I almost wished I was a bit weaker player so there would have been more of an effort to phase me out. I have always been one to survive, and there was no way I was going to let someone kick me out. I adapted and fought and made the coaches want to keep me. I couldn't see them getting rid of a hard-working, 3.8 GPA student who had shown signs of greatness on the field. However, I do wonder every so often if it would have been better if I had been pushed out. It would have given me three years at another program where I would have had a better chance to excel.

As I left to go home, I figured Mike Papili and I would battle for the starting left field job next year. I left thinking that next year was set up to be a star-studded season. How could I have been so blind and ignorant as to ignore Coach Hurbas's new recruiting class?

CHAPTER 15

I had about two days to get all of my sulking and reflecting out of the way. Less than a week after our devastating loss to Stony Brook, Jeff Dennis and I were due to report to Rock Hill, South Carolina, for summer baseball. There would be no vacation at home this time around. I had a few days to say hello to my family before Jeff and I made the 10-hour road trip.

Going away for my first summer was a bit scary, so I was glad I had a friend going along as it took us no more than 10 minutes after our arrival in Rock Hill to figure out that having a familiar face nearby was more than a luxury. A lot of the summer league teams seemed to have an extremely cheap owner and/or GM who tried to run a smooth operation but always forgot little things like ordering baseballs. Logistics were always a nightmare, and we were always given the impression that the team was one rainout away from being bankrupt. It seemed as if the planning for the team started a week before the season began. This was college summer baseball!

By the time we made it to Rock Hill it was very late at night. We had nowhere to stay and no one to get in touch with. We were told a hotel would be ready for us that night, but of course there were no reservations for us, and hotel staff never heard of the Rock Hill Sox.

Our general manager was nowhere to be found. Because of a NASCAR race in nearby Charlotte, N.C., every hotel within 30 miles was full – all except one. I could give you a description of the hotel, but I will just say I took everything out of the car that night: my TV, my clothes, even my snacks. I was sure that when we woke up the next morning the car would be gone.

The next few nights, we were able to stay in the hotel reserved for us. It turned out our GM failed to notify the hotel that some players were coming in the night before. Oops.

The hotel was only a temporary living facility. We still did not have a place for the summer, so for a week we pretty much lived out of our car. In another organizational disaster, our host family had backed out at the last minute and Jeff and I were eating McDonalds and snack packs for sustenance. Thankfully, a family stepped up and gave us a place to stay. More specifically, they gave us a house!

Gary, Fay, Chad and Courtney Martin went out of their way to make the summer one of the greatest Jeff and I ever had. They didn't ask a dime for it. They had heard about our situation and offered a solution. They owned the house behind theirs, and instead of selling it or renting it for a profit they let us live there for free.

I had heard horror stories about host families and dreadful living conditions, but the Martins were a dream host family. I am still in touch with them to this day.

The Southern Collegiate League was decent in terms of the power rankings. For a freshman, it was ideal. The players were not spectacular, but it was a competitive league. We played six games a week, but we had Mondays, Wednesdays and Saturdays off. It left time for a lot of fun. We were three 19-year-olds (Ryan Maxa, a player from Florida, also lived with us) who were on our own with a house and a hot tub. We were very respectful of the Martins' rules, but we definitely had our fun.

It would have been hard not to have fun. We lived in a golf resort community on a lake. We were given access to the pool club and spent many off-days lounging by the pool. Charlotte was only 10 minutes away, and we spent plenty of nights downtown. It was a dream summer. Off-days consisted of waking up whenever our teenage bodies felt like it and then either heading to the gym or doing chores for the Martins – the latter being much more strenuous and difficult.

I guess picking a weed/ivy patch as big as a medium-sized pool was a fair price to pay for having our own house and being guests of the nicest host family anyone could ever ask for. Jeff and I became great friends with Chad Martin, our host brother, from doing these "chores" together, and spent many hours in the evenings playing cards and drinking beers.

It became hard, however, to have any consistency on the field. On our off-days, there was no baseball at all, even if I wanted to try to practice. We were over a half-hour from the field and there were no hitting tees or balls. Getting extra reps was a pivotal part of my game, and it was a tough adjustment getting such a limited number of swings.

Game days consisted of waking around 11 a.m., watching some TV, and then heading to Ryan's Steakhouse and Buffet for our one free meal a day. (After two months I never wanted to see another Ryan's.) After eating pounds of greasy food, we would then head to our game.

After starting the summer out slow, I ended up hitting over .300 the second half of the season, and made some important adjustments at the plate. I was feeling very confident, and when the sun finally set on the summer, I was more certain than ever I was headed for a great sophomore year.

It was a magical summer. There was no school, and we didn't have the responsibility of a job. Twenty-five guys came together, played baseball and simply enjoyed life. Even with our field conditions most closely resembling a lava field, it was still a ball every day to go out there and play in the humid, 95-degree weather. I met some great friends and got to see a whole new part of the country. It was so much more relaxed than college ball, and the pace was a great change. After two months, I had started to feel the southern vibes. When I came back north in late July, I was officially a country music fan.

The entire summer had a Minor League feel to it. We would travel to remote parts of North Carolina, South Carolina, and Tennessee and play in old ballparks. The country music blared over the loudspeakers between innings and everything seemed to be sponsored by the local law office. For a first summer league experience, there was nothing more I could ask for.

Toward the end of the summer though, my body started to weaken. I had played over 90 games, and I could feel it starting to wear down. Mentally I was starting to fade as well. Visits from both my parents helped lift my spirits (and my batting average as well), but as August neared I could feel my body begging for a small break. I had only been home for three days since January, and I was out of gas.

During the last inning of the last summer game, I took a deep breath and allowed the scenery to fill my senses. I had gone through a lot of ups and downs in the last year, and as I stood alone in left field I reflected on all I had accomplished.

As the last out was recorded I took off my cap and began to jog off the field. I noticed a lightning storm flashing blues and golds in the sky. The lightning bolts blended with the fading orange sunset to form a mural straight out of a sunset painting. Thunder crashed, Earth shook. It was one of the most amazing scenes I had ever witnessed, and the perfect finale to my first year. I felt the warm air on my skin and muttered a quiet, "This is great." I knew I needed to keep this feeling with me. In a few short months it would be dark and snowing at 4:30 p.m. and I would have a test to study for.

And like that, freshman year was over!

PART 2
SOPHOMORE YEAR

CHAPTER 16

If someone told me a year earlier that going back to Binghamton would feel homey and comfortable, I would have told that person they didn't understand me at all. However, returning to Binghamton in the fall actually felt good. I was looking forward to having some stability and also to seeing some familiar faces in a familiar setting.

When I pulled into campus and was greeted by the small sign "Welcome to Binghamton University," I became excited. The sign looked as if it had survived both World Wars, but every year when I saw that sign for the first time, it made me smile.

Before heading back to Binghamton, however, I always got my much-needed break from baseball.

August was vacation month for me. After 90-plus games, I needed a few weeks to recharge my batteries. I went to St. Maarten in the Caribbean for a week and did my best not to think about baseball. I also enjoyed home life (and real homemade meals) and tried to see friends in town as much as possible. The weeks flew by, but by the time late August rolled around I was ready to hit both the field and the books.

I always thought it was funny that August was one of the major "down months" for a college baseball player. It was beautiful outside and a perfect temperature to play baseball, but because of the logistics of scheduling it was oddly an "off" month. Playing in March or October in 40-degree weather, however, was common practice.

Getting back into a routine took no more than a week. Baseball kicked off with the team's annual preseason meeting, and from there the days started to fly by. I was now one of the guys, joking around and trading summer baseball stories. The freshmen were not as comfortable.

In our initial meeting Coach Sinicki talked to us about our ultimate goal of winning a conference championship and what it would take. It was meant to get everyone fired up, but the speech also was designed to scare off the potential walk-ons. According to Coach Sinicki, up to that point a walk-on had never played a game for Coach Sinicki at the Division I level.

The meeting also offered a surprise that none of the returning players saw coming. With the change in assistant coaches the year before, lower priorities like gear and locker space got pushed to the bottom of the list. The result was, as coach Sinicki said, "a team that looked like a box of Froot Loops." This year, however, the entire team was issued official practice gear.

We were given a hat, four practice jerseys, and a promise that shorts were on their way. Coach Sinicki was very old school in some ways and did not care as much about gear and getting the latest style fleeces as the players did. Coach Hurba, however, was always donning the latest gear fresh from the factory. This trickled down to the players. From that day on, we would never again complain about not having enough paraphernalia. It was day one of my official Binghamton Baseball gear collection.

Looking like a team changed my entire outlook on the fall. We went from resembling a sandlot team to looking like the Division I program we were. We had matching shirts and hats and a field to call our own. After getting bused to assorted fields every day the previous fall, it was a pleasure to simply walk to the locker room, get changed, and then jog out to our own field. It was clear that Coach Hurba had already made a huge impact on the program.

What also made this fall different was the added "early work," better known as "mandatory optional work."

Early workouts were described as a chance for the hitters to get extra swings before practice began so that during practice we had time to work on "other" things. What early work actually turned out to be was an extra hour of practice.

Practices quickly ballooned into three- and four-hour marathons. We would work out hard for an hour, *then* stretch as a team. The order was a bit peculiar to me, but I suppose it had to be done this way to legally allow us to practice before practice. We would hit, bunt, and run bases – all before the team began to stretch at the start of the actual practice.

Along with extended practices, I also had school to focus on during those few brief moments not occupied by baseball each day. I was just getting into the School of Management curriculum and experiencing my first real challenges in the classroom. My high school taught only liberal arts courses, so trying to figure out even the basics of financial accounting seemed like a daunting task. The class itself wasn't very hard, but I was extremely intimated the first few weeks of the semester by all the new terms such as "credit" and "debit." As far as I knew, those were simply types of plastic cards that allowed me to purchase food and gas.

It was hard enough to learn a new subject in a traditional class setting but what made it even harder was the format of the class. Long gone were the days where classes met every day for an hour. One of my classes only met *once* a week for three hours. So like most every college kid, I simply closed my book after the three-hour lecture on Monday night and didn't look at it again until the following Sunday. It was really only after I took my first test and did well that I actually began to relax a little. Looking at the "A" written in red across my exam was the first time I remember thinking that I might not only survive the Business School, but that I had a good chance of excelling in it.

In baseball, my fall season was full of more ups and downs. Most days I was ripping the ball. The pressure of being an unknown freshman was gone, and I was much more relaxed. However, there were still days when college pitching made me look awful. One scrimmage during parents' weekend, I went 0-for-5 with four strikeouts against a subpar community college. It was the low point of the fall, but I managed to battle back to finish the fall season on a hot streak. I still had trouble getting over bad performances, but I was slowly learning how to recover much more efficiently. The cliché "every day is a new day" was starting to make some sense.

Our fall scrimmages, however, made practices seem brief. The NCAA states that you can only play 56 games in a college season, including the fall and spring seasons. It does not stipulate how long the games can be. Each day of competition counts as three hours of athletic time. A one-hour no-hitter or a marathon doubleheader both count as three hours of time. By NCAA rules, a team cannot compete for more than 20 hours per week and cannot play for more than four hours a day. (In the off-season you are only allowed to record 8 official hours of team sponsored workouts).[6]

Because of these rules, all three of our fall games lasted anywhere from 12 to 14 innings. No matter how long the game went, it only counted for three of our 20 hours for the week. Everyone got to play, and it allowed me to get a lot of solid at bats. With a lot of new faces on the team, I could begin to tell that taking advantage of every at bat was vital.

My fall season ended on a high note, and going into the winter season I was feeling confident and excited. I had only positive thoughts circulating in my head when the first snow fell in late October.

CHAPTER 17

I spent a lot of my free time over the winter trying to learn more about the mental side of baseball and did so by reading many brilliant books like "The Inner Game of *Tennis*" and "The Mental Game of Baseball." It almost became a hobby reading these manuscripts.

I had been a very typical freshman. On the surface it appeared to a lot of the players that I only cared about myself. Although this was not a fair assessment, I knew some of the older guys assumed this. They mistook my frustration for selfishness. Deep down I wanted to win as much as anyone on the team, but I also admitted to myself that I sometimes didn't show it.

It was an important lesson to learn early on because, as my career progressed, I would have to learn more and more to bury the negative personal feelings and pull for the team.

That winter I had a lot of "heart to heart" talks with some of the older guys about attitude and the team. It became my goal (in baseball and beyond) to be considered a valued team player. I wanted to be the guy who people respected for doing whatever was necessary for the good of the team.

I brought this challenge with me throughout that winter and carried it into my junior and senior seasons. Even when things got rough for me, I would not budge from my mission to always be a team player. I suppose you need to ask my teammates, co-workers, family and friends to see if I accomplished that goal.

The winter flew by as I once again packed my schedule. I was taking four classes, lifting, and training every day. Still, I made sure to find time to go out and to enjoy being a student, even if only for a few hours at a time.

Most of the year Bearcat baseball players did not fit the stereotypical image of carefree college students. We were usually way too tired and/or busy to be out on the quad throwing a Frisbee after class. Even if we had the time and energy to join a club or activity, we usually had something scheduled the next day that forced us to stay in and get rest. It made the off-season months precious. There were only a few weekends available to live as non-athletes.

The weight room became my favorite place in the off-season. After not working out all weekend (our weight room was *closed* Saturday and Sunday, so even if I wanted to be ambitious and work out I really couldn't), I was jam-packed with energy come Monday. Our team never got into steroids, but we did take supplements. Everyone claimed what he was taking was legal, but who really knows if it was all truly permissible? NO Xplode was passed around the locker room like candy. This energy drink made hour-long workouts flash by. The team was constantly getting "pressured" to finish up its workouts and clear the weight room for other athletic teams, so it was always scramble mode in there.

Most of the year it was our responsibility to find workout time on our own, but during the winter we got to lift as a team. The energy in the weight room was electric. I put on over 10 pounds in the off-season, and when spring rolled around I was a bigger, faster and stronger player. I had no doubt I was ready to have a breakout year. No doubt at all.

As I headed home for the long winter break I expected nothing but great things for the upcoming semester. I was more determined than ever to work hard and to be as prepared as possible come first pitch. Coach Hurba had even sat me down the day before the semester ended and told me that he wanted me to be the guy to anchor left field for three years. He did not want to have to worry if I would be a lifetime .220 hitter. I told him there was no prayer I would hit that low over my career if I was given a fair shake. I had no reason to doubt anything he told me. I was a very naïve sophomore.

I had been doing a pretty good job staying in touch with a lot of my high school friends through Facebook and AOL Instant chat, but gradually I was talking with them less and less. Winter break was the final nail in that coffin. I was so busy spending time with my family, training for baseball, and seeing my close friends that I felt it was nearly impossible to stay in touch with all the other friends from Connecticut.

Even with the ease of text messaging and the Internet, it seemed like more effort than I wanted to expend to stay in contact with all of these "casual" friends. During breaks as freshmen, everyone from high school would get together. However, it became very apparent over this Christmas break that this pattern was changing.

Every break seemed to separate my high school graduating class a little bit more. By my senior year of college, I only I talked to about four or five close friends. The grade-wide parties were a thing of the past. Eventually, even my best friends started to slowly move away for internships and jobs.

My new friends were my Binghamton teammates – the people I was about to spend the bulk of my time with.

CHAPTER 18

We were five weeks from opening day when Oregon State beat Hawaii-Hilo 5-0 on Jan. 25. Baseball could not have seemed farther away, and in fact Hawaii was about as far away as you could get. Binghamton was a different world in late January. Low grey clouds covered the city and snow blanketed the ground. I could not go outside without a winter jacket, gloves and a winter hat. It was hard to believe that Binghamton and Hawaii were both in Division I.

The five weeks of preseason dragged on just as they had the year before. The coaches tried to keep things new and fresh, but we ended up in a routine that made the 30-plus days of practice seem to crawl by. The only fly balls the outfielders saw before opening day were in a parking lot near our locker room – not exactly spring training in Dodgertown. It was tough as an outfielder having to endure a three-hour practice when I knew that all I needed was a half-hour in the batting cage. Indoor baseball became very dull and a chore. The team kept moving forward however as we knew our off-season would not last forever.

By the time March 3rd came around, many teams had already played a good portion of their schedules. In fact most southern and west coast teams had played well over 15 games. Can you imagine if the Yankees played 42 games before the Minnesota Twins ever played one? While the Twins would need to play six games a week, the Yankees could play only three games and just use their top three starting pitchers as their rotation. It wouldn't be a very fair setup – but this is exactly how college baseball was run before the uniform start date.

We opened with a Saturday doubleheader vs. Norfolk State in Virginia. They had played *only* 12 games before March 3, and that was on the low end of games played by a southern team.

When we arrived onto Norfolk State's campus on Saturday morning, it was a perfect early spring day, a truly great day to start a season. Unfortunately, the night before it had poured. The Norfolk coaching staff declared that the field was still too wet for any type of pre-game activity.

While I was trying to relax and stay focused, our team was stretching on an outdoor basketball court near the field. We had to loosen up our arms on this ridiculous concrete court. All the hitting was done in one cage and a tiny tee area. Fly balls were caught behind right field in a parking lot. It was a total joke. When my dad and sister drove up to the field, it must have been quite an odd scene to see the Binghamton outfielders shagging fly balls in a parking lot.

My dad and sister did not want to miss opening day. They took a short plane trip to Philadelphia, transferred to a Norfolk flight, then rented a car. Having arrived with 20 minutes to spare before first pitch, they looked extremely excited for the baseball season to begin. So was I.

And this is where my story really starts.

I sat in game one because, according to my coach, a lefty was supposed to start. He never did start, but still Mike Papili still got to play. I had no problem with it. I had assumed all year that we would be splitting time. I wanted to be able to play in front of my dad and sister, who had traveled so far just to see me, but I could wait until the second game.

Between games, our coach let us visit with family. I know in some programs that was frowned upon, but Coach Sinicki gave us a few precious minutes to greet our friends and family. I said hello quickly, but hurried back to the dugout so I could get ready for the second game.

I looked up at the lineup card to see where I was hitting and was shocked when I saw my name listed under the reserves. We had just gotten blown out 12-5, and I assumed that game two was mine, especially after Papili got yanked from the first game for a pinch-runner in the 6th inning and freshman outfielder Joe Charron replaced him in left field.

All I could think of was that my dad and sister weren't going to see me play. I shivered at the guilt I felt.

Throughout the fall season and the preseason, I figured I was the number one option in left field. Papili and Charron were very talented, but I knew how hard I had worked and didn't feel like I had showed any signs of laziness or poor attitude. When Charron got sent into the first game to replace Papili, I thought very little of it. I knew Joe was a quality player and also deserved time. But Joe starting game two left me totally befuddled.

My first thought was how it seemed that the coaching staff had failed in any way to communicate to me my role on the team. I figured that if the coaches had simply talked to me the season before, the month before, or even the night before about their strategy and my role, I would have been much more mentally prepared. Similarly, if I truly thought that I didn't deserve to be playing, I would have been much more able to deal with the situation. Unfortunately that did not happen.

I was so caught off-guard by not starting that I was left to wildly speculate as to what was going on behind the scenes. Having to sit through the entire doubleheader was the first true crushing blow to my confidence. Joe Charron was a terrific hitter and proved himself to be very deserving of playing time, but I thought it was wrong how they hung me out to dry that first weekend. I was totally taken aback, and it took me a long time to rediscover the confidence that they had stripped away from me.

They had no right to do that and sadly because of the lack of communication, it pretty much took me the entire season to fully realize that the coaches had decided to go with Charron as their number one guy, and that they had passed on me. I became their backup plan. It was a role I could not get away from, no matter how much I fought and struggled to escape.

If I had done something wrong I wouldn't have placed as much significance in that one doubleheader. But the suddenness of the unfolding story without any explanation or recognition by the coaching staff truly scared me and made me worry that I was in for a potentially very frustrating year. When a freshman is put in to start over you, it is never a good sign. Worse, the coaches never once said a word to me about it. Coach Hurba had recruited Joe and certainly was pushing hard for him to play over me during the coaches' meetings. It was clear where loyalties lay after just one day. I was growing up.

Right after the doubleheader, I was not that upset. I was bummed about not playing, but I did keep the perspective that it was only two games out of a very long season. But as the night wore on, I became more and more agitated. Every time I thought about the day, I became more infuriated.

I was in between tears and indignation as I lay awake in my bed that night. I had fought so hard to get to a position where I could succeed and, in a flash, it seemed to have all been taken away from me. All I could do was work harder and pray that the trend would swing back in my favor.

It was tough just going out to dinner with teammates and sleeping in the same room as them because I had to hide my true feelings. It would have been selfish and counterproductive to complain to them. Plus, I had a goal of being a team player this year. Still, I could never forget how my family had traveled hundreds of miles and only saw me for 10 minutes.

I slept uncomfortably but figured I was due to start on Sunday, so I tried to relax and get a few much-needed hours of sleep.

When I awoke the next morning, the weather had taken a turn for the worse. It was only partly cloudy, but the clouds hanging low over the hotel were heavy. When I stepped out into the parking lot, the cold struck me hard. It would be a long day in Virginia.

The game-time temperature was about 42 degrees, but with the clouds and wind it felt more like 30 degrees. Seeing my name in the reserves slot again didn't make the weather seem any warmer. Joe Charron was starting again in left field. I froze my butt off on the bench, unable to move or comprehend what was happening to me.

For about 90% of my games for the remainder of my career, I didn't know if I was playing until minutes before first pitch. *I hated not knowing!* Whenever I would get even a small hint as to who was playing, I was extremely thankful. Once I knew I was sitting, I could relax and change my mindset. Even if I was going to pinch-hit, I knew I had plenty of time to start preparing for that at bat. It was torture going through pre-game workouts without knowing whether I was playing. It killed me having to wait until 10 minutes before first pitch to see the lineup posted.

Joe Charron and Henry Dunn, another highly recruited centerfielder, were 0-for-14 after the first weekend. Now both were terrific players who clearly were good enough to start right away – and both did end up being impact players in the program. Charron actually started off very hot after the first few weekends. Still, it cannot be ignored how many at bats they were both given early on in the season and how much room for failure they were granted. They got the needed at bats to get going and to get into a groove while I was getting the short end of the stick/bench. This trend continued throughout the year and only got worse.

I never blamed Charron or Dunn because it was not their decision. They were just playing baseball. Instead, I resented this system that was cutting me off at the knees without ever allowing any room for error. I felt like I was in a no win situation where my effort and performance would never be considered good enough. If only the coaches had been honest with me at the post-season interview following freshman year, I would likely have moved to another program. I guess that is why they didn't tell me.

In game three, with the score 8-4 in favor of Norfolk State, I was asked to make my season debut as a pinch hitter. It was early spring and the sun was setting on the darkening field. It was windy and bitterly cold. My body was never so stiff trying to get "loose" for an at bat. I had not moved in what felt like days. Now I was at home plate with a 33-inch piece of metal in my hands. Tell me it wasn't a recipe for failure.

After fouling off a pitch, I got a fat 0-1 fastball. The second I hit the ball I knew it was gone. The ball left my bat on a beeline for deep right center. I put my bat down and headed for first base. I expected to look up and see the ball clearing the fence, but when I gazed into the sky I saw the ball tail-spinning down in deep centerfield.

When the ball finally landed, it was in the centerfielder's glove. The 30 mph winds had pushed a sure home run ball back into play.

I know everyone was impressed with my at bat off the bench, but it just angered me even more. The eight-hour bus ride home took forever and by the time we arrived at the Events Center in Binghamton late Sunday night, snow was on the ground. I craved my dorm room bed.

Next week would be better, I just knew it.

CHAPTER 19

The next weekend put us back in Virginia, this time to play Radford. After dropping the first game, we were 1-3. This team was supposed to be older and more mature and was assumed to have learned how to win close games. Clearly we had not. The proof lay in yet another game in which we blew a big lead, this time going from being up 5-1 in game four to being down 6-5. We got the lead back at 8-6 heading into the bottom of the 9th, but within seconds we again squandered the lead as freshman pitcher Murphy Smith gave up a two-run bomb. (Murphy had an amazing career, though, so I am willing to let this one go).

The game ended with a bases loaded walk-off hit-by-pitch in the bottom of the 9th. To make matters worse, I had to sit idly by and watch this play out. I just wanted to get away from the baseball field. I was in shock at how badly this season had started. I was like a deflating balloon, helplessly watching my precious air leak out.

On Saturday, I finally got my first start. I was determined to impress the coaches with a solid game because I was beginning to get the idea that these starts would be rare. I barreled a few balls up and got my first hit, a double to left field. That felt great, and took some pressure off.

I felt good after the game until we had our hitters meeting at night. There, Coach Hurba said that in order to win we were going to need guys to step up offensively and that 1-for-4 days were not going to impress anyone. I felt a little more air seep out of the balloon. I am sure Hurba did not mean anything too negative by what he said, and I certainly didn't think 1-for-4 was anything exceptional, but the way the words poured out of his mouth made it seem that my 1-for-4 had let the team down.

Sunday was yet another "off day" for me. Even when Jeff Monaco, a senior outfielder, went down with an injury in the middle of the game, I was not put in. I should have realized at the time how little they thought of me as an outfielder, but the thought never even occurred to me. I had been a superstar centerfielder in high school, so the idea that I was not capable of playing the outfield was so far beyond my comprehension that it never even dawned on me.

It should have when, instead of putting me in the game, they moved our third baseman, Ryan James, to left field (where he never played), moved Joe Charron to right field, and took Kyle Klee off the bench and put him at 3rd. All of this instead of simply putting me out there. It was a slap in the face and another example of how they built an assessment of my playing ability on several events during my freshman year. That picture lasted my entire college career and could not be refuted by my performance on the field.

The Radford experience left me with such a sour taste that for the first time I considered transferring. I spoke to my dad on a phone outside of a Burger King for about 30 minutes during our rest stop. We both knew the truth; my path at Binghamton was looking very bumpy. My dad recommended that I leave my new home and my new friends behind. It was going to be a tough decision, especially because I didn't have all of the facts about my current situation.

We headed back Sunday night with our record at a subpar 2-4. Our lack of games (and my lack of at bats) only continued to get worse. Our Radford series ended on March 11 and it would not be until March 24 that we played again.

The "Villanova Baseball Bash" was snowed out the following weekend, and the weather was a tough break for me. Jeff Monaco had hurt his shoulder diving for a ball at Radford and was out for at least the next weekend's games. However, those games were canceled because of the weather and so he never missed a game.

Rain erased our next two-game series vs. Bucknell. After every call from our captains about the latest cancellation, I would throw my hands up in disgust.

It was agony. When March 24 finally came around, many other teams had played over 25 games. I was 1-for-5 over six games! The next weekend at Lafayette was also on the cutting block as a "nor'easter" developed at the beginning of the week. The report was that the weekend might get wiped out even if the new storm missed us.

Thankfully, a solution was found to get the games in. Long Island University was equally desperate to get some games in. The plan was for Binghamton, LIU, and Lafayette to all meet at LIU in Brooklyn. LIU had a turf field, so the lingering snow was a non-issue.

LIU has a couple of campuses but its baseball field was located in the heart of New York City – one of the coolest fields I ever played on. The field was a big rectangle buried deep in the middle of the city. A huge dormitory nestled on one side of the field, city streets lined two sides, and an athletic center occupied the other side.

Yards away was a different world, filled with bustling New York City taxis and pedestrians. Within the chain link fence, though, was good old fashioned college baseball.

The only place to warm up was way out in deep right center field. LIU was playing Lafayette before us, so we had to make sure to get out of their way. Around the 7th inning, our coach told us to run out to loosen up. During a break from the game, our entire team set off for the warmup area at a decently quick pace. DH Jeff Wertepny was keeping up when the strap from his bag came apart and the bag crashed to the ground. Unable to stop and gather himself because the game was ready to resume, poor Jeff had to gather his fallen belongings and then drag his huge overstuffed bag across the entire outfield with everyone laughing at him. He took it like a champ.

We still had to wait to start playing long after we were loose, however, because the game went 13 innings. It seemed like this season would never get going. I was just waiting for a meteorite to hit the field and delay the season a bit more.

I started the first game but before I had time to do anything, I was yanked when after two at bats a lefty came in. Not only did I get pulled, but I got pulled after striking out on a 2-2 pitch in which the umpire made a horrendous strike three call on a ball 5 inches off the plate. I walked back to the dugout having left the bases loaded. The frustration was mounting.

Even though I was angry, poor Michael Quinn was much more outraged. I knew I was getting treated poorly but my roommate Quinn was getting an even worse deal. Quinn was recruited by the old assistant coach along with me, and he had *no* support. We only had two catchers at the time, Quinn and our starting catcher Pat Haughie, but our coaches wanted no part of playing Quinn. They had even less interest in trying to develop him.

Haughie had a lot of skills, but his bat my sophomore year was abysmal. As bad as Haughie struggled, however, he still got almost all of the innings at catcher, even catching both ends of most doubleheaders. It was fairly obvious that Pat was going to be the one and only catcher, but after the coaches' moves at LIU, it became crystal clear.

Pat Haughie went 0-for-4 in the first game. In the second game, Quinn finally got a start and was quickly 2-for-2. In the third game, however, Haughie was back catching. It wasn't just the brutal season-long slump that Pat was in that made the move ridiculous, but Pat had also seriously injured his finger the day before and was playing in pain.

I knew how wrong it was that Quinn was not playing, but what was I going to do?

Haughie went 0-for-3, and Quinn had to watch every painful pitch. It became very obvious that Hurba did not like Quinn as a baseball player. His fate was *written* his freshman year when Hurba saw something in Mike that he didn't like about him, but his fate was *sealed* at LIU. If he couldn't get in the game in this situation, he and everyone else knew he was doomed.

We both felt heartbroken the week after LIU. We had both been so excited and optimistic for the season. It was crushing. Mike and I were at a loss for words. Even though I got to play Sunday (and hit a nice double), it was becoming all too obvious that our coaches had other plans for us than to be starters.

We were frustrated and angry, and it was sadly the first time I remember seeing Quinn with the attitude of "whatever." Quinn cared dearly about the program and about baseball in general, but he was beaten down so many times that it became almost impossible for him to stay up. The weekend had been just one more major blow to his psyche. As bad as I was feeling about my situation, it hurt a lot to see the sparkle in Quinn's eyes slowly dim.

CHAPTER 20

One of the biggest perks of playing college baseball was getting to see new parts of the country. Before our spring trip to Utah to play Utah Valley State and Brigham Young University, I had heard stories about the snow-capped mountains of the Rockies, but I had never seen anything more than a picture or two.

The day before we left, the weather forecast was for snow over Utah. But Utah Valley and BYU were looking for an opponent and willing to help us financially with the trip, so off to Utah we went. As of March 28, we were one of only 3 out of 293 Division I teams to have played fewer than 10 games. BYU was 14-12.

Even with the "rocky" beginning, I was not about to let my early season situation deter my training regimen. I knew if I had any shot of turning this season around I would need to be in peak mental and physical shape. I had worked too hard all pre-season to just unravel now. Thus, I thought it was a no-brainer to skip my two morning classes on our travel day in order to lift and hit before our bus left for the airport.

Utah was absolutely gorgeous. We got into our hotel late at night so we could not see the mountains literally a mile or two away. When we awoke, we looked out onto towering mountains. They rose into the clouds and disappeared. The snow-caps made the cool morning air seem a bit chillier than the reported 55 degrees. But as Ernie Banks would say, it was an ideal day to play two.

BYU took advantage of its beautiful surroundings and positioned the field so that mountains loomed right behind the outfield. I had no idea Mormon country was so beautiful. (Not to mention all of the beautiful blond girls walking around).

Our games were at night so we were free until mid-afternoon. With my dad and step-mom Kathy, I got to explore some of Utah. I hated the idea of going to all of these cool destinations without getting to see the area. With my family around, I was able to explore. I would sightsee in the morning and play baseball in the evening, all on the dime of the university. Did it get any cooler than that?

We made the trip to see Olympic Park, where the 2002 Salt Lake Games were held. I also got to visit Sundance, home of the famous international film festival.

Our first game vs. BYU was an embarrassment. I don't like to use jet lag as an excuse, so I will just say our horrible execution was the reason we got trounced 15-0. I think we were intimidated by the size of some of their players and just folded. Many of their players undertake their Mormon missions during the college years and were two or three years older than the average college ballplayers. The first game showed it.

But baseball is a strange game. Good can go bad as quickly as bad can become good. You can have a 20-game hit streak and then go 0-for-20 after that. You can leave the winning run on base five nights in a row before being the hero. You can also lose by 15 runs one night and come back 20 hours later and beat BYU.

BYU was caught totally off-guard on Saturday night. It was an amazing game to watch and the hapless Cougars were left to figure out how a team from Binghampton (most teams got our name wrong) had just beaten them, 11-6. It would have been better to play rather than watch, but I was thrilled with the huge win.

The team was so excited about winning that we quickly loaded the vans to head back to the hotel. Everyone was clamoring and breaking down the game on the bus when our assistant coach, Andy Hutchings, answered his cell phone. In all of the excitement we had apparently left our trainer stranded at the field.

Everyone tried to contain the laughter, but it was pretty damn funny turning back into the stadium parking lot and seeing our trainer with her two big medical bags standing there. Sorry.

After a huge win, game three was back to the same old story; getting a quick lead and then letting the lead go even quicker. I sat around and watched us squander a 7-2 lead.

I knew I had struggled toward the end of my freshman year, but I was convinced I had learned a lot and was dumbfounded as to why after 12 games I only had 10 at bats. I was even more dumbfounded when I wasn't even starting game three. It was as if my "tryout" was over and the decision was made that I was not to be one of Hurba's guys.

With Dad and Kathy in attendance, it was just killing me inside to be sitting. It was a feeling of helplessness because I knew that without some consistent at bats, I was never going to start hitting well.

Jeff Dennis had given us 5 2/3 strong innings on the mound before transfer Gino Offerman came in to relieve him. The first time I saw Gino in the dorm parking lot in August, I thought I was looking at Mr. T. Gino was from the island of Curacao and had a Major League body. Just going off looks alone, it appeared he could either could hit the ball 550 feet or throw 95 mph. I may have overestimated his ability.

Gino was a great kid and we became very good friends, but he had a big issue on the mound – namely throwing strikes. Gino had overcome so much just to get to Binghamton, including a childhood filled with obstacles I couldn't really comprehend. He told me stories of his difficult childhood and how after getting off the island he had to move multiple times into different houses because of legal, financial, and economic reasons.

Unfortunately, Gino had a great deal of trouble getting used to Division I life and slowly but surely was falling behind. It wasn't just adjusting to college hitters, but also adjusting to college life in general that caused him heartache. And once the coaches decided he was "uncoachable", it was all but over for him.

A coach only has a player for at most four years, so when he sees someone like Gino who needs extensive time and attention to be successful, there may be a tendency to take the easy road and just find a replacement. Gino's performance at BYU did not help his cause.

Gino faced five batters. He walked one and gave up hits to every other hitter he faced. He never recorded an out. It was painful to watch.

Ironically, none of his runs were earned. A one-out errant throw by Ryan James down the first base line had prolonged the inning. I actually had a perfect view of the play and saw the tag being placed on the runner in time, but the umpire ruled that our first baseman missed the tag. BYU put up a 9-spot after that call, and the game appeared over. But not yet. We loaded the bases in the last inning with only one out. It was as good a time as ever to give me my first at bat of the weekend.

I was not good enough to play any of these three games, but now I was the man they wanted hitting. It made no sense to me then and it makes no sense to me now.

I took a first pitch low and then on the next pitch took a good outside fastball for strike 1. At 0-1 I decided to swing at a slider which I missed by a good five feet. The final pitch was another slider that stayed away but this time it also stayed up in the zone and I absolutely ripped it right at the shortstop. Before I placed my DeMarini bat on the ground the shortstop caught it, stepped on second and like that the game was over. Boom, double play.

That evening Quinn and I went for a walk. We talked about how we seriously thought that they were going to cut us both. It seemed so obvious to us. Little did we know that cutting us was never their idea. Their strategy was for us to remain as backups. In time I learned to deal with this situation. But early on I spent many nights wishing that they had just cut me. If they had, at least I could have found another program before it was too late.

That was not my fate. I was meant to stay at Binghamton and grow up.

After taking off Sunday (the Mormons can't play on Sundays), we had a two game series vs. Utah Valley State, an average independent ballclub which played right next door to BYU – in a gorgeous Minor League park that 95% of affiliated Division I teams would kill for.

We were very confident we would handle a weaker UVS squad, and going into the 8th inning with a 6-2 lead only confirmed our thoughts. But then it was déjà vu all over again. UVS scored eight times, and we blew *another* game.

Coach Sinicki remained calm as he told us to go into the locker room. We assumed we were about to get yelled at – nothing new to us. He came in calm, collected and cool. His back was toward me. He put his hat on his head and said simply, "35 minutes to the next game." And then he lost it.

I've never seen a coach get angrier quicker in my life. We probably deserved it, but I have never before or since heard anything quite like it. "This ain't high school ball anymore." He yelled that this "was Groundhog Day," that "we have no pride" and that "we were an embarrassment to the state of New York."

He ranted and raved. He was trying to get through to us while also getting rid of his frustration, but every time he made a comment it just seemed to get him angrier. His face grew beet red. The Incredible Hulk appeared before us. Players feared one of us was going to be thrown across the room. Instead, the helpless victim was his innocent stopwatch. It smashed against the wall and broke into pieces. The room was dead silent – and then he chewed us out some more.

We were all stunned. No one knew what to do or say. After an awkward moment of silence, Coach Sinicki told the position players and starting pitcher to go back out to the field to get ready. Our other pitchers didn't appear at the field until the game had already started. They got yelled at for another 20 minutes in the locker room.

We had no prayer of winning the second game. We were so demoralized and shaken up that we felt totally numb on the field as we yet *again* blew a lead and lost a very winnable game.

CHAPTER 21

About five to six days before every game, I got into the pattern of checking weather.com. It was like waiting for my grades to load up on a webpage. The anticipation would kill me. Seeing 80 degrees with sun was like seeing an "A." But when that D in Spanish popped up it was just devastating. On the Monday before Albany, the beginning of conference play, the weather forecast listed highs of 40 with snow showers and clouds. It was worse than a D. This was an F.

Our first game at Albany was set for 3 p.m. Friday and, being only two hours away, we made the drive Friday morning. Part of me loved being able to take a nap on the cozy and warm bus, but it made getting changed into my uniform and transforming into "game mode" very difficult. As the bus pulled up to Albany's field, I gathered my bag and snack bar and stepped off into a wall of frozen air. It felt like we had entered Dante's frozen 9th circle of hell. I was amazed at how similar Albany's campus looked to that of Binghamton's. It had a similarly boring field, plain buildings and a cold climate!

Thankfully, our coaches let us hit indoors before our game as no one wanted to be outside any longer than necessary.

I wasn't in the lineup which was bad enough. But it meant I would have to sit in the dugout all game and freeze. I had six layers on when the game started – my cold-gear Under Armour, Under Armour t-shirt, Nike long-sleeve t-shirt, jersey, fleece, and then my jacket. I also had on my winter hat on top of my ball cap and two pairs of batting gloves. This was my outfit for four games.

As I sat freezing on the bench, I couldn't help but think of the long term damage caused by keeping me out of the lineup. The year before I felt as if I was given the at bats I needed in order to learn from my early failures and to understand how to correct them. Without a healthy portion of at bats my sophomore year, I feared that I would not get the opportunity to further develop my hitting to the next level. Without someone investing the time in me to learn, to fail, and to help me develop, I just couldn't see how I would ever get to the place I wanted to be as a hitter.

With Coach Collins long gone, I felt like I had *no one* backing me up. It seemed that any mistake I made was counted against me twice while I watched others go 1-for-10 with no consequences. As I stood shivering in the dugout that day, I sensed that if I stayed at Binghamton there were going to be many, many more games where I would be freezing on the bench wondering what the heck went so wrong.

I was the odd man out. Two freshmen were playing the outfield, causing me a log jam. As I said many times, they were both excellent ballplayers, but I was good too. If I couldn't compete at the level, I figured I wouldn't have constantly been asked to pinch-hit on a moment's notice in key situations.

The coaches never stopped playing me entirely. At times throughout my career I became a starter due to injuries or slumps and in some spurts I would play as much as 75% of the games. Still, time and time again someone would regain his health or complete his penalty time off for slumping or there would be an influx of lefties, and my playing time would once again be cut.

I truly believe that if I was given 100, 75 or even 50 at bats in a row I would have much more quickly become the hitter that I eventually became late in my career. But without someone really investing in me, getting that chance was not a possibility. It was a textbook Catch-22: I didn't get the at bats because I wasn't a great college hitter, but I wasn't a great college hitter because I didn't get the at bats. Thus, the self-fulfilling prophecy became a reality.

Albany had no answer for us in the "ice bowl series" and dropped four in a row. We walked all over them and boarded the bus laughing all of the way. We could only hope we saw them again in the playoffs. On paper there wasn't one aspect of the game in which they were better than us in. On paper...

By mid April I only had 18 at bats in 22 games. I was stressed out about my classes and had very little time to enjoy myself. Being out on the field was supposed to be my enjoyment, but it was just the opposite. The field was where I was feeling the most anguish. I had no one to vent to except my dad and my computer. I poured my heart out on paper, trying to cope with everything. I felt alone. I didn't have time for a girlfriend and even though Quinn and I would *always* talk, I still felt alone.

My heart was hurting. It scared me to see my passion wane even just a little bit. It was disheartening to watch the season unfold. It seemed impossible that I would ever truly enjoy baseball again.

A snowstorm arrived, eliminating a mid-week game in which I was slated to start against Siena. As I heard the news I broke down. It took a big hit out of me internally as every break seemed to be turning the wrong way. It was so hard to believe in myself without my coaches believing in me, and I was still too young and inexperienced to generate the confidence from within. I felt my foundation crumbling.

One bad thought led to another, so I immediately focused on the fact that I was not placed on a summer team yet. Most guys got placed early in the fall, when the majority of summer teams filled their roster slots. This was April, and I had nowhere to go. Quinn and Kyle Klee, both Collins' recruits as well, were also summer-league homeless.

There was no possible way to ignore what was happening to my recruiting class. Tom Carberry and Bobby Warner were gone. Junior college transfer Mike Papili and Jeff Wertepney (both Collins recruits), Michael Quinn, Kyle Klee and I were all getting buried deeper each day. The only Collins guy thriving was 6"6" lefty Jeff Dennis. It is tough to bury a 6"6" lefty with a good fastball and curveball and a winning temperament. They later tried and failed, and Jeff had a terrific college career.

During the snowstorm Kyle Klee and I went to eat at the nearby Texas Roadhouse. In the parking lot before dinner, we discussed transferring and how both of our fathers were outraged about how we were being treated. Guys who came into the program after my sophomore year had no idea how they treated Kyle before their arrival, and I am sure they would have difficulty believing that our future captain actually had this talk with me. Nonetheless, before injuries and the exodus of Sinicki's older recruits, Kyle was going through a similar story as the rest of us Collins' recruits.

CHAPTER 22

My saving grace was a volunteer coach who joined the Bearcat staff at exactly the right time for me. Assistant Coach Edward Folli came aboard my sophomore year. He was recently retired from his teaching/coaching job at a local high school and wanted to be part of the program. He threw batting practice for the Binghamton Mets in the summer, but in the spring he spent a lot of his free time with us.

Coach Folli is one of the top two coaches I have ever had. (Biff Schumitz from my hometown is right up there). Both of these guys should have been professional coaches. They understood "it." The respect the entire team had for Coach Folli was amazing. He earned every ounce of it with a seemingly effortless style. The man taught me a lot about baseball and life in very short amount of time.

Folli got paid a total of $0. He was simply a volunteer. The man loved baseball and his love for the game was contagious. The passion and care he gave to me on the field was invaluable. He probably doesn't realize the impact he had on me, but he taught me so much more than just hitting. By example, he showed me the importance of having a good attitude and of treating every day on the field as a blessing.

If I do become a coach or manager, I will do my best to model myself after him. I just watched him every day and noticed how happy he was to be on a baseball field. It made everyone else, including me, happy.

He instilled the confidence in me that I had trouble finding. He showed me how to enjoy the game when I hated everything about it. I could be wrong, but I truly believe he knew how good I was and how screwed at times I was getting. Of course he could not say anything like that to me, but I always got this feeling that he was really happy for me whenever I succeeded. He was always so positive and encouraging. It wasn't fake rah-rah posturing. It was real. There was never a panic attack or temper tantrum from him. He was honest and respectful. And he knew a ton about the game.

Unfortunately, he had little influence on the lineup, on how practices were set up or the team dynamics established by coaches Sinicki and Hurba. I am sure that if he had been head coach, the Binghamton program would have truly excelled. It seemed that everything he touched turned to gold.

After two midweek games were canceled due to snow (no longer a shocker for me), we headed a few hundred miles south to play conference foe UMBC. Thankfully, by the time we got to Maryland there was no more white stuff.

Our Friday game deviated from our original plan for a blowout, but we hung on for a 4-3 victory. I sat on the bench until once again I was asked to pinch-hit – this time in the 7th inning of a one-run game. Having 10 days off in a row without an at bat was a death sentence for me and my pinch hit at bat did not end with the result I was looking for. The first pitch, a fastball away, was called for strike one. Then I swung at a decent curve for strike two and finished my bat off by missing on a dirty curveball. I was angry, but in the 9th inning I righted the ship and hit a solid line drive base hit. I was still above water, if just barely.

Saturday was a doubleheader. I sat out game one and sank lower. I wasn't sure how much more my foundation could take without cracking. As I stared out at the field between games, Coach Folli took me aside. I don't know if he saw the pain in my eyes, but he took me to a private area and talked to me man-to-man. He told me very calmly that the "old regime" was out and that players like me wouldn't "rot on the bench" as we had been. He said that he knew what was going on, and he was fighting for guys like Klee and me.

Never once in my four years did Sinicki or Hurba really talk to me like that and help me understand the situation at hand. The communication I needed was not there. Folli respected me enough to talk to me and for that I am eternally grateful.

I started in game two. In my first at bat I ripped a fastball to right for a single. All game I hit the ball hard. I played game four on Sunday as well, this time in front of my dad, Kathy, Eric, Jaclyn, Mom and Bob. I smashed the ball.

I don't think that getting hot directly after Folli's speech was an accident. I felt so light and free at the plate and had this extra confidence. Even with a lefty in the game, I ripped the ball all day long. I did what I had visualized all year. I was relaxed and got good fastballs to hit. I kept it simple and as a result I had the best weekend of the short season.

CHAPTER 23

Timing is a funny thing.

On Saturday night after the UMBC doubleheader, my dad and I went out to eat. Before we went into the restaurant, however, we sat in the car and talked about the season. He then handed me a large manila folder. It was just like in the movies where two politicians pass along a secret packet of papers in an abandoned parking lot.

On the cover was the word "Transfer." He had gathered all of the papers and information on transferring as well as possible options for me to explore. At this point there was no rule that would have forced me to sit out a year (as long I didn't transfer to another America East school and as long as Sinicki OK'd my release), so I was taking the situation very seriously.

Every point my dad brought up was correct. There was no way I could have argued against the fact that at Binghamton I was always going to be fighting an uphill battle. But timing is a funny thing.

Out of all the days to go over this, my dad chose the very day that Folli had talked to me. From his speech and my day's play, I was convinced things were going to be different. I was confident I was going to start playing a lot more. I knew that our designated hitter, Jeff Wertepny, was graduating along with starting right fielder Jeff Monaco. The other reserves were fairly weak, and I was somewhat sure there were an ample amount of slots opening up next year.

Any other day that year I probably would have said, "Yes, I am leaving." But this wasn't any other day, and I wasn't in the same mental state as the day before or, as it turned out, shortly thereafter. My dad couldn't have picked a worse time to bring up transferring.

I didn't want to leave my friends, my school, and my life. I was feeling good about baseball (for the first time all season!), and so I took the folder and kind of placed the thought of transferring way back in my mind. If I had just gone 0-for-4 or if Folli hadn't talked to me.... I really don't think I would have graduated two years later from Binghamton University.

After UMBC the season went into ultra-drive. Going into our home series against Hartford, we were 9-2 in conference play. The weeks of school were just flying by. We would get home late Sunday night and, before we knew it, it was Thursday and either travel day or pregame day. It was hard to believe it was May.

Hartford was once again at the bottom of the standings, and these were important games for us to take. After I had committed to Binghamton, I visited BU to watch a game against Hartford. The players looked so much older and bigger then. The game looked faster. As we took the field for pregame that weekend, I realized how natural it was to look at the next level and be intimidated. When I was in 8th grade, I felt the same intimidation watching high school games. Everything looked so daunting. But now being on the field felt natural. Thinking that the Hartford Hawks could ever have made me uneasy was comedic.

I went 1-for-10 against Hartford.

It had nothing to do with "intimidation," however, and, in fact, it was probably the most valuable 1-for-10 in my career. For the first time in over a year, I got 10 at bats in one weekend. After a double in my first at bat, they peppered me with breaking balls low and away. Even the fastballs were kept off the plate. I couldn't make the adjustment to sit soft and away and perished as a result.

I was not yet advanced enough as a hitter to see either how they were pitching me or to figure out how to deal with this knowledge during the game. But if nothing else, I got 10 at bats to start to figure this all out. After failing for nine straight at bats, something in my brain said, "You moron, they are killing you with the same pitch. It is time to make an adjustment."

As obvious as it sounds now, without grounding out five times in a row I just couldn't see the pattern. Furthermore, not only did I begin to see these patterns in action, but I also got my timing back. Every strikeout and soft groundout on a low and away change-up taught me that much more about what adjustments I needed to make.

I needed the 10 at bats. My season really took off right after the Hartford series (in which we won all four games). It was not an accident. I had finally gotten the reps I had been begging for. Even though I had a bad weekend, I was feeling upbeat after the Hartford series. Our team was performing well, and I thought good things were to come.

The next Tuesday we played at Le Moyne College, in Syracuse. It was dark and cloudy, and all morning I feared the skies would open up. Thank goodness they never did. In an offensive, bloodthirsty, no-holds-barred match, we lost 21-16!

Le Moyne's field was small, and balls flew out of the place left and right. I did not have any home runs, but I did have a 4-for-4 day. Again, I truly don't think the timing was an accident. After my talk with Coach Folli *and* those 10 at bats against Hartford, I felt at peace in the batter's box. Everything I hitting was hard and in a hole. It boosted my spirits. It was especially gratifying getting two of those hits against a lefty who in high school had dominated me.

All of our pitchers got hit hard at Le Moyne, but for Gino Offerman it was the last straw. Coach Sinicki came to take him out after he allowed all three batters he faced to safely reach first base. Coming off his disastrous BYU performance, Gino was all but done. Coach patted him lightly on the butt as Gino made his last walk off the mound. He never pitched another inning as a Bearcat.

CHAPTER 24

I had been working out in the weight room fairly hard all spring, determined to maintain as much strength as possible because inevitably as the season waned I would lose some body mass. Every winter I tried to put on as much weight as possible because I knew that in the spring the combination of not lifting as much, being on the field for 10 hours some days, and not eating well on the weekends would cause me to lose at least 10 pounds. The primary purpose of in-season lifts became simply to minimize weight loss. I would stretch, run, and then lift. It was an intensive workout, but I was sure my body could handle it. Seeing my spike in play lately, I became more convinced that my regimen was working.

It was a Thursday afternoon and I was feeling good. I had just done some squats when all of a sudden I felt some tightness in my lower back. I went down for a stretch and POP!

A loud noise resonated from my lower back and immense pain shot through my body. I went into paralysis for a moment. I knew it was bad the second I tried to move again. Immediately the thought crossed my mind that I was out for the weekend series vs. Stony Brook.

I hobbled to the trainers' room and lay down in pain. I was depressed and upset as I couldn't believe the lack of luck I was having. How could this happen after I just got into the lineup and started mashing the ball?

I went to see coach. I tried to downplay the injury, but I knew it was bad. Once I was convinced that I was out of commission, I quickly called my dad after practice. The injury was similar to others I had suffered periodically throughout my career, and I thought he could help. Before I started lifting and stretching, I would pull my back out about once every two years. Ever since I started intense training and prehabilitation though, my back had held up fine. This was just a bad break at a horrible time.

The first night after the freak injury was one of the most painful of my life. I got an hour of sleep, and when I woke I thought it was about 11 a.m. It was only 5:30. During the weekends' games I could barely get off the bench to congratulate my teammates.

We won the first game 3-0, but lost both games on Saturday. In the first game, we had only one hit, which came with two outs in the last inning to break up a no-hitter. We did not fare much better in the second game. We saw righties the whole weekend, and I had to sit on the bench barely able to move.

Thankfully, though, it was the worst injury in my four years. I was blessed. To miss one weekend in four years was pretty damn good.

I dressed Sunday and took a few swings, but my back was still killing me and I did not play. I took off a full week from baseball and spent most of my time lightly stretching or getting rehab in the training room, pretty much doing anything to get back on to the field. I had a doctor massage it out. I iced it. I stimulated it. I heated it. I put Ben-Gay on it. I took Aleve, and I used a back brace.

Thankfully the next weekend was our "bye" weekend from conference play so there was no pressure to rush back. We were playing New Jersey Tech in a four-game series at home. NJIT was 11-20, a new Division I team, and ripe for the picking.

I was cleared to practice on Thursday, which gave me two days to get ready. It was like boot camp trying to prepare in such a short time period. I also had finals coming up so I had to really budget my time well to assure that my grades would not fall. It became so difficult finding time to study, practice *and* rehab that it almost caused me to miss my managerial accounting final.

The exam was on Thursday night. I had just gotten rehab and somewhere in the process, I had forgotten the test. I went up to the dining hall after treatment and got a nice meal. I was chomping on a burger when all of a sudden I got this feeling that I was forgetting something. From that moment of realization until I was seated at the exam took less than four minutes. I sprinted across campus at full speed (or as fast as I could run with my back still hurting) and made it to the classroom only 20 minutes into the exam. I got an A.

NJIT was a lefty haven. They had three lefty starters (and many more southpaws in the bullpen), and even though I didn't start any of those games, we did such a number on them the first two games that I got in as a substitute. My first at bat I hit a hanging curve for a base hit. I was back.

We won three of four, and I had another very solid outing. The good games were now far outnumbering the bad ones. Things were clicking.

Even better, with the weekends' games school was officially over! There was still one more weekend of games before the tournament, but I was now halfway done with my higher level of education. With school being over, I didn't mind having to make the great eight-hour hour trek up to Maine. We were already playoff bound at 15-4, so a split of the four games would guarantee us the No. 1 seed.

Without classes I enjoyed every single second of the trip. I watched movies and read books and was surprisingly entertained. Before I knew it we were in Maine – in the middle of a downpour. The bad weather had followed us once again.

It rained. And it rained. And then it rained some more. We sat in our hotel Thursday night, most of Friday and almost all of Saturday. We never got on the field.

Maine was an outlier for the America East in terms of facilities, having by far the nicest baseball complex in the conference. Their field was a true stadium, a rarity in the America East, with a clubhouse and even a patio for fans down the third base line. Maine had the feel of an Atlantic Coast Conference program, but the Bears' 20-26 record (11-8 in America East) was a huge disappointment for them. They were fighting for their playoff lives.

I suppose they needed these superior facilities to recruit because of their extreme weather, but the fact is Maine did it right. The school even had an entire indoor bubble for live batting practice. It also had a batting cage with a screen that simulated an actual pitch. The screen would show the pitcher going through his motion and at his release point, a real ball came out. It was a cool little toy.

So instead of playing games, Friday and Saturday consisted of baseball practice in a bubble. At any other America East school we would have been in a hotel room, so we considered ourselves lucky. The bubble quickly brought back memories of indoor winter workouts when I played AAU travel ball where we would have unnecessarily long five-hour practices in cold, poorly-lit bubbles. Maine's bubble, however, did give Kyle Klee an opportunity to hit one of the most amazing balls of all time. From a tee 75 yards out, Kyle hit the ball right into a garbage pail on the other side of the bubble. It would have been hard to accomplish this feat by accident, but we were actually trying to hit it into the pail. A one in a million shot!

Finally the rain subsided, and we managed to get onto the field. My dad and Kathy had come to see me play, and I feared this would be Norfolk State all over again.

We battled hard in game one but lost 5-4. As I was on the bench, my dad and Kathy decided to leave halfway through the game because they both had to get home for work on Monday. After spending days up in Maine, they had never gotten to see me play. At that point I was so bummed that I didn't even care about playing in the second game.

The funny part of my sporadic playing time however was how I was managing to stay locked in despite everything. In my first time up in game two, I worked the count to 3-1. Then, on my first swing of the weekend, I got a flat fastball and hit a deep home run to right field.

After being treated so poorly all year, it felt great to round the bases and shake Sinicki's hand at third base. Of course, all of the other parents called my parents to tell them that I hit a home run. I am sure it was bittersweet for my dad when he heard the news.

We won the game 5-3. I was 3-for-4 with two runs and an RBI. We were now 15-6 in conference play and rolling into the playoffs. We still had two games left vs. Maine, but if we won the first game, we would clinch first place and get to go home early. We were one game away from our first regular season title.

We had been in Maine since Thursday. Now it was Monday. Every other team was done playing so the playoff scenarios were black and white. If we won one, we'd clinch the No. 1 seed and Maine would be the No 4 (1 plays 4). If we lost both, we'd be the No. 2 seed and Maine would be the No. 3 (2 plays 3). No matter what happened, we were going to play Maine on Thursday in the playoffs.

Maine threw another lefty, so I never got into the game. No matter how hot I was, all the other team had to do was throw a lefty, any lefty, and I would be pulled.

Nonetheless, we won 3-1 off a stellar pitching performance by junior Gio Yannuzzi. We needed to set up our playoff pitching, so it was only Gio's second start of the season. He did a fantastic job, striking people out left and right with a 78 MPH loopy curveball. It was devastating.

We were regular season champions at 17-5. The bus ride home was full of happiness and excitement.

As good as the bus ride felt, being a regular season champion in a mid-level conference was like winning the "best effort" award in first grade. It felt good but it didn't mean much. The only way to make it to the NCAA Regionals was to win the conference tournament.

Also, there was no playoff advantage resulting from our championship. The No. 1 seed was supposed to get to host the tournament – the conference's "reward" for being best in the regular season. The major stipulation, however, was that the team hosting the tournament had to have either have a lighted field or access to a lighted facility nearby. We had neither because the Binghamton Mets were playing a home series at NYSEG Stadium that weekend. We were ineligible to host the tournament.

If the No. 1 seed was ineligible, it fell to the second seed. I know this isn't an issue that Virginia and North Carolina face, but being up north the plain fact is that many programs did not have Division I quality fields. I always thought there should be a major stipulation that to call yourself a Division I baseball program, you had to commit to having Division I facilities. For example, a team would have 10 years from when it became Division I to build a stadium approved by a panel before its construction.

No such rules exist, however, so Stony Brook (the #2 seed) got to host the tournament. It didn't have a field with lights either, so instead we had to travel four hours to Long Island to play *near* Stony Brook. And with only four teams in the playoffs, the difference between No. 1 and No. 4 was minimal. We truly had no advantage being the top seed.

We got back from Maine early Tuesday morning. We got to sleep as quickly as possible, got up, ate, lifted, and had a light workout before packing again to leave for Long Island at 5 p.m. Instead of having all of Tuesday to relax at home with a light practice on our own field, we had to drive to Long Island and get ready to play in an unfamiliar stadium. Lastly, we lost our 10th man, the Bearcat fans – all because our field didn't have lights.

CHAPTER 25

The trip to Farmingdale (Long Island) started off badly. It was a hot day, and on short notice, the only bus we could get was a mini. Everyone had to double up. The AC was non-existent, so it was painfully hot and sticky on the bus. To top it off, the traffic turned a four-hour drive into a six-hour trip.

Every team at the tournament was given one hour of practice time on Wednesday. It pretty much limited us to having batting practice, and getting a very brief feel for the way the field would play. Farmingdale, a Division 3 team, had a newly-built turf field with a stadium capacity of 1,000 and brand new lights. It would have made many Division 1 programs proud. Neither Binghamton, Albany nor Stony Brook (all State University of New York schools) had fields half as nice.

The America East put us up in a Hilton. It was a tradition for the conference to host a banquet the night before the tournament started, and we gathered in the hotel's banquet hall for a well-earned feast. It was a classy act and showed the teams a little bit of appreciation for all of their hard work. All four teams gathered for dinner and a presentation of the yearly awards.

It hurt a little watching guys win awards and knowing under the right circumstances, I at least would have made a hard bid for some recognition. I had to keep my emotions in check though and focus on the upcoming game. It was nice, however, to see our first baseman, Brendan Hitchcock win player of the year after hitting a whopping .366.[7]

Hitchcock was one of the best pure hitters I ever saw. In his four years he hit .305, .399, .366, and finally .366. He also happened to be one of the best defensive first basemen to come through the program. Brendan didn't have a natural position though as according to professional scouts, he did not have the power for first base nor the speed for the outfield. Hitchcock never got drafted. It was a shame. Our coaches did not have a lot of contacts to help him, and he kind of got pushed aside.

Hitchcock was not a big power hitter and to demand that he become one went against everything he stood for as a hitter. His approach was the most advanced I had ever seen first hand. I believe at another school he would have been a solid 20th-40th round pick. At Binghamton, he was just another really good player not to get drafted.

Still, he taught me more about hitting than any other teammate. If anyone wanted to listen to him, he would quickly understand why Hitchcock always hit for a high average. He was constantly one step ahead of the pitcher. People would watch his lackluster batting practices and mistake him for a lackluster hitter. He was always working and fine tuning his swing and approach in practice. Without fail, he got the job done.

We were due to play Maine at noon. The tournament was double elimination, but we would come to find out over the next three years that really it was a "who can go 2-0" tournament. If you went 2-0, the tournament was all but yours. At 2-0 it meant that a team that had already lost would have to play in the morning to get to the championship series. If it won that game, it would play the 2-0 team at night. If it somehow won that game, the team would have to beat the same team *again* the next day using its "fifth starter" and a weary bullpen. Go 2-0, and you were likely the champion.

Playoff baseball is intense. Every pitch matters. Every moment can change the outcome. Whether it is a Little League game, an All-Star game, a conference championship game, or a World Series game, everything matters. It is the ultimate stage, and the most fun to play in.

Unfortunately for me, Maine was throwing another lefty. I knew the night before that I was going to be a sub. At least it allowed me to prepare for a potential pinch-hit appearance. The playoffs were no time to be selfish.

We fell behind 1-0 in the top of the first inning but responded with a run in the bottom half. Zach Groh and Greg Lane then shut down the Black Bears the rest of the way, and we posted a convincing 9-3 victory.

At night we watched Albany play Stony Brook. We had already beaten Albany four times, but Stony Brook scared us. Our prayers were answered with a win by the Great Danes, and we were set to play Albany. How much easier could this get for us?

After hitting well the second half of the season, I got the start in the biggest game of the season. Every playoff game that goes down to the wire has turning points. The turning point of this game came in the top of the second. Kyle Klee was on third base, I was on second, and Pat Haughie was at the plate. He got a fat fastball and punished it. The ball was clearly leaving the park; the only question was whether it would be fair or foul.

As it sailed over the fence, it swept ever so slightly into foul territory. The umpire hollered "foul." Instead of a huge inning, we got only one run. At the time it didn't seem important, but it was a huge play. It is indeed a game of inches.

In the third we put up three more runs and were in control at 4-1. I was looking clueless at the plate, struggling to find my timing. I wish I could have put just one or two more balls hard in play.

Up 7-2 going into the bottom of the eighth, we were starting to feel very confident. After starting pitcher Mike Van Gorder gave us five solid innings, reliever Murphy Smith was continuing the mastery of the Albany hitters. Even when they scored a run in the eighth we were still very confident entering the last inning.

We were just three outs away from the victory. It seemed a mere formality.

Murphy was rolling and looked to easily have three more outs left in his right arm. However, coach decided to go with our more experienced closer, Khalid Afify. As I watched Khalid's warmup pitches, it looked as if his usual high 80s fastball was clocking in at about 83. I think he had some arm issues he was concealing, but to even a casual observer it was fairly obvious he was not throwing well.

After Khalid recorded the first out, though, my concern quickly turned to joy. Some of the guys in the dugout were joking about warming up the "V's." Instead of shaking hands after a victory, we would form a V with our fingers and tap the tips of each others V's. It became known as the "V's."

The next batter struck out swinging. Two outs. Our closer was on the mound, a pitcher who had a 5-1 record and six saves. We were up 7-3. This game was over.

Except it wasn't.

Konstanty was the first to strike. He slammed a fastball over the left field fence. Khalid laughed off the home run. Not because he didn't care, but because that's how he dealt with adversity. And he certainly thought – as we all did – that the run was meaningless. No run ever is.

Wood was up next, and grounded to third. Kyle Klee had a cannon for an arm. It was usually accurate, but once in a while a ball would float on him. Kyle scooped up a routine ground ball and firmly tossed the ball over to first base for what on any other night would have been the final out. This ball had just a little too much on it, though, and was just out of Hitchcock's reach. Wood was safe at first.

Barbato singled. Corvino singled. Now I was starting to panic. But no one was warming up in our bullpen. Khalid was shot, but our coach was sticking with him. The bases were loaded with two outs. The tying run was now at first. We all feared a grand slam.

I remember the pitch so vividly. It was in slow motion. I heard the ping of the bat and saw the stitches making contact with the metal alloy of the barrel. For a split second the ball was frozen on the sweet spot of the bat. Then, boom – everything went back into normal time.

The ping was so loud you just knew the ball was headed for the deep parts of the outfield. The only question was whether it had enough juice to make it over the fence. The ball finally landed a few feet short of the fence but in no man's land. Three runs crossed the plate. We were now tied, and Khalid was still in the game.

We decided to walk Hill to face Donovan. I could hardly believe what I was witnessing. When the next pitch was laced up the middle for a game-ending, walk off base hit, I just continued to stare in disbelief. Game over.

The Great Danes stormed the field. We were shell-shocked.

I sat on the bench for 20 minutes. Coach had to yell at me to leave the field and get on the bus. My mom and dad had nothing to say when I saw them outside the field. What could they say?

Our season was still technically not over but it sure felt like it was. We would have to now show up in the morning and beat Maine. Then we'd have to try to beat Albany again in order to survive until Sunday, where we would have to beat Albany yet again.

The bus was silent on the way back to the hotel. It was only a game, but on that night it felt as painful as anything as I had ever experienced.

The night still had one more eventful incident, however. All of the restaurants in town were closed, so we ordered pizza from Domino's, which then had the 5,5,5 deal — three or more pizzas for $5 each. We ordered a whole bunch of pizzas and bread sticks. The bill should have been about $40, but when the delivery man arrived he handed me a bill for about $65.

I argued that the bill was wrong, but the man told me I had to call the store to argue. I was already outraged and overtired from the game, and decided to take my anger out on Domino's. I called and yelled at the manager for 10 minutes until he conceded and sent back the delivery man, who I yelled at for five minutes more. I feel awful to this day about my temper tantrum, but it did help get my anger out. And I got free bread sticks! My friends still make fun of me to this day about the "Domino's Incident."

CHAPTER 26

We walked all over Maine on Saturday morning. The 13-4 romp was the program's record 28th win of the season.

We now had 6-foot-6 lefthander Jeff Dennis going against Albany. I had no doubt he would rise to the occasion, and I was right. Jeff was brilliant. He gave us six strong innings with only one earned run.

Greg Lane gave us the last three innings without surrendering a run. The Albany lineup looked clueless at the plate. The only problem was that we were doing even less with the bats than they were.

I was back on the "do not play" list. After a poor performance against Albany the previous evening I pretty much knew I wasn't going to be in the lineup on Saturday. As the game progressed, however, the coaches told me to stay loose and be ready for a late-inning at bat.

I got my call to lead off the top of the ninth inning. We were down 1-0, three outs from elimination. The first pitch was an outside slider. As a pinch-hitter, I always swung early in the count. First because I hated getting down in the count, but also because pitchers always wanted to get ahead of pinch-hitters and thus left way too many balls over the plate.

I took a clean cut at the slider and roped it into left center. I got out of the box quickly and was thinking double right away. My legs felt heavy as I trucked down the line. As the ball was coming in to second I tried to kick my body into turbo-drive but was shocked to find the tank empty.

The throw came in a split second before I arrived at the bag. I was out. I jogged off the field, mortified.

It was the right decision to go for two. The kid made a great throw. I was disgusted about the base-running, but it didn't escape my mind that I once again came off the bench cold and ripped the ball. Joe Charron, who was up next, hit a triple, so we still had a runner at third base with one out.

Pat Haughie came up after that. Pat was a terrific leader and great captain, but he struggled at the plate his senior year. He led our team in strikeouts with 40 (The next highest was 30). All we needed was a sacrifice fly. We didn't pinch-hit for him, though, and he once again struck out. So too did Smucker after a Henry Dunn walk – and just like that our season was done.

We watched Albany celebrate. After beating them four straight times in the regular season, they had come back and shocked us twice. It was a crushing loss that took a long time to recover from. I think it took Coach Sinicki at least two years, if in fact he ever got over the loss.

It was crushing to see our seniors cry after the game. They were done. It was a fantastically talented class, and they deserved a championship. Sinicki broke down in tears. We were losing a lot of talent, and I wasn't too sure that there would be another chance to get to a Regional in the next two years. My chance might have just slipped by for good.

The great thing about being a fan is that when your team wins you get to celebrate. It also means that if your team loses a heartbreaker, you can shut off the TV and go on with your life. For the players, there is no remote control to shut off the loss. We were still hours from home and still needed to go back to Binghamton to get our end of the year administrative tasks done.

I could hardly believe my sophomore year was over. To come that close and fail hurt so much. It was easy to analyze the game and season and second guess the decisions, but I knew it would not change the outcome. I had to move on and take the positives from the experience. I had overcome a great deal of adversity and managed to get back up every time I fell. I managed to hit over .300 and really thought I had solidified myself as an everyday player. I was wrong.

Our tears turned to cheers and smiles when we got to Binghamton. It wasn't that we were feeling any better about the loss, but we also knew that we had only one more night together. We decided to celebrate great memories and even better friends. We drank hard and long at the baseball house. We took shots at the bar. We drank more when we got back to the house. The party even poured onto the streets, where we played touch football into the wee hours of the morning.

Afterward, Quinn, Jeff, and I went back to the dorms and talked outside until the sun came up. All of the other students had already gone home for the summer, so the dorms were ours to roam. Looking at the campus in the summer gave me a weird feeling. It was so empty and quiet.

Like the sun that had just risen, college was cyclical, full of ups and downs. As I decided to call it a night at 8 a.m., I couldn't help but think that my days were slowly counting down.

Three hours later, I had my coaches meeting.

It went well. Too well. I hate to say that they intentionally lied to me, but they certainly put a nice coating on not only the season but also on my future. They talked. I listened. And for the most part, I naively believed. I had no reason not to. When I left the meeting, I thought that everything was great.

With hindsight, it was clear in my coaches' minds that I was going to be a "part time starter." I was a solid hitting lefty off the bench who could start when someone was hurt, ineligible, sick, or simply hitting badly. The coaches began their speech by saying how even though I had started slowly, they were impressed by how I had turned it on at the end.

As they talked, I was thinking, "This is total bullcrap." Their scenario just wasn't reality. The fact is that I had a paltry 20 at bats spread out over the first month plus. I got squeezed. I only started "slow" because I was getting two at bats a weekend.

I am *not* making excuses for failing to crush the ball the first half of the year, but for them to just say I had a slow start and leave it at that was ridiculous. Once I got consistent playing time, I started to heat up. I am not saying I deserved to play every inning of every game, but it should have been obvious to me that they were *never* going to give me the chance I needed to get to be the everyday player I knew I could be.

From the UMBC series on, I hit .384. With Coach Folli's support, some injuries throughout the team and a hot streak when some of the other players were in slumps, I finally got the playing time I needed. I was the perfect gap player. They were in dire need of a hot bat in the lineup, so I was given the chance. If our other DH hadn't slumped, I don't think I ever would have gotten the opportunity to hit like I did the second half of the year. Next season proved this point all too well.

If I had been told the truth in that meeting, I would have never returned to Binghamton. I had just come off a great half-season and finished the year playing a lot. I was totally confident I was ready to really shine. Things ended so well that I almost assumed that I would finally be given a starting role.

How could I have been so blind and ignorant as to ignore Coach Hurbas's new recruiting class?

After the meeting I packed up my car, cleaned out my locker, said my goodbyes and drove home. My dorm days were over, or so I thought. I still did not have a summer team so I just drove home. I had nowhere to go. I was on standby until my coaches could place me somewhere.

For 10 days I just chilled out at home. Finally my coaches called and said they had found a spot for me in the New York Collegiate Baseball League. The Vermont team needed an outfielder. I was headed for Bennington, population of about 36,000. It was a cozy little New England town filled with old Victorian homes and bed and breakfasts. Not much of anything ever happened there.

My summer life revolved around tiny Southern Vermont College, enrollment of about 450 students. The entire school was located in a mansion. It looked out on a gorgeous view of the famous Green Mountains. It was a spectacular place to visit for an afternoon. For a summer, not so much.

The day I arrived (one day before the season was to start), the field looked like an overgrown, abandoned downtown park. Weeds were everywhere. Mounds of sand were piled high where first base should have been. The dugouts were half-completed. There were no bleachers and no pitcher's mound.

Southern Vermont College was not exactly a baseball powerhouse. That year's team went 1-11! Our coach was SVC's head coach – a great guy, but definitely better at drinking beer than coaching baseball.

Our field started out as a mess and only got worse. We had yet another cheap GM, so the infield was made out of sand, as compared to the standard clay infields. After constant complaining from the team, the GM finally put clay on the field. The only problem was that he never took the sand off. When it rained, the sand and clay clumped together and made the field unplayable.

It was quite embarrassing when the other team had to get back on the bus and go home. I am sure our seven fans weren't too happy either.

What looked at first to be a disastrous summer, however, turned out to be a lot of fun. The operations of the NYCBL were shaky, but the level of ball was fairly good. I got to see a ton of lefties, and by the end of the summer I was hitting lefties better than righties. After seeing so many lefties and taking batting practice every day off my friend Tristan Hobbes, another lefty, I was learning to hit them very well.

I also got the treat of playing with a whole bunch of America East players. Even though I had to deal with some Albany guys' stories about the Regional, we still got along great. For the next two years, whenever we played Albany, Vermont, or Maine I had friends to greet. It was a cool little bonus.

We got all the food we wanted, got to hang out in the dorms, and bum around. It was a huge summer for me because I got to lift and got a ton of at bats. I batted third and, after another slow start, turned up the heat. I was hitting lefties and righties alike with authority and learning a bit more each day.

Still, the summer dragged on. Living in a small rural town and playing in other no-name towns wore on me. For two months I lived a life very similar to that of a Minor Leaguer. I would wake up, eat, watch TV, lift or hit, eat and then go play a baseball game. There wasn't much else to do. It is hard to look back now on my "dream summers" of college baseball and ask how I could have ever wished them to end. But I don't live my life in the past. At the time I was tired and wanted to go back to my life. By the end of July I was ready to go home.

Our last game was a road game vs. the Glens Falls Golden Eagles in which I went 3-for-4. I really wanted to end the summer on a hot streak and was thrilled to be going out hitting so well. Still, I couldn't help but laugh after my final at bat. Glen Falls brought in a pitcher from the outfield named Mike Konstanty to pitch the final inning. On a 3-2 pitch with the crowd chanting, I got a soft changeup. It looked at first like a fastball to me, and it wasn't until about half way through my swing that I realized in fact that it was an off-speed pitch. I did a sort of half swing/fall over my flailing body for the final out. It was embarrassing.

It would have been bad enough to end the season on that note. When I found out after the game that Mike Konstanty was the same kid from Albany who threw me out at second base from the outfield in the final game of the tournament, I was not too happy. Even worse, this was the *first* inning he had pitched all summer. I guess he just owned me.

Besides my final at bat however I was feeling good when I left for home. I once again was positive that the upcoming season was going to be special. Soon that dream would turn sour.

PART 3
JUNIOR YEAR

CHAPTER 27

When junior year came around I was a veteran Bearcat. I finally moved out of the dorms and into the infamous baseball house – though it was actually just a floor of an apartment building. The first floor was a restaurant. We inhabited the second floor, lacrosse players the third floor, and Pi Lam, a fraternity, took the top two floors. You could say that there was a decent amount of socializing at this address.

From day one, Jeff Dennis and I wanted to be part of the crew at the "RE." I don't know who named it, but I assume the name comes from the fact that it is located on 23 Henry Street.

The RE was an interesting place to live. Just imagine the ultimate frat house. Our coach hated it so much he claimed he never went inside, even in the summer. I always felt though, that he must have snuck a quick glance inside at least once. He wanted to stay as far away as possible from any trouble and that meant the RE.

Picture an old red brick building with crumbling blocks and huge cracks along the side, with soot from a past fire covering parts of the exterior. Now walk up the rusty fire escape and enter our apartment.

The first units you see as you walk down the hall are the bathrooms. Passed those rooms is the huge common area with a flat screen TV and some random seating arrangement. (We went through about 10 different couches/chairs in my two years.) Fifteen bedrooms surround the common area. Our bedrooms had high ceilings, so we were able to build lofts and sleep "upstairs." I loved climbing up my ladder and crawling into bed on a cold night. Sounds good so far, huh?

The lofts were great, but the RE was a dump! The heating was so poor that whatever temperature it was outside, it was that temperature inside. The trick was to figure out how to get the lights off and still make it up to the loft and under your blankets without getting frostbite. I would hit the lights and, fully clothed, run up to my loft. Once under my four blankets, I would undress.

Some winter mornings I would wake to ice on my windows. It didn't help that the furnace broke for a month during one of the famous Binghamton winters.

Aside from the fact you could hear *everything* your roommate said or did, which sometimes I definitely did not want to hear, the bedrooms were decent. The common areas were not. Our kitchen wouldn't pass an inspection if we spent a week cleaning it. Crud was everywhere; the sinks were clogged (sometimes dead mice were found in them) and there were no working smoke alarms.

I was one of the few brave souls to try to cook pasta in there. We had a great table for "flip cup," though. "Flip cup" is a drinking game in which two sides competed to see who could drink their beer and flip over their cups quickest. It was a great ice breaker when girls were around, and it got you drunk quickly. However, it left one untidy mess. The "flip cup" table also served as our dinner table and food preparation table.

The table also was our backup garbage can when our two actual garbage pails overflowed. However, our maintenance man, Izzy, would come around once a week and make the place appear somewhat habitable. No matter how trashed the place got, Izzy fixed it up just good enough so that we could live there for another few nights and wreck it again.

The bathrooms aren't even worth mentioning. Imagine what the Guantanamo Bay prisoners had. Now imagine that without locks on the doors. Those were our bathrooms.

Thank God the common area carpet was black, because it was the only color that could cover up beer, vomit, tobacco spit, and old

Chinese food. The couches were just an extension of the carpet, but even grosser because you knew that sickening substances were constantly spilled on them and left to rot.

The common room did not have windows, and it always seemed that at least two of the four lights were out. And thank goodness for the dark. Any light would have exposed the true extent of the filth.

The "best" part of the RE was our landlord. His name was Prince. He was Greek and lived in New York City. To manage the building, he hired a firm called SALS. Enron had more accurate accounting records. These guys at SALS had no clue what was going on. They were always getting the tenants' payments wrong. Sometimes they overcharged and sometimes they undercharged. During my senior year they never knew about occupants of a certain room, so they never charged them. It was the worst run business operation I ever saw.

Did I mention how much I loved the RE? I would not trade one moment of my two years living there. We had the place to ourselves with no one to bother us. It was our refuge. I have memory upon memory of hanging out with the guys and just talking baseball. I wasn't a huge drinker, but you could count on at least one or two guys drinking some beers on any given night. It was the team hangout. I got to live with my 15 best friends.

The RE was a disaster, but it was our disaster. It was a quick 10 minutes to campus and a five-minute walk to all of the bars. It was perfect for 15 college baseball players, not to mention an ideal place to have legendary parties.

The RE got a reputation for being party central. And yes we had lots of fun. But so many people (especially the parents) assumed that every night we held a rave. In reality, most nights were fairly quiet. Many people did their work in their rooms behind closed doors. Some guys played a lot of video games, and we chilled out a lot. We got our work done and were responsible (for the most part).

In fact, only a few nights ever got out of control, but if we ever had a game or early practice the next day you could pretty much guarantee that the place was going to be quiet (at least our floor would be).

When Jeff and I moved into the RE in late August, we were ecstatic. Mike Quinn was a bit less animated, but he had nowhere else to live so us dorm guys stuck together. I was thrilled to have my two best friends living with me. We kept joking about the fact that this was *our* place. We were on cloud nine.

My parents helped me move into my new room, and after a nice meal they once again said their goodbyes. It got more routine saying goodbye to them, but not any easier. My dad had given me his old Toyota Highlander for school, and it was an extremely weird feeling seeing my dad drive away with that car still in the parking lot. Times were slowly changing.

Classes began, and once again I was in full swing. School, baseball, lifting.

Being a Division I athlete required a time commitment than extended beyond the playing field. We had the occasional charity event, team meeting, or camp to work that always added to our long list of activities each week. We had just gotten back to school, and on day one we had to report for a prospect camp from 9 a.m. to 3 p.m. We were all tired from the night before, but we survived the day.

I felt bad for the campers. I remembered how just a few years before I was going to these types of "tryouts." It was nothing like playing a real baseball game, and I hated them. I always saw the college players at these camps who looked so comfortable. I was quite envious of them. I so badly wanted to be one of them. Now I was that guy.

Jumping from being a sophomore to being a junior year was a huge leap. One second I was a younger guy on a senior laden team, and suddenly I was a veteran on a freshman heavy team. It was clear that things were different for me this year. More than half of the guys I "grew up" with my first two years at BU were gone. There were a lot of new faces. It was a totally different team, the first one primarily filled with Coach Hurba's guys. It was not something to be ignored as the upcoming season played out.

Hurba had brought in some good talent, but we had lost a lot of talent as well. One of the departed players was junior Scott Diamond, who had recently signed on with the Atlanta Braves. Diamond was highly scouted at Binghamton, and everyone was sure he would be drafted. He never was.

Perhaps it was Diamond's average numbers his junior year that left the scouts less than enthused. Perhaps it was simply pitching for Binghamton, a northeast program that had few connections with the pros. Regardless, when Diamond went south to play summer ball, he was furious with Binghamton. He was seriously considering transferring when late in the summer the Atlanta Braves offered him a generous contract. The little lefty from Canada whom Binghamton couldn't get drafted became a top prospect for the Atlanta Braves and now has a chance to be on the Minnesota Twins 25 man roster.

As I gazed around the room, some very familiar faces were absent. Some very gifted players had graduated and, having gone undrafted, were completely out of the game. What chance did I have of playing at the next level if these talented ballplayers weren't considered good enough? I had seen literally thousands of players in my 15-plus years of baseball, and I knew that some of the players buried in the "non-drafted cemetery" were good enough to at least get a shot in the minors.

BU has managed to get just enough guys drafted or signed (Diamond) that it masks the volume of very talented players who never get signed to professional contracts. A lot of solid ballplayers never had a chance of playing professional baseball from the day they first stepped on to campus. Being an exceptionally good ballplayer was not enough if you went to Binghamton.

Most northeast schools do not have the exposure that southern and western teams get. It was easy to spot the few northeast schools that kept getting guys drafted at a higher rate than the norm. It wasn't just that these schools were recruiting and developing better players. They also had connections. Either the coaching staff knew a lot of scouts or there was some other connection that allowed and/or convinced scouts to draft guys from certain programs.

Just watch a live Major League draft. There are hundreds of late round picks from no-name schools. Recently graduated Binghamton players like Brendan Hitchcock and Matt Simek could have easily been late round picks. Perhaps if they had ended up at larger programs or at least ones with some solid connections things would have turned out differently for them.

I understood that most schools did not have powerful connections with scouts, but it just seemed that so many players at BU slipped through the cracks that something must have been wrong. Looking back now, I see that there were simply too many good ballplayers playing college baseball for every good player to get drafted. And I believe this happens at a lot of places across the country. If you didn't throw 90 MPH or hit 20 home runs in a season, you went by the wayside. Once I started to realize the immense talent pool *worldwide,* I truly began to understand just how tough it is to make it to the Big Leagues. Unless a player is "A-Rod" like, it would be wise to study hard in school, because the chance of an individual being good enough to compete with Robinson Cano at 2nd base is slim to none.

Nonetheless, every fall we had a scout day where some local scouts came by, but it was usually a mere formality. They were there almost always there to see one pitcher. Watching everyone else showcase their skills was a courtesy more than anything else. The don't know how other programs worked, but I saw *so* many players, many of whom I played with, get drafted who I knew weren't as good as some of our undrafted players.

With so many players having departed, there were now only three remaining seniors – captain Ryan James, lefty pitcher Gio Yannuzzi, and 5th-year, co-captain, Zach Groh. Our last captain was Kyle Klee, the kid who a year ago was getting treated like a third-string string walk-on.

Gone along with Scott Diamond and the seniors was sophomore Val Ardini, who was from Virginia. The dreaded Binghamton weather was just too much for him. He said he couldn't fight through another winter and then play baseball games all spring in 40 degree weather. With him went the starting second base job. Justin Smucker graduated, leaving a vacancy at shortstop. There was a dramatic shortage of infielders and veteran players and an abundance of outfielders and underclassmen. Amazingly, they were still considering moving one of our few infielders, Ryan James, to the outfield.

As the fall unfolded, the first inkling that I had been duped creeped into my head. These guys were determined to keep me out of the outfield. Were their plans to also keep me out of the lineup?

As bad of a recipe as it was for me, it was the opposite for Kyle Klee. Another Collins recruit, Klee undoubtedly deserved to be the starting shortstop. Still, he happened to be fortunate to be in a situation where there just weren't a lot of Hurba infielders on the team. He was a terrific ballplayer and deserved every accolade he got, but he also was in the right place at the right time.

Klee was never a vocal leader. He led by example and was a great captain in my eyes. It still amazed me, though, that he was named captain just one year after being taken advantage of to the point that he was considering transferring. The truth was that in his first two years the coaches didn't need him. His junior year they did.

Ryan James was well deserving of the honor of being a captain, but I found it irritating over the years that the coaches picked our captains for us. (I would have voted for Ryan regardless.) I have always thought that being a captain should be an honor determined by peers.

The outfield was stacked with Hurba recruits. Even with star centerfielder Henry Dunn ineligible, there was still a traffic jam. Sophomore Joe Charron was in left, freshman Corey Taylor in center, and freshman Pete Bregartner in right. This was decided in the early fall at the latest. I just failed to recognize it until it was way too late. I was at best a fourth outfielder. My only hope was at DH, but that too proved to be a clogged position.

CHAPTER 28

Entering my junior year I was on a very generous scholarship. Considering that I was an out of state student, I was paying well below the tuition of an in-state student attending Binghamton. Because Scott Diamond had left so late (he signed in August), the coaches still had his scholarship money available. Their solution was to frontload both Kyle and I on scholarship money in our junior years. We both got increases.

Coach said he did this because he knew that we had been around for a while and that we understood that there was no funny business going on. I knew there wasn't any problem with the arrangement, but I also knew that this really wasn't a favor to me or Kyle. It was business. By giving us more money this year, it would free up more money for next year in order for them to spend it on new recruits. It was all about the business of college sports.

The arrangement worked out nicely for me though because the next season there was some extra money left over again. As a result, Coach Sinicki *very generously* gave me more than he was required to. I was getting money to play baseball; it was still very cool.

Even if I never got a dime though, I still would have given the game everything I had. I always knew how important training was. I put in my time in the batting cages and in the weight room to get my body in top physical and mental form. I failed, however, to spend much time training on the track so my 60-yard dash time remained average. It's not that I got slower as time went on, but I never got much faster. There are plenty of factors that caused my time to stagnate right around 7.2, but I always assumed the major factor was my training style.

I definitely sacrificed some flexibility and speed for strength. I know that. I was never a big power hitter, but I believed (accurately) that I needed to continuously train with weights and remain strong if I was going to succeed as a Division I hitter. If that meant losing a few tenths off my 60 time, I thought it was worth the sacrifice. I needed to be as strong as possible to avoid injuries.

Taking steroids does not directly make someone stronger. They help one to train and recover to build the superhuman strength. The reason some professionals took steroids was to get really strong. They realized the benefit of being stronger than the guys next to them.

I never took anything illegal, but I did focus in the off-seasons on getting as strong as possible. I got my squat regimen up to 8-10 reps at 355 pounds. Considering that just two years before I was doing six reps at 185 pounds, it was apparent I was a much stronger and more mature athlete.

The winter following my sophomore season, however, I tried a different training approach. I figured I had nothing to lose and was curious to see what the results would be. I hit less and lifted lighter weights, and I ran a lot more. I got to the point where I would run four or five times a week. And it worked. My speed increased dramatically. I was lighter and faster. I was amazed how much more fluid my sprints became.

However, over the course of the spring and a full 50+ game schedule, I ran less and my form began to slowly break down. With four-hour practices and games it was impossible to keep up my sprinting regimen.

My suspicions were confirmed when I ran 7.2 60-yard dash at tryouts the first day of my junior year. It would have been easier to stomach the slower time if I knew I couldn't do better, but I knew that with proper training I could get my time down to where it needed to be. I had done just that 6 months earlier. It was a crushing blow to know that I had lost all of my newfound speed so quickly.

I knew that with a 7.2 my chances of getting drafted were almost zero. I needed to be under 7. But I could never find it within myself again to train like I had that winter. I felt that even if I did it again, I would see the same results the next fall.

It didn't help that I *hated* running. It was always a grind to get myself to sprint. I loved lifting and obviously hitting, but I had no desire ever to run sprints. It was like doing homework for a subject I despised.

As my subordinate role on the team became increasingly clear, I think I deep down knew that I wasn't going to get drafted. The exposure was simply never going to be there. Yes, I had my summer leagues, but the odds were just not in my favor. And if I wasn't going to get drafted, then why was I going to kill myself in order to shave a paltry two-tenths of a second off my 60-yard dash time? At least that is how I rationalized it.

Given my situation, even running a 6.9 wasn't going to get me drafted. I did a simple cost-benefit analysis and decided it was much smarter to focus my time on hitting and lifting and accept a 7.2.

When I would run for a fly ball or run out of the box for a double, I was quick and free. When I was running a 60, I was slow and tight. Sprinting just wasn't a natural thing for me. I am going to force my kids to take running lessons. It is so important to learn how to run correctly and, if you can learn to run well at a young age, it will help you tremendously when you get older. Speed is key in baseball. It makes and changes games.

I accepted running as the "weak" part of my game and focused on the other components. It was probably a mistake. I was never going to be Usain Bolt, but I was not the "old geezer" my coaches saw either. I was a good base runner in high school and when I was allowed to steal in my summer leagues, I always swiped a good amount of bags. At Binghamton, though, it was just another part of my game that didn't get fully developed.

My arm was very weak at the beginning of high school. I identified and worked on this weakness, and by the end of high school I was timed throwing 87mph from the outfield at recruiting camps. Then flash-forward to my senior year at BU, when during "fall tryouts" my first throw from right field to third base was a low line drive that still had *a lot* of oomph on it when it smacked into the third baseman's glove on a line. The arm strength was there. It just took a while to find it.

Similarly, I used to be an awful breaking ball hitter. Flash-forward to my senior year, when I would actually sit on breaking balls at times because I thought they were easier to hit. Hours of hitting breaking balls off a machine and studying the proper approach to hitting curveballs had led me to find what had always been there: I was a good breaking-ball hitter.

Even my ability to relax and just have fun playing baseball was always within me, despite the fact that at times early in my college career it looked as if I was wound as tight as a rubber band. Flash-forward to my senior year, when I can honestly say I felt total bliss in the batter's box.

It was all there! I just needed the time, the patience and most importantly the coaches who saw all of these features in me. I needed the freedom to develop these skill sets. I needed people who saw past my immediate weaknesses and wanted to work with me to improve my game. At the end of the day what I needed were coaches who believed in me and didn't accept that my deficiencies were unalterable. Being around Coaches Sinicki and Hurba, I truly got a sense that they underestimated my potential. For quite a while, that became a self fulfilling prophesy.

Before I blinked, half of September was over and with it half of our fall season. Our practices had become absolute marathons, consistently stretching into the third and fourth hour. A few practices even went five hours!

It felt like we covered every facet of the game in every practice. I used to joke that we were one of only four teams in the country to have ever mastered four bunt pickoff plays in a single practice.

I loved baseball but some of our fall practices just dragged on. There was one particular practice when we did a tandem relay drill, which consisted of the outfielder receiving a ball near the fence and throwing it into the cutoff man as runners were racing around the bases.

Depending on the situation, the infielders and catcher had to figure out where to throw the ball. Good drill, right?

It was good except that after every throw, the coaches would pause the drill and talk. And talk. And talk some more. Every one of our four coaches had an opinion on how the play should have unfolded. We went through about one ball every seven or eight minutes on average. I was ready throw my glove at the huddle of coaches.

We always used to complain about our lengthy practices, but our coaches would always ask, "What do you think Georgia or LSU are doing right now?" I used to jokingly answer (to myself) that I am sure they were not catching fly balls off of a machine and hitting fungos to each other in the outfield.

Coach Hurba had us do this drill where we would stand about 75 yards away from a partner and hit fungos to each other. It was a drill to get your top hand involved in the swing, but for me it did not do anything, which is fine. Not every drill is for every person. Nonetheless, I always thought it was comedic that while we practiced hitting fungos, other teams like LSU were more likely working off a tee or in a cage.

The other point I liked to make (to myself, of course) was that a lot of other schools got to play fall intra-squad games. At most, we would play once a week and get two to three at bats. While schools like Pepperdine would have a Blue vs. Orange World Series, we simply did abridged scrimmages.[8]

Still, it was hard to complain too much about *having* to play baseball for a school that was "paying us" to play. We were almost all scholarship players who obviously had a responsibility to give a lot of our time and effort to the program.

By this point I kind of already knew I was a designated hitter, yet there were many days in which I had to endure a four-hour practice and get only 15 swings. Worse, the four coaches rotated throwing batting practice so at least 25% of the time my 15 swings would come off Coach Folli, a lefty. We didn't do a lot of hitting drills or even hitting in the cage, and perhaps that is why I disliked our practices so much. I knew the fielding drills were a waste of time for me. All I wanted to do was hit.

My most vivid memory of that fall, though, was a great one: Coach Folli's speech to me. He got right in my face and told me that I could do anything on this field, that I was special player and that I should never limit myself to anything but my best. As he was instilling confidence in me, coaches Hurba and Sinicki seemed to try and drain it out of me. They never said anything bad to my face, but they didn't have to. It was the way they handled me.

A prime example was during our fall game at Cooperstown, home of the Baseball Hall of Fame, just one hour from Binghamton. We scrimmaged Le Moyne at legendary Doubleday Field, and the plan was to visit the Hall of Fame in the morning and play in the afternoon. My day didn't exactly go according to plan in more ways than one.

First, we were making great time on the way to the Hall of Fame when our bus driver turned one road too soon. It was a small side road, so he decided to try to turn the bus around on the street. We got perpendicular to the road when we heard the tires screeching and churning. The front of the bus had fallen into a small ditch and the wheels were turning on air.

We all got off the bus to look at the damage. The bus was literally at a 90 degree angle with the street, blocking traffic in both directions.

I thought this was just about the funniest thing in the world.

A tow truck finally came and got us back on the road to the Hall of Fame – but we were extremely late now so our time looking around the museum was short. To really appreciate the Hall you need a weekend. I had been there before, so I didn't mind just glancing through. It is an amazing place. You feel awestruck every time you enter the chambers.

We played Le Moyne in a simulated game later on in the afternoon. I left that day feeling like an inferior player. In one afternoon, months of confidence gained over the summer was washed away.

I was the last position player to enter the game. The freshmen, the last pitcher on the totem pole – everyone got in before me. I finally entered in the 6th inning as the DH. I wasn't even given an inning in the outfield. I was going into my junior thinking I had a chance to be a top starter and here I was in a fall game as far from the starting lineup as possible.

I batted twice. My first time up, I hit soft liner to center field. There was a runner on second with no one out, so in an ideal world I wanted to hit a ball to the right side of the field to help advance the runner to third base. My mindset was to look for a pitch on the inner half to drive. What I got was a 3-1 pitch well out and over the plate. I could have taken the pitch and hoped at 3-2 to have gotten something more over the center of the plate. Alternatively, I could have tried to pull the outside pitch in order to get the man over. In hindsight, this probably would have been the best route. But when I saw a fat 3-1 pitch where I could get my barrel on the ball, I decided to take a chance and look for the RBI. I didn't hit the ball great, but I did get enough to line out to center.

When I got back to the dugout, Coach Hurba muttered how that simply was not going to get the job done. I knew where Coach Hurba was coming from, but we were also winning the practice game about 7-0, so I just assumed that playing for an extra run was not of the utmost importance. I knew I was going to get only two at bats and I wanted to make the most of them. I should have done anything to sacrifice myself to get the guy over, but in the moment I didn't want to waste one of my precious at bats by being too perfect with a runner in scoring position. I got the sense that Hurba was expecting/looking for me to do something wrong.

Maybe I interpreted Coach Hurba's words and tone incorrectly, but Mike Quinn, who was there, attests that I did not. The way the words came out made it sound so demeaning and cruel. It hit my nerve. I took my helmet and smashed it against the bench. Thankfully, though, I did it in such a manner that no one noticed except for Quinn.

That game really damaged my confidence. I was really made to feel like an unvalued player. It was almost as if my lowly place on the team was made public that day. I knew from that day on it would be an absolute grind to make it into the lineup for any extended period of time.

I knew I would be in trouble come spring. My whole family agreed. I needed to talk to the coach, but I also knew that it wasn't going to do much good. It was a crappy position to be in. I now knew that I had been somewhat deceived during the end-of-year meeting in May.

I hit well during the fall, but my frustration was mounting off the field. I had desperately wanted to play summer ball in the New England Colligate League. I told coach Hurba this early on because I knew how quickly the rosters would fill up. As the fall pushed on though, I could tell it wasn't going to happen. In my coaches' defense, I didn't have superstar numbers, but I just got the feeling that there was a minimal effort being made to place me where I *wanted* to go. Rather, it felt as if players were getting placed on teams that would open or continue connections that the coaches wanted.

Coach Hurba offered Kyle and I spots on a team in the Jayhawk League – in Kansas! I respectfully declined. Coach was trying to open a connection there, but I wasn't going to be his pawn.

Worse, Henry Dunn, an outfielder, got placed in the NECBL. *Worse yet* was that Henry wound up being ineligible for the spring, and so with him went his roster spot in the NECBL. I loved Henry Dunn and wasn't angry at him. I simply was angry that he was placed there when the coaches knew how badly I wanted to be the in that league.

The roadblocks continued throughout the fall as freshman Corey Taylor worked out as Henry Dunn's backup in center field. As a wall was being built between me and the outfield, my frustrations were mounting, assisting in my outfield play starting to slide. Corey proved himself to be a terrific baseball player, but the fact remained I wasn't granted even one inning out there.

I suppose I became so frustrated during the fall because in such a short amount time all those summer hopes came crashing down. I saw the player who I was in the summer and hated that I couldn't be him at Binghamton. The summer player hit third, played the outfield, and roped lefties. Now I was a backup DH/OF on a team that seemed to breed negativity into me.

My previous summer in Bennington had been fun but there was no way I was going back there. I feared that if I did not act, it would be déjà vu all over again. Thankfully, I remembered a conversation with a kid I played with my freshman year in Rock Hill, S.C. He said he originally was going to the Hawaii Collegiate Baseball League, but that his family's financial situation had changed and he could no longer afford to go. The economy was already starting to tank, and I thought that a lot of kids might be in similar situations.

I took the initiative and had Coach Sinicki send out a recommendation for me. He gladly obliged. I heard nothing from the people in Hawaii for months and assumed it wasn't going to work out. Then one morning right around Christmas I got an e-mail labeled "HCBL acceptance." A simple click and it was done. I was going to Hawaii!

What a place for my last summer of baseball. I knew there wasn't going to be a ton of exposure out in Hawaii, but I didn't care. I was going to have the time of my life.

All year people said how lucky I was to be going to Hawaii. But where was the luck? I had made the contact. I had put up the numbers my sophomore year. I was the one who kept e-mailing the HCBL every few weeks during the fall.

As the snow once again replaced the autumn leaves, I did my best to forget about the rocky fall and focus on the upcoming spring. I decided to try to get as strong as possible and see where it took me. I took NO Explode, Protein, four vitamins per day, and Cell Tech, a creatine supplement that helped build muscle mass. (They were all legal for the NCAA). I stayed busy lifting, having fun at the RE and doing my classwork. By junior year I was into my core business classes, so I was starting to really get a handle on my major. Taking Operations Management, Marketing, and Management Information Systems all in one semester definitely made for some long nights though.

I turned 21 in November. Another milestone. As weird as it was to buy my first legal drink, it was gratifying to know that I would never have to worry about not being 21 again. Unfortunately though, becoming 21 meant new responsibilities as well. Everything has its trade-offs.

(The 2008 Binghamton Bearcats.)

(Studying for a final in my dorm room.)

(Binghamton University on a warm, spring day.)

(Best friends Michael Quinn (left) and Jeff Dennis (center), and me (right) eating a true Cajun meal during our New Orleans trip.)

(Looking very happy (and tan) after a game for the Hawaii Aliis in the Hawaii Collegiate Baseball League.)

Going with the Pitch 149

(By senior year I had transformed my swing into a much more compact and simple one.)

(The infamous "RE". The second floor was the "Baseball House", accessed through the shaky fire escape.)

(At the plate at the University of Hartford. It was always a treat getting to play in my home state.)

(Winning the America East Championship at 3 am!)

Going with the Pitch 151

(Going with the Pitch at Varsity Field.)

CHAPTER 29

First semester classes ended in early December, but I decided to hang around school for a week and enjoy some downtime. While I was lounging around, my girlfriend decided to break up with me. It really sucked at the time. I liked her a lot, and even though we hadn't been going out that long, the inevitable feeling you get when you break up with someone crept into my body. I missed her, and I felt a bit lonely without her.

Looking back, it was for the best, but during those vulnerable moments strikeouts and home runs didn't seem to matter.

But then something else happened that was much, much more painful.

I was busy playing *Medal of Honor* on Jeff Dennis' Playstation 2 when Mike Quinn came into my room.

"What's up, Mike?" I was staring at the screen so I didn't look up to see his face. If I had, I would have known what he was about to say: "I just quit."

It took a second for the words to register in my mind. I hit the pause button and looked into his eyes. He was hurting.

He explained how he just didn't have the love or passion for the game anymore. He said he had talked to coach and told him he couldn't give it his all anymore. Everyone could see his lack of enthusiasm during the fall practices and during our winter team lifts. I think most people just thought that he had a bad attitude. I knew better.

Many people wrongly assumed that Mike had committed baseball suicide, meaning that he had voluntarily quit as opposed to having been cut. From my viewpoint it was the complete opposite. It was more like someone had shoved him to the edge and said jump or we will push you. As I see it, Mike had little choice.

I knew Mike as a freshman and as a sophomore. I saw the love he had for the game. As my roommate for two years, he inevitably became one of my best friends. I was there when we took hours of extra batting practice before games. I was there when Mike, Jeff Dennis and I would talk baseball nonsense in the dorms for hours. I was there when we would run out to practice together just so we could hit some balls early.

I was also there when time after time he was beaten down. He kept getting up, but every time he would have just a little larger limp. I was there each time he was passed over during a weekend series. I was there each time Coach Hurba said he wouldn't have recruited him. I was there whenever one of the coaches would comment that he just didn't know what, if any, of Mike's skills were good enough for Division I baseball. I was there every time Mike got shot down.

It was a shame to see his love of the game stripped from him. The Bearcats were losing a catcher. I was losing a best friend. To see the spark in his eyes dim a little each day hurt me. He knew what I knew. Under this coaching staff, he was always going to get back far less than what he put in.

Mike wasn't dying. For that matter, he wasn't even transferring. But with my full schedule and the fact that he was moving out, I knew that we were going to see each other a lot less frequently. There were two freshman catchers coming in, and Mike knew what lay ahead for him. He couldn't take another year of just 16 at bats, and I didn't blame him.

I gave Mike a big hug and watched him leave. Then I lost it. Tears watered in my eyes. Mike hadn't told anyone but me. He was too sad and uncomfortable to tell others. It was my responsibility to spread the news.

Within 48 hours I had just lost my best friend and my girlfriend. I decided it was time to leave Binghamton for winter break.

I went home and took some time to relax. Included in my break was a 10 day trip to Israel. When I returned I was ready to get back into shape.

The NCAA Division I rules had changed. Now the starting date for *all* Division I teams was the third weekend in February. That meant our season was set to begin on February 23rd. When I got back from Israel, it was only a month until our first game.

Baseball was my anchor in life. It was always there. Baseball gave me direction, purpose and something to focus on. I couldn't see a life without it.

It was because of this feeling that I was so worried going into the spring of '08. I knew how much I wanted to have a good year, but I also knew that there were going to be inevitable lows. I tried to focus on just getting ready for the season, but it was not easy.

Unlike my first two years, upon returning to school the winter workouts in the gym just flew by. Instead of having over five weeks of training, we now barely had three. By NCAA rules we couldn't start practicing until February 1. It was a lot easier to get through the indoor workouts when I knew that in just a few short days I would be outside playing a real game.

However, working out as an outfielder inside was the *biggest* waste of time of my entire college career. Even if I was going to *play* the outfield, which I knew wasn't going to happen, it would still have been a waste of time. There isn't much you can do with a basketball court-sized indoor area. We would do meaningless little pop up drills and ground ball drills that met the definition of tedious. Our defensive drills indoors were generally awful, and the poor lighting didn't help.

We would do team defense once or twice a week, and it was always 50/50 whether we would get through it without having to run. After a few poor throws from our catchers, everyone would start to get worried. Coach became a ticking time bomb. You never knew which bad throw would set him off, but you knew that enough bad throws were going to make him explode.

After a week of wasting away with the outfielders, the coaches decided to move me to first base. I officially became the backup there for Ryan Holley, a junior college transfer from the Chicago area. He was an excellent ballplayer, and it was clear he should be starting at first base. But they needed a backup, and I was that guy. I said I would do it because I really did want to help the team, but also because if Holley ever went down it would have been a way into the lineup.

I was being used. I knew that, but I had little choice. Most drills needed two first basemen. I was a pawn. I would show up early to practice to work on various things such as footwork and ground balls. I put hours upon hours in at first base – and I played one half of one inning there the entire season.

After a few weeks inside, we finally boarded the bus and left town. We were to open our season against James Madison University in Virginia, so the day before the game we made the eight-hour drive.

Due to the weather, we played only one game Saturday. My dad, sister and brother drove down, and I was excited that they were there to see me play. It was about 45 degrees, not horrible weather but definitely chilly. As game time got closer, my nerves really started to kick in. By the second inning, though, everything felt at peace again.

I was the designated hitter, and in my first at bat of the season I got down early right away. I managed to fight off an inside fastball and hit a slow grounder to second base. Normally I would not have reached base, but the second baseman made an error and I was aboard.

My next at bat I got an outside fastball and slapped it for my first hit of the season. In my last at bat, I ripped a fastball over the center fielder's head for a double. So far, so good.

Things were great as I went to dinner with my family at night (and got to pocket the 21 bucks!). We were supposed to get $22, but the team had decided to donate our last dollar to Coach Folli. He was a volunteer and deserved some compensation. If it was up to me, I would have paid him a full salary.

Things went to shit (literally) about 2 a.m. Sunday morning. I awoke feeling weird. Five minutes later I was coughing up blood, throwing up and dispensing of waste in an efficient manner. I re-woke at 7:45 a.m. feeling worse, and quickly ran to the bathroom. My back also had stiffened up from playing in the cold weather and had locked up over night. I felt like death.

I will never forget that Sunday, and the pain. From warm ups, to sitting in the dugout freezing, to shivering through an eight-hour bus ride, it was a miserable day. I was as sick as they come.

I sat out the first game, so my family left in order to get back home at a reasonable time. I just couldn't see myself playing that day. So there I was, cuddled up in the corner of the dugout in about five layers of clothing. In the 7th inning JMU led 2-0. I was still suffering from a combination of nausea, back pains, and shivers.

I thought I was starting to have hallucinations when I heard coach ask if I could hit. It took him repeating the question for me to realize that he actually wanted me to go up there and hit. Of course I said YES!

One minute later I was in the batter's box. I took a swing at the first pitch and fouled it off. I have a very vivid memory of all my other at bats, but for this one I had to look back at the box score because I have limited recollection of it. All I know is that the next pitch came hard and in, and even though I was well behind the pitch I still caught enough barrel to dump the ball into center for an RBI single. It was a miracle.

In the 9th I managed to get another hit. I was somehow 2-for-2. We lost 3-1 but we played well, and to be honest my only concern was to get on to the warm bus.

The ride home was painful. I was thrilled with my hitting, but I would have traded my bed for all four hits that weekend. I was sick and hurt, yet the coaches still asked me to hit in a big situation. It was a huge compliment, and I thought that maybe I had overreacted during the fall and winter.

I hadn't. The situation only made it that much more puzzling when later in the year I couldn't get consistent at bats. How could I go from the player chosen to hit in a huge situation to one who would go a full weekend without getting a single at bat?

CHAPTER 30

I was fully recovered the next weekend when we returned to Virginia to play Virginia Military Institute. After we won a close first game, I played in game two as the DH. In my first at bat I ripped a fastball down the right field line for a clean double. Feeling good, I was determined to get at least two more hits that day. What came next was an event that caused me to be teased to this day.

On an 0-2 count, I got a breaking ball in the dirt well short of the catcher's mitt. I did a little check swing, but I didn't think I was even remotely close to swinging, so I stepped out of the box to refocus on the next pitch. Then, without even checking with the field umpire, the home plate umpire screamed "Strike three" in my ear and punched me out.

From home plate to our dugout was about a 50-foot walk. I walked slowly, ranting, "NO WAY!" Now if I said it once or twice, it would have just been another uneventful strikeout. But I wouldn't stop yelling: "NO WAY!" "NO WAY!" NO WAY!" "GIVE ME A CHANCE!" "NO WAY!"

I was already angry for even thinking about swinging at such a bad pitch, but then to get screwed over on the call made me lose it. As I reached the dugout, Coach Sinicki (rightfully) hollered, "Enough, Ken!" My teammates were dying laughing.

I am glad I brought some comedic relief to the team. It was the closest I ever came to getting thrown out of a college baseball game.

We lost two out of three to a very good VMI team, and even though I hadn't seen any time in the field I was still very happy with my play during the first six games. I had another big RBI against VMI and almost all of my at bats were productive. My season had started out very well. We were only 2-4, but I felt good about where the team and I were headed.

We had another game scheduled against Virginia Tech on Sunday. The weather was absolutely gorgeous, about 65 degrees with sunshine. I was feeling loose and finally had just a t-shirt on under my jersey. I was even getting to play the outfield for a game. My host family from South Carolina was making the trip to see Jeff and I play. Everything seemed in place for a great day at the park.

We lost 12-1! Virginia Tech was an Atlantic Coast Conference team, so we knew they were going to be good, but we played so badly that I doubt we would have beaten most Babe Ruth League teams. We had no timely hitting, played sub-par defense, made poor base running decisions, and had awful pitching. Worse, I lost a fly ball in the high sky and it allowed an extra run to score. I felt awful. There are few worse feelings in baseball than when you know a fly ball is headed your way but you can't pick it up. The ball bounced 50 feet from me. So much for making a bid to play the outfield.

After the game we got reamed out. We were accused of not caring and not having enough leadership on the team. When you lose, it makes everything seem worse, and at 2-5 things seemed pretty bad. Coach said his job was on the line, and the time commitment that the coaches put in made this loss sickening. Coach Sinicki wasn't particularly happy about his team laughing and discussing dinner plans in the dugout when we were down 10 runs, either.

After another long drive home to Binghamton, I had to defrost the windshield of my car for 10 minutes and scrape off the ice before I could drive back to the RE. It was strange to be in two completely different worlds in the same day.

Feeling a bit down, I decided it was time to get in touch with some friends playing ball around the country.

Once the season got going, it became a daunting task to stay in touch with high school and summer ball friends. Thank god for Facebook and AIM, or I would have never talked to them at all. I did make sure, however, to call my friends on various college teams every once in a while to see how they were doing and how their seasons were going. I loved being able to share stories and hear about their experiences. They always helped me get through any struggles.

My high school had produced some pretty special ballplayers over the previous few years, and I enjoyed calling them. Brian Irving was pitching for Yale; Nick Lefeber was a catcher/captain at Middlebury; Jeff Musante was in the starting rotation at Babson; Craig Cooper was the starting shortstop/captain at Colby; Sam Schreiber was playing at Emory, and Will General was playing at Davidson. It was an impressive resume for a small, northeast private school (that didn't recruit for sports) to have all of these college baseball players in just a few short years.

I found comfort in talking baseball with these guys. It was nice to know we weren't the only team struggling against southern teams and that other guys were going through the same issues I was.

The next weekend we again headed to Virginia. At this point I felt like I could have driven there blindfolded. This time we were playing independent Longwood University. The bus ride took a whopping 11 hours, and I loved every moment of it.

I had my movies, my book, my audiobook, my homework, my mandatory naps and card games. I could have sat on the bus for a few more hours if needed. I loved the bus rides! Plus, how could I complain about stopping at Ryan's all-you-can-eat-buffet on the way down? I soaked in every moment of it. I just had to make it a point to sit far away from the bathroom on the bus following our food stop. The buffet food always seemed to stir the team' stomachs just about two hours after finishing the meal.

Longwood was another roller-coaster weekend. We were swept in the Saturday doubleheader to make our record an abysmal 2-7. We once again blew a 5-0 lead, giving up six runs in the last inning to lose 6-5. Once again, Coach Sinicki tried to figure out why this kept happening and, once again, no one had any answers. I saw a lack of sturdy defense and a weak bullpen. I didn't think it was that much of a mystery.

We also lost game two, 4-3. Once again, all their runs came in one inning. Longwood had been shut out in all but two innings and yet we had lost both games. Baseball is a funny sport.

Thank goodness we won on Sunday. As a team, we figured we had won a few games against some good southern teams and there was nothing to worry about going forward. I had played in all three games at DH and, even though we weren't winning, I was playing good baseball. Still, it was time to get out of Virginia for the season.

CHAPTER 31

After three weeks of intense travel, our days in Virginia were over. With so much road time, I felt like I had pretty much been ignoring a little thing called school. To my amazement, though, my grades remained pretty high. After two-plus years of college, I had finally developed a system where I figured out what work *needed* to be done and would focus on that. I was happily on my way to a 3.8 GPA while keeping my reading to a minimum. I made sure to get to every class I could, and any work I missed I would do on the bus ride. It helped as well to be taking marketing and finance classes which I found fairly interesting. It made the work a lot less painful. It was hard to believe, but we were already one third done with the semester and 10 games deep into my junior season.

When we headed to Philadelphia, it seemed like a walk around the block. After three straight weekends in Virginia, we were all ecstatic to only be traveling three hours. Due to weather, the Villanova Baseball Tournament was changed so that instead of playing Temple, La Salle and Villanova, we would only play the first two. Of course, Villanova was the team I really wanted to play against.

When I was a senior in high school I had gone to an invitation-only showcase camp at Villanova. I had talked to the coach prior to attending, and he really liked me. He wanted me to come to the camp to play in front of him one more time, so I made the drive on a Saturday morning. Unfortunately, the day before I had just begun my lifting program (a very dumb move), and I was extremely sore. My throws were weak, and my swings lackluster. The Villanova coach never spoke to me again.

I wanted to play in front of him on his field and dominate. But that just wasn't in the cards as the rain again played havoc with our schedule.

The weekend was much ado about nothing for me. After playing in eight of our first 10 games, it was like I had failed some divine test. I hadn't hit great at Longwood, but I was stroking the ball and getting RBIs and did not foresee the events at Philly unfolding as they did.

Once we hit Philadelphia, everything changed. I started to play much less, and my aggressiveness and comfort level at the plate diminished. There was no communication from the coaches about this shift in my playing time, and before I knew it, I sank into a mild slump.

We got to the Philadelphia area Friday around noon. The game was scheduled for 1:30 so we had to hustle to get ready. The weather turned out to be pretty nice, probably in the 50s. I had a marketing test to take on the road, but I decided that instead of taking my test on the bus in the morning, I would sleep and be rested and alert for the game. What a waste. The other team was throwing a lefty.

I talked to my dad for over 45 minutes after the game and got some perspective about my situation. I was in an extremely awkward role on the team because sometimes I was treated as a starter and at other times I was more of a bench player. As always, my dad was right when he told me that I had to stop fighting it. At this point, I needed to accept my role and do whatever I could to help the team. I had to change my entire mindset.

Like an addict, however, I was simply not ready to make that adjustment. I needed to bottom out first. That would come in a few weeks.

The problem was that I knew that I had the potential to do great things on the field, and it took a big step of maturity for me to accept my role. When I finally fully committed to my role, which really wasn't until late junior year, I started to really enjoy playing again. It was at that time that I started to hit the ball really well again. I think the process could have been expedited if the coaches had communicated to me what my role was and why it was important. I doubt if they had defined it themselves, and my eventual success occurred after finally stumbling to the conclusion that team success was the singular objective and that I could be an important tool for achieving that goal.

I got into one game at La Salle the next day but was 0-for-2. It was the first time in a long time that I thought I had to be perfect up there or else I would be benched. Looking back, it is still hard for me to accept the truth that hitting became a chore during this stretch. Everything I did was mechanical. It was a recipe for poor performances. The opponents' pitchers were awful, and our team punished them, winning 6-1 and then 9-1. I was one of the few guys to not hit well.

When the year began, I was free and easy at the plate. Then I was benched for a few games, and my mindset changed. I thought if I wasn't textbook perfect, I wasn't going to break into the lineup again. Until I could overcome my fear of making mistakes and being pulled, I wouldn't be successful. How stupid I was. How could I not enjoy each and every pitch?

As time went on, words like "perfect" and "must" vanished from my vocabulary. I warn you that if you ever hear a coach say, "You *must* play a *perfect* game in order to win" quit that team. It is simply the wrong mindset to be in as a player or person. I spent way too many games and at bats thinking that I *had* to hit my goals. Well, what if I didn't?

I failed many times, and each time I got back up, learned and moved on. If someone is going to tell me I must be perfect, the consequences of my actions better be much more severe than simply striking out. It better be life or death.

Once I was able to change my mindset from *must* to *want to* and from *perfect* to *full effort,* I quickly relaxed at the plate and realized that the worst-case scenario was in fact not all that bad. A Do-or-Die attitude is not a sustainable one and was a major cause for my mid-season slump during my junior year. Thankfully, as time went by, I understood this and it became a welcome relief when after a rare 0-for-4 game I was able to say "oh, well" and move on.

"You can't buy anything at the store with hurt feelings" so get over it and make the best of it. Overcome. It was the mindset I was going to have to have for the remainder of the season. Joe Charron was hitting well in left field, even if he did have the occasional defensive blunder. Freshman Corey Taylor was patrolling center and, even though he wasn't hitting well, it was obvious he was getting more comfortable with every at bat, and that he would be terrific. Even with average range in the outfield, he was still out there every day. (As it turns out Corey Taylor is on pace to be one of the best hitters the program has ever had, so my projections for him were pretty accurate.) Freshman Pete Bregartner played right field. Similarly, Pete wound up having a terrific year as a freshman, winning Rookie of the Year, but again it still irked me that he was decreed the starter from day one of the fall. There was just no room out there for me.

These guys were recruited by Coach Hurba to play the outfield. I wasn't. It made a big difference.

The only spot open for me was DH. The problem with that was that whenever a bench player played a game, it was usually in the DH slot. I had to compete with a lot of guys for the last spot in the order, and when transfer Tom Baileys, a local kid who played at nearby Broome Community College the year before, got red hot it was game over for me.

I love Tom Baileys and we got along great (becoming very close friends as time went on), but it seemed so unfair that because he was hitting well I was marked "unplayable." In my coaches' eyes, I couldn't play the field, couldn't run, couldn't bunt, and couldn't steal, so if I wasn't killing the ball or if someone else *was* killing the ball more than me, it meant I was a dead duck. I was playing with a losing hand.

I knew it was going to take a new level of mental toughness to get through the rest of the season. Similarly, I knew that complaining would just be counterproductive. My dad brought it up to me all the time. My complaining to teammates and him complaining to other parents would have been childish, inappropriate, and simply pointless. It was a full-season, full-out effort to mask my anger and do whatever I could to help the team. I *needed* to be the first kid out of the dugout to cheer one of the guys when he hit a home run.

The most challenging moments though, were after games back at the RE with my teammates. It was tough not show my bitterness. If we won, I was thrilled and I was never bitter at *them*. It was directed at the situation I found myself in. I was thrilled when they succeeded, but it was tough at times to have to keep my feelings bottled up. I desperately missed Mike Quinn, who had been the only person I could talk to the year before. I had to keep working and getting better, or I would have crumbled. It was the only way I knew how to do things.

Any time I gave the opposing pitcher credit I was selling myself short; any time I believed in the nay-sayers I was selling myself short. No, I would continue to work hard and try like heck to rebuild my shattered confidence. Many people never do.

We got back from Pennsylvania on Saturday night because the Sunday games had already been canceled. It was a rare weekend night to go out in Binghamton, and the team took full advantage of it. We drank the town dry. About once a month we needed a huge party night to blow off some steam. I woke up the next morning ready to get back at it.

CHAPTER 32

On March 20, we flew to Kansas for our big, wild and crazy spring break trip. It was my first trip to the middle part of the country, and Kansas was *exactly* what I had imagined it to be: miles and miles of flat farm land.

Kansas State's campus was a few hours drive from the airport (which was located in Missouri), so I got the opportunity to stare out of the window and watch corn grow for four hours. Actually, that wasn't so bad.

After a long day of travel, it was a good feeling to finally arrive at the hotel across the street from the Kansas State campus. Normally, when visiting a new school, I would try to see as much of the campus and surrounding area as possible. I was always curious about how other schools went about things, and I loved to see other universities in full swing. My wandering mind was almost always put to rest whenever I did get a decent tour of another campus. Maybe the buildings were a bit nicer or a bit bigger, but 95 percent of the colleges were similar in many ways.

Even though I didn't get to see much of the campus on this trip, I did get to explore famous Aggieville, *the* true college town. The town had the standard local bars, the school store, the Buffalo Wild Wings, and the local spirit shops. Purple and grey Wildcat banners hung out of windows and flapped in the cool spring air. I don't know if the town stole its image from the movies or if the movies stole the image from this town, but Aggieville *was* Collegetown, USA.

To no one's surprise, the Wildcats' baseball stadium was remarkable, with purple box seats behind home plate and green trees lining the outfield fence. The school had just installed a new turf, and the stadium, opened in 2002, looked brand new. I know it was common for a big time school in a conference like the Big 12 to have facilities like this, but every time I went to one of these schools I was simply amazed.

Kansas State was a solid Big 12 program. The Wildcats never overpowered us in our three-game series but instead just steadily beat us down. We did not get embarrassed, but they were simply a better team.

The weather was the worst part of the series. During the middle part of the 7th inning of game one, snow began to fall! It was like we had never left Binghamton.

We finished our Kansas trip with two games vs. Wichita State. My dad came west by himself to see me play, and I kind of felt bad for him being on his own and having to drive around by himself. When I wasn't in the lineup it hurt a little bit because I knew how far he had traveled to watch me. I wasn't ready at the time to fully understand the commitment and pure joy he had in watching our games.

Today, now removed from the game, I already know I will travel the globe twice around in order to watch my son (or daughter) play. It is one of those things I know I will not fully comprehend until I have a child of my own. My parents always used to say how it was the time of their life traveling around and watching me play. Now I am starting to get that.

Wichita State has one of the best college stadiums in the nation. Eck Stadium is nicer than *most* Minor League stadiums. Head Coach Gene Stevens took the program over in 1977 when baseball did not even exist at the school. The program had been shut down for seven years and there was no history of success. In 30+ years, Stevens has changed all that. His track record is remarkable.[9] Under his leadership, the Shockers have been to seven College World Series and countless NCAA tournaments. His most impressive feat, however, may be overseeing the program when Eck Stadium was built.

Eck stadium is the holy grail of college baseball facilities. I am not sure what else a college stadium should have. In 2008, the Shockers averaged 4,168 fans per game, 12th best in the country.[10] Behind home plate were the normal 10-deep box seats that wrapped half way around the base paths. However, above those blue seats was a large section of green seats, followed by another section of yellow seats. Acting as the roof to these seats was the floor of at least 10 luxury suites.

There was also an entire extra section of seating down the right field line, just in case the normal seating was all filled up – and an area behind the outfield fence for the hard core hecklers. Wichita didn't have everything, but it had college baseball.

What really topped off the stadium were the two extra levels of seats directly behind home plate. First there were the press boxes and then on top of that was the All-American Club exclusively for members. These suites and boxes could have easily been confused with the Yankees elite Audi club in the New Yankee Stadium.[11]

After our game we were invited up to the All-American Club for dinner, and it was nicer than any hotel ballroom I had ever seen. We were served a full course meal with a pristine eagle eye view of the turf field way down below. What an awesome atmosphere to play a ball game.

Even for a non-conference game against a no-name northeast school, the stadium was still fairly packed. We were extremely intimated. It didn't hurt that their third basemen, Conor Gillaspie, was the 2007 Cape Cod MVP and would eventually be the Giants supplemental first round pick, soon signing for $970,000. Sixteen players from their team wound up being drafted or signed. They were pretty solid.[12]

Upsets are one of the best aspects of sport. There is always the slim chance that on any given day a lesser team can take down a greater force. The strategy for taking down the king is usually to just stick around as long as possible. Make it close going into the fourth quarter, into the third period, into the final set, into the 7th inning and maybe, just maybe, you have a chance.

The worst thing that can happen to a team looking for an upset is to get down big early. Our dream of a big upset was instantly shot down when, before we blinked, we were down 9-0 in the second inning to the No. 11-ranked team in the country.

Now there were great ballplayers in the other dugout, but as bad as we were getting plummeted after the first two innings, we did begin to realize that as good as these guys were, they were just college baseball players and we were good enough to compete with them. Most of the kids playing at even a baseball factory like Wichita St. would be done after college, and most of those who did get drafted would be done two years thereafter. These guys still made mistakes and had brain farts. The difference between a Wichita State and a Binghamton team was small when looking at narrow factors, but very large overall.

The difference is between running a 6.7 instead of a 7.0. Throwing 92 instead of 88. Hitting the ball 400 feet instead of 380. Barreling the ball up once every three times instead of once every four. Cleanly fielding nine out of 10 grounders vs. eight of 10.

Each time the level gets higher, the difference in play between "us" and "them" grows just a bit larger but the difference is still fairly slim between a mid-major program and a top 25 Division I program. That is why America East teams can beat ACC teams on any given day but why it is still so rare. The slight difference in ability, stature, and talent are magnified when there are nine guys on one side who are all just a little bit better. It adds up and suddenly you find yourself down 9-0 in the second inning.

The rest of the game was uneventful as we settled down and lost 9-2. At the very least, we competed. I was hitless but I battled at the plate against very good pitching.

We lost the next night, 13-8. This time we played Wichita State much closer and proved to the thousands of fans that we could play with a nationally-ranked team. I didn't expect to play, but got into the game midway through when Joe Charron botched a groundball in the outfield. I used the opportunity to rip the hardest hit ball of the season to dead center, but all it was good for was a sacrifice fly.

I was thrilled. Finally I had ripped a ball. It had been far too many games since I connected like that. And hey, it was pretty cool being at the plate and seeing myself on the video Jumbotron in left field.

We went 0-5 out west, but it was a huge learning experience playing two top 25 teams. We were not getting into the NCAA tournament as an at-large team anyway, so it really didn't matter statistically how we fared outside of conference play. Most of the other America East teams were not doing much better. Also, we had Fairleigh Dickinson on our schedule the day after we landed back east. We nicknamed Fairleigh Dickinson "Fairly Ridiculous."

Their baseball team was in shambles. In 2007 they finished 9-45. The year before that they were 10-43.[13] If you saw their field you would begin to understand the root of the program's problem: funding. We had just played at one of the top 10 facilities in the country, and it's safe to say that Farleigh Dickinson's field was one of the worst five facilities in the country.

When I stepped off the bus Saturday morning in New Jersey, two things entered my mind. One was that it was ridiculously cold. The other was the condition of the field.

It resembled a Babe Ruth field that hadn't been watered or raked in about a month. Goose droppings were everywhere. It had to be in violation of a few health codes. We went from two state of the art stadiums, seating about 5,000, to wooden bleachers that sat about 50 (not including the geese).

I don't think a team ever intentionally dogs it during a game or goes into a game not wanting to win, but there are definitely different levels of intensity and urgency that a team exhibits. This was never truer than during our weekend series vs. FDU.

The weekend was a recipe for disaster. We were tired and we were playing against a poor team on a horrific field. It was all too easy to overlook FDU in anticipation of the next week's conference opener vs. Stony Brook. The freezing temperatures were the finishing cap. No excuses, but I know all of these factors played a role in our sub par 2-2 weekend.

FDU was stacked with decent lefty starters. Because of rain on Friday, we played two seven-inning games on Saturday and two more on Sunday.

We snuck by in game one, squeezing out a 4-3 victory. I was 1-for-1 and Joe Charron, Pete Bregartner, and Bryan Ivan all added RBIs.

We weren't very happy after game two. We had just two hits and lost, 4-3. I had seen and heard an angrier Coach Sinicki, but I never saw a more disgusted one. After everything he had put into the program, to lose to a team like Farleigh Dickinson must have burned his insides. I know it burned mine.

My at bats were again getting more sporadic, and it was beginning to show. I was doing everything possible to stay locked in but wasn't having much success. That hard sacrifice fly in Kansas appeared to be an aberration. I had no punch in my swing. Whenever I got into one of these funks, I would try just about everything to get out of it. There were the usual remedies such as extra batting practice, but I also explored more unique solutions such as drinking a full Gatorade before every game and hitting with my batting gloves un-velcroed.

One treatment I could do the night before a game was to do some dry swings in the mirror. It just so happened that a convenient time to do my mirror swings was when I was in my sliders waiting to take a shower. With three to a room, there was always a wait to take a shower. When Tom Baileys got out of the shower and saw an almost naked person taking swings in his boxers, he started to laugh hard. To this day, we joke about my dry swings in my boxers at FDU. It was a great remedy. I suggest it to anyone not hitting well.

Sunday was even colder than Saturday. There was even more goose shit on the field, and we had even more trouble beating the Knights. We were losing game three going into the 7th inning, but managed to squeak a late run across to tie the game and force extra innings. We were down to our final out when Pete Bregartner singled in the tying run. Whew.

In the 8th inning I pinch-hit with one on and two out. I got an outside fastball and punished it to deep left field for a game-winning RBI double. It was that quick and simple. One second I was on the bench freezing my butt off and the next second I was standing on second base, having just struck the game-winning hit.

We carried none of the momentum to the next game though and got beat 3-2. It was time to get out of New Jersey as quickly as possible.

I don't think any of us minded Monday morning when classes began. We needed to put our 2-7 road trip behind us.

Even though we were only 7-15, we were 0-0 in conference and that's all that mattered. It would have been nice to have some confidence going into our opening weekend in Stony Brook, but we weren't living in a perfect world. We were living in the northeast.

CHAPTER 33

I had always known that to hit well I needed consistent at bats. By my senior year I had mastered my craft enough so that instead of needing 10 at bats, all I needed was three to four to get going. Every year it seemed like I needed fewer at bats to be a good hitter, but throughout my junior year I still needed a solid two or three games to get in the groove.

Whether or not I was ready, we were about to begin conference play at Stony Brook. Two years ago we had blown the tournament play-in game on the same field, and the guys who remembered that game wanted a little revenge. Instead, we got swept.

Stony Brook beat us in every facet of the game. We had a lot of young players who had heard about our dominant record the previous year, and I think a lot of them just assumed we would walk through the regular season.

In game one, we were down 7-1 before exploding for an 8-spot in the eighth inning. It felt like sweet justice. I was partially responsible for our 7-1 deficit, going 0-for-3 with three strikeouts. However, I was also a big part of our comeback.

In the eighth inning I once again faced Tom Koehler, who had already sent me back to the bench three times. With 2 strikes on me and flirting with my 4th straight strike out to start conference play, I buckled down and focused on my 2 strike approach. All it took was one mistake by him for me to win the battle on that day. With the bases loaded, I ripped a three-run triple over the center fielder's head. As I slid headfirst into third base a rush of adrenaline overcame my body. I had been one strike away from my fourth consecutive strikeout. Now I was the hero of the game – at least for half an inning until our inconsistent bullpen wasted no time squandering the lead. The game gave us some confidence that we were never truly out of a game, but it was still difficult to have had the victory within our grasp and then let it slip away. It's not every day that a team overcomes a 7-1 deficit and loses!

We had a half-hour between games to hit the reset button and "salvage the series." Due to the rain on Friday, we were playing two games both Saturday and Sunday.

Game two was as deflating as game one. We had another lead going into the last inning and once again our bullpen blew it.

With the team at 0-2, I could already feel the panic button being hit. Amazingly, instead of responding to the pressure, we blew *another* lead in game three by surrendering seven runs in one inning.

Baseball works in funny ways. The one constant is change. The year before we beat Albany four straight times in the regular season and lost to them twice in the postseason. This year Stony Brook had three come-from-behind wins against us and was virtually unbeatable all season. The next year we would have three walk-off wins against them. The conference was always changing. This particular year seemed to be Stony Brook's as it put the seal on the weekend in game four when we gave up an early 5-spot that was insurmountable.

The bus ride home after the series was as bad as you can imagine. The first hour was basically grim silence. Worse, even after we won a game, Coach Sinicki never seemed to be hungry, so it usually took a lot of convincing to get him to stop the bus for food. After a loss, no one dared ask him about eating.

Our weekend food situation was always interesting. We awoke around 8 a.m. to eat a continental breakfast in the hotel. Normally, we would have a waffle and yogurt or perhaps indulge in a cinnamon bun as well. I always tried to get something down, but I often felt nauseous while trying to eat pre-game, so it was a fight to consume a decent breakfast. I did learn as a veteran to pack an apple or small box of cereal for the games, but those only went so far.

We would get to the field at 10 o'clock, play at noon, and the game would end around 2:30. Then it was time to pray that some of the parents got together and brought us lunch. Most days the parents were very generous and provided subs or pizza. But on some days there was no food, and you were stuck with Nutrigrain Bars and a bag of old peanuts.

Sometimes we didn't get to a restaurant (or dining hall for home games) until after 6 o'clock. I was constantly living off sunflower seeds and beef jerky during the back end of doubleheaders. Thank God for convenience stores.

If there was food provided and I knew I wasn't going to be playing, I would stuff my face. Even if I did get subbed in, I figured most of the greasy pizza would have been digested by then. But I always thought it was funny that after working out all fall, lifting and hitting all winter, practicing all spring, preparing all year for these games, and doing anything to get an edge, we ignored the simple fact that a hungry player will not hit as well as an adequately fed player.

During my senior year we took this idea to a whole new level by introducing "senior bagels." If any player ever complained about being hungry, the seniors would ask him if he had his bagel yet. On trips when we left early in the morning, the coaches would buy us bagels and cream cheese. We would teasingly ask teammates how they could be hungry 10 hours later on the way home if they had eaten their bagel that morning. One or two bagels was so far removed from a good pre-game meal that we had to make fun of it.

After hours of driving in the dark, we arrived in Binghamton late Sunday night with a conference record of 0-4 and a dismal season record of 7-19. That is a .269 winning percentage. People all over campus and within the athletic department had written us off. We were now considered to be in a rebuilding year. That was nonsense though, because if you looked at our starting pitching and the amount of close games we had lost, you would have realized that we were as good as any team in the conference (well, maybe except for Stony Brook).

I was never able to do homework on the way home from games, so I stuck to movies and reading ESPN The Magazine. On that trip I read a fascinating article about Ryan Howard that changed my hitting approach for the next season and a half.

Ryan Howard crowded the plate in order to be able to hit the outside pitch with authority. Anything inside that missed by an inch or two either hit him or was left over the center of the plate. He controlled the strike zone and forced the pitcher to make a perfect pitch. I toyed around with that in my mind. From my next batting practice session on, it just felt right. I got on the plate and took my mind off everything else. All of a sudden everything I was hitting in practice was on the barrel. It felt great.

After sampling countless ideas, simply getting on the plate was the secret that got me feeling comfortable again. It all of a sudden made so much sense to stand close to the plate in a league that constantly threw outside to me. Now I slowly learned to take inside pitches and go after anything out and over the plate. Not only was it was one of the rare moments of my junior year where things made a lot of sense, but the adjustment caused a major breakthrough in my mind. A seed was planted. The idea that there wasn't a black and white separation between a physical adjustment and a mental adjustment started to take hold. It was Ryan Howard who helped me begin my epiphany, but it would be another (this time older) professional baseball player a few months later who would help me complete this idea.

CHAPTER 34

Our season was on the brink of a total collapse. Already four games out of first place after just one weekend, our wiggle room was now down to nearly zero. We needed a turnaround, and right away.

Throughout baseball's storied history there have many instances where a team started out dismally but based on one key game or series, magically turned it around. On May 22, 2003, the Florida Marlins were a dismal 19-29, averaging fewer than 16,000 spectators per game. On May 23, 2003, the Marlins defeated the Cincinnati Reds in a 5-4 battle. From that day on, the Marlins played .632 ball, going 72-42. They won the World Series.[14]

Then of course there were the "Miracle Mets" of 1969 who on May 27 were 18-23. Then on May 28, 1969 the Mets pitcher Jerry Koosman threw 10 scoreless innings before Tug McGraw got the win in the 11th inning. The next time they would lose, their record stood at an impressive 29-23. Their final 100-62 record led to an eventual World Championship.[15]

Not every turnaround results in a championship, but almost every turnaround season does have a key moment. Ours was against UMBC. We were feeling down after our disappointing weekend against Stony Brook. Our mid-week game against Cornell had fallen victim to inclement weather. But from UMBC on, we played at a 22-8 clip.

Every year we would alternate which America East team hosted the weekend series. This year we were home, which meant an extra day of classes and an extra day of practice (on Thursday) and, most important, an extra day to sleep in our own beds.

Home series were dream weekends. I didn't have classes on Fridays, so when I got out of class every Thursday afternoon, I felt a wave of relief. Even if I had a lot of work to do on the weekend, I would either have a long bus ride and hotel room for doing my homework or, if I we were home, I would just bang out most of the work Thursday night. The rest of the weekend was all baseball.

Having a home series meant I was able to wake up Friday around 10 a.m. and relax in my own room. It was infinitely better than a hotel room with two or three other guys. I would just relax and surf the web until I was up to date on the world's news. Then I would go to the dining hall for a big pre-game meal and head to the Events Center to get ready. By 1 o'clock we were on the field and taking batting practice.

I was feeling very excited for the weekend series. Because of some cancellations, Friday's game against the Golden Retrievers on April 11 was our *first* home game of the year. If that didn't get me excited enough, I had had a huge series against UMBC the previous year that became the turning point of my season. On top of that, I had been creaming the ball in batting practice with my new approach, feeling fresh and new at the plate.

I was locked in all weekend long. From my first at bat, I was barreling up pitchers' mistakes, leading off the weekend with a line drive straight up the middle. It deflected off the pitcher's glove before he had any time to get out of the way. The ball bounced oddly up in the air and fell right at the foot of the pitcher. This all happened in a fraction of a second, and I wasn't even out of the batter's box by the time pitcher picked up the ball and threw me out at first. Still, it was what baseball experts call "a good sign of things to come."

The team played poorly, but in spite of our efforts to throw the game away, we managed to pull out a late victory. It was our turning point. We had no business winning a game in which we stranded 15 runners on base, and we were down three runs going into the bottom of the ninth. But freshman outfielder Pete Bregartner led off with a clean base hit, and a late rally sent the game into extra innings. We won in the 10th.

After going 1-1 on Saturday we had to change our goal of a sweep and try to win three of the four. I continued to crush the ball all day Saturday and could not even sleep in anticipation of three at bats on live television Sunday.

Time Warner Cable had something of a monopoly on cable television in the southern tier of New York. One cool feature, though, was the local Time Warner Cable Sports Network, created to broadcast local sporting events. Our conference game vs. UMBC was selected for the game of the week. It wasn't ESPN, but it was still kind of a cool deal. Better yet, we were going to get to play at NYSEG stadium, home of the Binghamton Mets.

NYSEG stadium was one of the few modern structures in downtown Binghamton, and was literally a three-minute walk from the RE. A few times during the spring, a couple of us would walk to a Mets game and relax. (That's right – we watched baseball during our time away from baseball.) The stadium also was just 10 minutes from campus by car. Though the stadium wasn't going to be full, or even close to it, and the game was on TWCS, not ESPN, all of the guys were very excited about Sunday's game.

For so many of our games played in the cold, we were at the whim of Mother Nature. No amount of layers could stop the cold from penetrating to our skin. However, on this cold April day, we were all toasty warm in the dugout. Very generously, the Binghamton Mets had lent us their super jet-powered heaters.

The heaters were about as far as our team went in having a relationship with the Class AA Mets. We never tried to take advantage of having a minor league team in town, and I always thought that it was a lost opportunity. Maybe it would have been logistically impossible, but I thought it would have been a nice treat for us to get to interact with the players and perhaps even work out with them every once in a while. I would have loved to practice with those guys and learn from some of the best players in the world.

We never got to play at NYSEG stadium unless there was a special circumstance, such as this TV game. I would have loved to make NYSEG our "second" home field and play there whenever the Mets were out of town. Instead, we played on campus at Varsity Field, all the while patiently waiting for our new stadium that was now pushing five years in the planning.

Game four of the UMBC series was an exciting, fast-paced, hitting exhibition. For the hundred fans at the game (primarily parents, girlfriends and the entire drunken lacrosse team which came out to support us) and the 56 fans watching on TV, we put on a show and won 10-8. My new strategy at the plate had added four more hits to my season total. I was starting to get my batting average up. In just a few games we had saved our season, and I had turned mine around as well. We were now 3-5 in conference, I was creaming the ball, and we were starting to roll,

The mid-week game against Siena, which we dropped 6-2, seemed almost like a practice game. The intensity that existed during the conference weekends was absent and the teams' attitude was relaxed. However, to Dan Steers, Pete Bregartner and myself, it felt like a real game.

For me it was a cheap shot and one that went deep. I just had come off a really good weekend but after warming up for the Siena game and ignorantly assuming I was the starting designated hitter, I scanned the lineup card and did not see my name – even as a reserve! I know it was not malicious, but the coaches had simply forgotten to write my name on the lineup card, even as a substitute. It didn't exactly make me feel very rosy or important.

Junior Matt Simone, who by all rights deserved to get a start, was given the nod instead. As always, he was placed in "my" spot. Matt Simone was both a pitcher and a hitter and always gave a maximum effort. Our coaches never really considered him a starter either on the mound or at the plate, but he was a great teammate and an even better person. He would eventually be a team captain. With his work ethic and team-first approach, Matt earned the occasional start.

Matt was one of my close friends on the team (and my business school partner when it came to homework assignments), so I never had a beef with him. If it wasn't Matt taking my place it would have been someone else. Plus Matt was a great "team social director." Whenever we needed to organize a party or create a mixer with a sorority, we could count on Matt to get everything together. How could I get mad at a kid like that? Still, time and time again I was the player holding the short straw.

For Dan Steers it felt like a real game as well, as it was one step closer to his eventual departure from the program. Dan was a good kid who just couldn't seem to get college hitters out. His stuff just wasn't ready for Division I competition as a freshman. He probably needed some time to develop his pitches and his mechanics, but he would never get that time at BU.

After one more forgettable start later in the season, Dan's future was sealed. The Siena game was just one step closer to his pink slip. It wasn't a practice game to him.

For Pete, his school record-tying 14-game hit streak ended. Pete was one of those players who could tell you every stat about himself, about the team and about our opponent. He got crap for caring a little too much about his own stats and not enough about the team, but I didn't blame him for wanting to break the hit streak record.

He would have done it, too, if not for a bad call by the first-base umpire. In the first inning he punched Pete out on a bang-bang call. He was pretty pissed off that his streak had ended. The game seemed real to him too.

CHAPTER 35

When Albany came to town, last year's misery was still fresh in our minds. We knew sweeping Albany would not rectify the disaster, but it was the best we were going to do. The past wasn't going to change.

As the progressed, it became apparent that the heightened level of emotion was an extension of the previous year's playoff games. There was no love lost as we battled Albany very closely in three of the four games.

I did not start game one, but by now I knew I had to be ready at some point to hit. With the team down a run and with a runner on second base in the bottom of the eighth inning, I was called upon to pinch-hit. It was a huge situation. I got a decent 0-1 pitch to hit but was a tick too slow and popped it up to second. I had started to get the reputation as being a clutch pinch hitter but with so little room for error, having only one at bat, it was far from a guarantee that I would get a hit.

We still won the game in the bottom of the ninth. I was unhappy with the at bat, but after the game I put baseball in the back of my mind and went out with my family for a great meal at a real restaurant. It sure beat dining hall food. Afterwards, I headed back to the RE. I was in college now and that meant that I had to go back to my place and my family had to go home. That was life.

The next day we wore our hitting shoes. It was a total team effort in which the offense gave the pitchers 16 runs to work with in game one. I contributed my first home run of the year, which came in a very odd fashion. After ripping two line drives in my first two at bats, I was anxious to get another hit. The first pitch was a cutter that came flying in at my hands. The pitch moved so much that when I started my swing, the ball was in the strike zone but when it crossed home plate it was merely inches from my fingers. I realized the ball I was swinging at might hit me. I attempted a check swing but it was a futile effort. I was so embarrassed that I dropped my bat and headed off to first base, trying to play it off as a hit by pitch. The umpire wasn't blind though, and called me back to the batter's box. I argued that the ball hit me, but it was more of an argument to save face.

The next pitch I drove over the left field fence.

Game two was an extension of game one. We didn't put up as many runs, but the entire team played quality baseball in a 4-3 victory. We faced my ex-summer league teammate, Josh Willimott, and it was both exciting and challenging to square off against him. He knew how I hit, and I knew how he pitched.

We had great battles all day, and though I didn't have any hits, I did manage to come up with a huge RBI. I was as hot as a Texas chili pepper.

After our 30-minute ritual of cleaning the field which included raking, grooming, watering, and putting away the equipment, I walked back to the Events Center beaming. Finally I was locked in *and* getting to play every day. Plus, we were winning, and a championship was starting to pop into my mind. I couldn't see how things were going to go wrong. If I only I could have looked 24 hours into the future.

Streaks cannot last forever. Inevitably, you slowly return to Planet Earth. Deep down most players can accept this, if only just slightly. No one can stay locked in forever.

Whenever I managed to get into a hot streak, it was a special time. I never hit 20 homers in a month, like Sammy Sosa once did, but when I was hitting well my food seemed to taste better, math problems seemed easier, and balls flew farther. Every ball I hit was a missile. It felt good to see my hard work paying off. Each at bat was a fun and exciting adventure.

Though one can never depend on a hitting streak to save a season, I did learn from two years worth of college games that streaks are a necessary component to ending a season with worthy stats. Hitless days were inevitable, so 6-for-10 streaks were needed in order to offset the bad days. Simply put, the hot streaks neutralized the cold streaks.

So why do hitting streaks come and go? There are so many variables at work that it is a futile task to try to identify the combination of factors which are decisive in getting a good or bad streak going during a given period. Sometimes a player needs to completely overhaul his swing, but sometimes it is just tweaking the smallest of things, like moving three inches closer to the plate. The trick to being a good hitter is to limit the duration of the cold times and ride the highs as long as possible. The older I got, the better I was able to do this.

If why streaks occur is a mystery, it is much more troubling why they disappear and how they can end so randomly. But whenever the streak ends, it ends. A player accepts the great run and moves on.

I would have loved to see to how far I could have taken my streak. I was becoming a good enough college hitter that I don't see any reason it wouldn't have extended deep into conference play. However, I never got the chance to finish off my hot streak. Instead, I was slowly moved to the bench and had to observe most games during the frigid April and May months as my streak shriveled away.

Here is how my greatest hot streak of the season came to a screeching halt:

Going into game four of the Albany series, I had only positive thoughts. Nothing could seem to stop me at the plate. Then my entire season was altered.

I was 0-for-2 going into the bottom of the fifth inning. We were down three runs with a runner on base and I was facing a two-strike count. I stepped out of the batter's box and took a deep breath. I clearly remember thinking that I was way too hot and locked in to go 0-for-3. The next pitch I put off the left field fence for a double. I was on Cloud 9.

For my next at bat, Albany brought in Dave Noble, a lefty, so the biblical command was to take me out of the game. Tom Baileys was a big righty bat for us. Being new in the league, there was no scouting report telling the defense where to play him or what the pitchers should throw to him. He feasted on average fastballs.

In one pitch, Baileys turned the game around, and with it my season. The second ball met bat everyone in the park knew the result – a pinch-hit, game-tying home run.

We piled on him as he stomped onto home plate. Baileys added another RBI single in his next at bat in our 13-10 victory. It was a huge performance, and I was thrilled for the kid. He deserved to be the star on that day.

Was it the right move to bring in Baileys? Maybe. The result cannot be disputed. Nonetheless, taking me out after I'd just hit an opposite-field double off the wall ticked me off.

My season was never quite the same after that. Out of our next 10 games, eight were against lefties. The result was that in between my double off the wall at Albany (on April 20) and my single to break up a no hitter at Hartford, 20 days had passed in which I only played in two games.

A string of left-handed pitchers and Tom Baileys getting red hot was enough to kill my hitting streak. Over the 20-day stretch I batted nine times.

My misfortune turned into Baileys' riches. He got to face lefty after lefty who fed him fastball after fastball. He mashed the pitching, leaving a lot of sore necks on the mound. Even the balls he didn't crush seemed to shoot through infield holes.

I was never resentful of Baileys. We were good friends and I loved to see him succeed. But I was agitated that I had been taken out of the lineup during my hottest streak ever as a Bearcat and that there was no effort made to get me back into the lineup. Even if Baileys deserved to be hitting every game (which he did), there were still eight other spots in the lineup I could have hit in.

On top of that, I was extremely frustrated about how I was handled with regard to lefty pitching. Instead of trying to help me become a great hitter against both lefties and righties, the coaches simply decreed during my freshman year (incorrectly) that I would never be able to succeed against a lefty.

I never did really get going again during my junior year, and I never fully got back into the lineup for the remainder of the season.

CHAPTER 36

Ever since I arrived at Binghamton and became a part of the America East Conference, it seemed that we were in a constant search for more teams to play. In the northeast, it seemed a lot of schools had cut baseball in order to save money. Years earlier, America East members New Hampshire and Boston University had decided to do without baseball. Then, in July of 2005, Northeastern left the America East for the Colonial Athletic Association (CAA). It left America East baseball with seven teams – thus the need to play four-game series on weekends. It also meant that there would always be a team having a bye weekend.

We had our bye weekend sandwiched between Albany and Hartford. After playing such good baseball, no one was excited about a weekend off from league competition. Because of midweek games, we had six games slated in between conference play.

The first was against rival Le Moyne. The Dolphins threw a lefty. I sat. Then we played four games against New Jersey Institute of Technology — which threw four straight lefties. I played once.

My double against Albany felt like a millennium ago, and I was growing impatient. I was thrilled about our team's newfound life, so I had to bite my tongue, but I could feel the icicles growing on my body.

We beat Le Moyne, swept NJIT and all of a sudden were riding a nine-game winning streak.

The most memorable part of the NJIT weekend was the unforgettable bus ride. NJIT played its home games at historic Bears and Eagles

Riverfront Stadium, home of the Atlantic League's Newark Bears. As we approached the stadium, we started to get our things together. The stadium was 100 feet away.

Still, our bus driver somehow got lost after literally being just across the street from the stadium. Apparently, he tried to turn the bus around to let us off on the right side of the road but instead took a turn going the wrong way on a one-way street, and before we knew it we were back on the highway!

It took 25 minutes to find the stadium again. On the way, we got a tour of some bad parts of Newark. We were all pretty sure that we had found Newark's version of the RE. It was an old, abandoned building that clearly had not been occupied in 15 years. Everyone got a great laugh at comparing the decrepit building to our baseball house. The comparison was a bit too close for comfort, but still hilarious.

Le Moyne came to our park on April 30 for our last midweek game. The weather was hot (for April), our team was hot, and I was – ice cold. After having just three at bats in the last 10 days, I was visibly off my game.

Midweek home games were always hard because it meant I had classes in the morning and did not have a bus ride to catch up on sleep. On most weekday games I had an 8:30 or 9:40 class, so I would have to wake up early and go to school. It was very unsettling to sit in a class and watch a professor go over stock dividend ratios and debt to income charts while the only chart I wanted to read was the pitcher's chart for our day's opponent.

Our midweek games started at 3 p.m., so after class I would run to Appalachian dining hall. When I lived in the dorms, I could run to my room and take a nap. Now I no longer had that option.

Now that I lived off campus I had to settle for using the "group study room" in the basement of the dining hall to catch a quick nap. The library had a few couches, but I liked the dark basement area much better. It had a better couch and was usually quieter. Soon news of my secret sleeping place spread, and you usually could find at least one or two baseball players dozed off on one of the couches at any given point in the day.

The drill became synonymous with game day. I would run to the study area, set my alarm, and go to sleep. I would wake up after a cat nap feeling as dreary and out of it as you would expect. I would then run to the dining hall, get some food, drink a Vault energy drink, and head to the field for batting practice.

Usually by the first pitch, I was alert and ready to go. Against Le Moyne, though, my schedule was all messed up. First I had a mid-term exam in the morning. Then I had to attend a group meeting for another class. I had to sprint to the field by 1 p.m. with no nap, and having only eaten a snack bar. I was out of my routine. It wasn't an excuse for my 0-for-4 day, but it didn't help. Every student athlete has to deal with academic issues which inevitably interfere with baseball.

Freshman starting pitcher Dan Steers must have missed his nap as well. In what would be the last start of his career, Dan allowed eight earned runs on seven hits. He faced only 13 batters. By the end of the second inning we were down 9-0.

Le Moyne ended the massacre with 21 hits and 18 runs in an absolute annihilation. Just one week after we had broken up Le Moyne's nine-game winning streak, the Dolphins did the same to us. Sweet justice, I suppose.

Coach Sinicki always used to give us speeches after games and soon they became a sort of a joke with me, Morgan Smith, Jeff Skelhorne-Gross and Walker McKinven. We weren't being disrespectful to coach and we always did it in a private setting, but being baseball players we had some fun with the speeches in our downtime. After Le Moyne beat us, Coach Sinicki yelled about how a recruit was there for the game and now he had to somehow convince this kid to come play here. (Perhaps he used the card that we obviously needed some sound pitching.)

The rest of the season, the guys would joke after a bad play or loss about how we could possibly convince the "recruit" to come to this awful, embarrassing program. We got a few too many laughs out of Coach Sinicki's serious point, but his message was clear: Playing that badly was simply unacceptable.

Reflecting back on it, the situation had some irony because the recruit that day was a pitcher named Billy Hurley who after his freshman season would also be released. Weird.

The Le Moyne game had to be quickly expunged from the team's memory. I was especially upset because not only did we get embarrassed, but I had allowed the coaches to negatively affect my play. I was so angry about my recent playing time that I went into the game convinced my rhythm and timing would be off. Of course with that attitude, it was easy to prove myself correct.

If baseball was not enough to think about, school was starting to heat up as well. Thankfully, I had one easy class to give me a small but needed break. It was the type of class I imagined a bunch of football players from Texas (no offense, Longhorns) took in order to stay eligible. Just to give you an example, our final consisted of 25 multiple choice questions – that were given to us ahead of time!

There were no essays or critical thinking questions. I got a 100 on the final which lead me to an "A" in Marketing 480E "Strategic Retail Management." No one had to know that this difficult sounding class was a breeze.

I did have two real tests to worry about, though – one in Corporate Finance and another marketing test for my other tough class "Marketing 480D – The Mechanics of Strategic Pricing in today's Global Market." It was a bit challenging but not nearly as hard as the name suggested. I managed to get another A!

CHAPTER 37

We were 7-5 in conference with 12 games remaining. I was wrestling with my emotions all week after the disastrous "Le Moyne Massacre." I knew I needed to go talk to coach, even if it was going to get me nowhere. My dad had wanted me to go talk to him for a long time, and I was very hesitant to do so. I believed that by performing on the field everything would just fall into place. It was becoming very apparent that this was not so. I thought a conversation might iron things out a little bit. I stood by the coaches' door deciding if I really wanted to have a talk in which I knew how it would turn out. Finally I decided "what the hell" and went into his office.

I talked to him about playing the outfield, and my role as a hitter. One thing coach hinted at was that if I played the field then Joe Charron would have to DH. *When* they pinch hit for me, the left field position would then be vacant. My 7.2 60-yard time also didn't help my case. So I was officially a DH. Coach Sinicki said he and Coach Folli were in my corner. It was as if he made a point by not mentioning Hurba's name.

Nothing substantive came from the meeting, but I was glad I went and talked to him about how I was feeling. It was a bit intimidating, but I stayed respectful and, though it never really helped me, at least I took the chance and told him I wanted to do more. As I left, he told me the plan was the same as before; for me to get as many at bats as possible versus righties. I guess that is why they are just called plans.

I know there was no direct connection between my meeting and the way things turned out in our next series against Vermont, but it did just so happen that my lowest moment ever as a Bearcat occurred right after I talked to coach.

Traveling to a conference team's campus during junior year meant that it was the last time (aside from the playoffs) I would play there. Stepping off the bus at Centennial Field in Vermont marked the beginning of the end in a way. It was the first of our conference foes that I would oppose in a place where I would not likely play again.

Centennial field was as old-fashioned a stadium as any in America. It had hosted decades of both Minor League baseball and UVM baseball, and the chipping green paint and rusted support beams revealed its age. It was a part of New England history. It reminded me of the stadium from the classic baseball film starring Tom Hanks, "A League of their Own."

I usually had a decent idea from batting practice on day one of a series whether I was locked in or whether the weekend was going to be a dog fight. Ultimately, I did come to learn that pregame batting practice and game results were not as closely linked as I once thought. All batting practice could tell me was if I was super hot or super ice cold. With anything in the middle, it was anyone's guess how the game would unfold. It really was only a few rare days that I felt an extreme response in the cage. Thus I began to treat pregame BP as a warmup for my body, mind, eyes, and nothing else.

Still, after I finished BP at Vermont, I was sure I was going to have a great weekend. I was crushing balls as hard and far as I had all year with practically no effort. I left the batter's box feeling great. I had spent over a week agonizing about losing my swing and hot streak and now, to my surprise, I was back to feeling comfortable.

Game one matched two powerhouse pitchers. We sent out old reliable Zach Groh. They again countered with lefty Joe Serafin, the eventual 37th round pick of the White Sox. On this cloudy Friday, Serafin out-dueled Groh, adding one more to the list of dominant games he threw against us. He was throwing so well that I was extremely content watching and cheering from the sidelines.

Bouncing back from Friday's loss, we won the first game on Saturday. It seemed like every game brought a new hero. It was fun to know that anyone could be that hero at any time. This time it was senior captain Ryan James, who drilled a two-out, game-winning, bases-loaded double.

After seeing seven lefty starters in eight games, we were finally getting to see a righty. This was my one chance. For all I knew, I wouldn't get another start for at least a week. I was feeling so confident from my batting practices, though, that I really wasn't nervous. I was sure I would have at least one line drive in the game.

I felt amazing at the plate. I dug into the back of the box and sat there waiting for an early mistake. I attacked the first pitch I saw in a week (probably not a smart idea) and hit the line drive that I had envisioned for 48 hours. The only problem was that I failed to prophesize where the ball would land. Halfway to first base, I saw the ball tail right and land about 10 feet foul. Back to home plate. Strike one.

At 1-1 I got another fastball in. I was just a tick late this time and grounded out to shortstop. I was not concerned. Keith Rakus was a great pitcher for me to face, and I was eager to see him again a few innings later. He threw hard and challenged lefties, and I had a feeling the next time up I was going to get him.

However by the fifth inning he was out of the game and his replacement was a soft throwing side-armer who tossed the ball in at about 76 mph. On the second pitch from the "poop slinger," as slow side-armers became known to our team, I saw a fat changeup and took a hack at it. I was way too overanxious and hit a 200-foot pop-up to the leftfielder. I slapped my helmet hard in disgust, slammed my bat down and ran out of the box.

I never got another at bat all weekend. Catcher Jeff Skelhorne-Gross pinch-hit for me as we eventually went on to win another close game, 6-5. By winning twice on Saturday, we had significantly improved our prospects for making the playoffs.

After games the team would board the bus and return to the hotel to shower and get ready for dinner. It usually gave me five minutes of peace to reflect on the game and gather my thoughts. I considered the day's events. I knew that two lefties were throwing Sunday and my weekend was done. After suffering weeks worth of mental anguish about losing my swing, it had magically resurfaced. But all I had to show for it were two lousy at bats and six more days without any hope of live action.

I kept it together through dinner with my dad and step-mom, Kathy. We talked and ate a fantastic meal of lobster and crabs. I was upset, but they had the right words to calm me down and put everything in perspective. We were winning (11 of 13) so it was hard to get too mad.

We left the restaurant as the sun was setting. I don't know what the heck entered my mind as I walked out of the restaurant, but I just lost it. I was a few feet ahead of my dad and deep into my own thoughts when some foreign salty and wet substance rolled down my cheek. I am not sure exactly what thought triggered the first tear, but all of a sudden my eyes watered up.

I had had so much frustration bottled up that I had nowhere left to bury it all. It all came out. The tears, the pain, the frustration. I am ashamed to say that I felt sorry for myself. I just couldn't believe that events had unfolded as they had. This was my career. This was my one trip around the block. Things were supposed to be so different.

I thought of how much bad luck I had. Little did I know that I was far from the only player in the country in this situation. It is one of the main reasons why I wanted to share my story. It is all too common.

It seemed like a bad dream. As I let everything settle in my mind, I finally accepted my situation. That is not to say I was okay with it, but I became at peace with it. It wasn't worth fighting the situation anymore. I was so bent all the time on proving to my coaches that I was an all-star that I let every small thing get to me. Every strikeout, every pinch hit, every little comment. It was killing the game I grew up loving.

The tears came first. Then came my epiphany.

I realized right then and there that most likely I was going to be done with baseball in a little over a year. It was time to enjoy every second on the field and make the best of my situation.

I finally began to accept my situation. I promised myself I would stop fighting it. I had hit my low point and was ready to acknowledge my circumstances. If I went 0-for-2 in a game, then that was the day's result. If I had prepared as hard as possible and still had come up short, that was life. Worrying about getting pulled after every strikeout was futile.

Externally there was no change. I was already determined to show a good face and cheer as hard as possible for my teammates. I really, really wanted the team to WIN. I hated losing. But within myself, I swore that I was going to do the most with the chances I was given and that I would only focus on what I could control. The rest was up to the Baseball Gods.

That night in the parking lot were the last tears I experienced over baseball (well, except for when I watched the last game ever at Yankee Stadium) until my last day in organized baseball more than a year later. I wiped my eyes and pledged that I wouldn't feel bad for myself anymore. I would prepare and then compete.

Baseball had slowly become less and less fun. What had had happened to Quinn was now happening to me. That night in the parking lot, I was saved. Even though the next day I was on the bench, my entire outlook was different. Baseball made sense again.

For the next year plus I loved going out to the field every day. The last year or so of my career was the most fun I ever had playing the game. I had years before where I absolutely dominated the game, but I genuinely enjoyed my last year more than any other. I *know* that without my struggles and their resolution, I would not have attained the passion and appreciation for baseball I have today. It made me realize how wonderful an honor and privilege it was to be part of the greatest game in the world.

CHAPTER 38

We won Sunday and with eight games remaining left Vermont in striking distance of Stony Brook for first place. All of a sudden another regular-season championship looked possible. First, though, we would have to dispose of Hartford.

I was pumped to be able to go back to Connecticut. It was rare to play in front of hometown fans, and always a treat to come home. The entire family came Saturday. Once again, rain had postponed Friday's game and created Saturday and Sunday doubleheaders. America East weekends were marathons, though it always seemed when Monday morning came around that the weekend had somehow flown by.

Saturday was just an awesome day. We won both games, and I got to play in front of my family. We were getting no-hit entering the sixth inning when I singled up the middle to break the spell. After my hit, the offense came pouring out and we won convincingly. I finished the day 2-for-7 but felt good about my play. I had once again rebounded from a long period of down time.

Sunday was a different story. It was Mother's Day, and it killed me when I wasn't in the lineup for either game. I wasn't upset about sitting. I was upset that I was clueless as to the logic behind my coaches' moves. My mom was there, and I am sure she would have liked to see me play. Hartford was throwing two righties, and all I could think about were two distinct conversations I recently had.

The first was my talk just one week before with coach about getting into the lineup against as many righties as possible. The other was my conversation with dad in the parking lot at Vermont. I wasn't going to let this get me down. I rooted hard from the bench.

We left Connecticut taking three of four. The bus ride home was a happy one. I was handling adversity and, just as important, I was formally done with my junior year of school! I did not have any exams during the upcoming finals week, so I was officially a full-time baseball player.

Also, our team was finally over the .500 mark at 25-24 and, with four remaining game against Maine, another regular-season title was well within our grasp. With our solid play at Vermont and Hartford and Stony Brook's late slide, entering our last series (which started on a Thursday because classes were finished), we were now tied for first place with Stony Brook.[16]

With so little of the season remaining, I started to seriously think of how things would likely shape up for my last season at Binghamton. Tom Baileys (DH), Joe Charron (LF), Corey Taylor (CF), Henry Dunn (CF), and Pete Bregartner (RF) were all coming back. I didn't know what freshman were coming in, but I could assume they would be getting at bats as well. I wondered how I was going to try to prepare all winter for a season that looked so bleak. I had to snap myself back into the present and focus on Maine. One day at a time.

In game one, our offense raked in the runs, and we won 12-4. After the game I had to go up to the dorms to say goodbye to my girlfriend, Corey. She was heading home for the summer. I was going to Hawaii in a few weeks, and I just wasn't ready to try to make the relationship work. It was sad to say goodbye, but I thought it was the right thing to do. It's tough when a relationship ends because of timing and distance. I almost would rather have a relationship end because of an internal problem. When the thing that ends it is logistics, it kind of sucks. But that was the way it was.

My situation was far from rare, and I truly believed that the other players and parents on the team who had been around for a few years knew what was going on. I'd be surprised if deep down many parents weren't thinking "better him than my son."

That being said, thank goodness my parents were smart enough and mature enough not to complain to other parents. It still felt good when a parent made a comment to me or my parents just acknowledging my situation. I never expected them to lose sleep over it, but positive comments from the other players or parents went a long way. It made me feel like this situation wasn't something that I had created in my own imagination. The comments solidified what I believed; that I was a very talented player at the wrong place and the wrong time.

The fathers of Ryan James and Greg Lane become pretty close with my dad over the course of watching dozens of games together. All three parents truly rooted hard for the others' children. So when I hit an absolute mammoth home run in game two of the Maine series, Mr. James and Mr. Lane were the first to congratulate me. They probably didn't think much of the gesture, but it stuck with me throughout the years. It was just a firm handshake from the both of them, but to me it meant a lot more than that.

To me it was a deeply encoded message, "Great job. That a way to overcome so much adversity."

In my first at bat of the game I had hit a high chopper to third base and was thrown out by half a step. I was frustrated because I was convinced that if I had gotten out of the batter's box just that much quicker I would have been 1-for-1. I had no idea what was coming the next at bat.

I always had streaky home run power. If I was allowed to play in every game when I was hitting well, it wouldn't have been odd for me to smack three or four in a short period. In summer ball I usually ended up with four or five wood bat home runs. During the college season I rarely parked a ball. When I did, it simply was a line drive that kept going.

The ball came over the plate perfectly aligned down the middle. If there was ever a pitch to belt, this was it. The ball exploded off the bat like a bullet leaving an M-47 chamber. As I trotted around first base the ball cleared the fence and exploded into a tree, taking branches down with it.

The second game was yet another classic Maine-Binghamton matchup, but this time we were on the losing side in a 7-6 dogfight. Still, if Stony Brook lost we were regular season champs. Our celebration was on the fritz and now lay in the hands of Stony Brook. We cleaned the field, headed to the locker room and sat impatiently waiting for the Stony Brook score.

When coach finally broke the news that Stony Brook had been defeated, we all gave a small cheer. It was great being regular-season champions but there was just one small problem: We still had no lights!

This once again meant that second-place Stony Brook would host the conference tournament at SUNY Farmingdale — the field where our cataclysmic loss to Albany occurred roughly 360 days earlier.

The possibility of redemption was great, but having to go back to that graveyard was a total disadvantage. I am pretty sure the cheers were more for our party, now officially on for that night, rather than for winning the title.

Because all of the parents were in town for the Maine series, we held a parents party at the RE. Liquor and beer flowed from every corner of our apartment. Our parents played beer pong with us and took shots of liquor off the ice luge, a huge block of ice that chilled the alcohol as it rolled down a chiseled path until it finally arrived at the bottom where your mouth was.

I tried to freeze (no pun intended) that night in my mind as best as I could. The time was flying by, and the beer only made it seem to go quicker. But it was a magical night of fun. It didn't hurt to have our parents' expense cards at the bars, either.

I woke up Sunday at about 3 p.m. We had three days to get ready for the conference tournament.

When I woke on Friday, I peered outside and could tell it was nasty. Sheets of rain were falling, so there would be no baseball. Stony Brook, however, did get its games in and went a surprising 1-2 on the weekend. It meant that if we either went 1-1 on Saturday and Stony Brook lost or if we went 2-0 we would be regular-season champions regardless of what the Seawolves did. If there was a tie, we would have to play again on Sunday. And that couldn't happen. We had our big "parents party" scheduled Saturday night which meant we *needed* to clinch on Saturday afternoon.

Our games started at 10 a.m. on Saturday. I was not a fan of energy drinks, but having to be on the field at 8 o'clock left little choice. I chugged a Monster Energy Boost and trekked to the field.

The first game was a classic Maine-Binghamton battle with us getting in the last punch. Tom Baileys hit a walk-off single in the bottom of the 10th for the 6-5 victory, as he once again seemed to be in the middle of a late-inning rally. I was relaxed on the bench. I had a coach when I was 16 who said that a person's nerves can only withstand so much. It's hard to be at your best when you are nervous and tense hours before competition. I got better and better at relaxing until right before it was my turn to perform. Like going from zero to 60 mph in 3.5 seconds I learned to hit the ignite button only when it was time to actually race.

Luckily we had characters on the bench like Jeff Dennis to help me relax. Jeff had plenty of help, but he certainly was the leader of practical jokes on the bench. He probably pissed the coaches off from time to time, but I loved having a guy like him keeping everyone loose. His most famous joke was called "water hands".

When a player would be sitting with his hands exposed, Jeff would come by with a full bottle and dump the ice cold water over the poor guy's helpless hands. It didn't feel good on a chilly and windy afternoon, but it was small, dumb jokes like this which went a long way in keeping the bench relaxed during tense games. It was such a stupid joke, but every time he pulled it off the entire team laughed.

After Matt Simone and I fell victim to Jeff's little prank, however, we decided to get back at him at practice one day. While Jeff was standing near the dugout entrance we both took full water bottles and dumped them on his feet. Jeff had just fallen victim to "water feet." Making him run around all day with damp socks was sweet justice.

Jokes aside though, with the most recent victory we were now just one win away from repeating as champions. I was ready to play, and although I was unsure if I would, just being a part of such a high stakes weekend made me happy to be there.

CHAPTER 39

The conference tournament setup was eerily similar to the year before. In fact, everything was way too comparable to the previous season's playoff setup. We once again had the banquet the night before the tournament, and I once again had to watch other people, who were very deserving, receive awards while I considered how things could have easily played out differently.

I have always loved playoff time. With every pitch having the potential to make or break a series, everyone is constantly on edge. You just never know when a big play will come that may make all the difference.

We took care of Vermont in game one without a hiccup to match up with Stony Brook in the second round. It was a night game, and the place was packed with over 1,000 fans. It was a great atmosphere. I thought we had a better chance to win with me playing – every competitor should have that attitude – so I was unhappy when the coaches decided to go with Baileys as the designated hitter in game two against right-handed Gary Novakowski.

Baileys had one hit in his last 15 at bats. I had faced that pitcher numerous times, I had playoff experience and loved big games. But that's just the way it was.

At my end-of-year meeting the next week, the coaches told me it was a gut feeling that they went with Baileys. It was an insulting excuse. I wish they had just said they wanted to go with their guy who admittedly wasn't hitting well over the last few games but was still having an excellent season and deserved the start.

I still wonder what would have happened if I played. We lost 1-0. We had a few chances to score, our best coming with runners on first and third with Ryan James up, but we chose to hit away as opposed to bunt or hit-and-run. He grounded out to third base.

Stony Brook scored in the bottom of the eighth when Steve Mazzurco led off with a bunt single. Dennis pitched another masterful game, but Mazzurco scored in a most unusual style. He bunted his way on, stole second on a hit-and-run, advanced to third on a wild throw, and scored on a wild pitch due to a mix-up between pitcher and catcher.

With our back to the walls and just one out remaining in the game, my coaches decided it was now time for me to get my first at bat of the postseason.

I had not batted for six days. Now, with our season on the line, I was being asked to save the day. I had only one thing in mind: destroy a baseball.

I got the count to 3-2. I fouled off a fat first pitch, so the rest of the at bat I was battling from behind. At 3-2 the pitcher, Jordan Purington, came back with a slow fastball/change-up. Whether it was the juices flowing within my body or simply a very good pitch, I did not get a good read on the velocity. I was slightly out in front of the pitch and hit a mile-high pop up straight to the second base area. A quarter of an inch lower on the bat or an eighth of a second later and perhaps that ball leaves the park…

And just like, back in the losers' bracket, our season was all but done. We packed up our bags and headed for the bus.

My mom or dad couldn't make it to the game, so once I got back to the hotel I called them and went over the game's events. My dad tried to find the right words to settle me down, but there were no words to say. I hung up and went straight to my room and went to sleep. We had to play Vermont again the next morning.

When we knocked out Vermont the next day, it was our 29th win – a season record for the school. It also meant that we again were matched against Stony Brook in the nightcap.

In Joe Torre's "The Yankee Years." pitcher Mike Mussina is rumored to have quietly thought before the team's game 7 American League Championship Series loss to the Boston Red Sox that there was no chance the Yankees were winning that game, not with Kevin Brown on the mound. Our "game 5 starter" had much better support from teammates than Kevin Brown, but unfortunately he was not that much more effective than Brown had been on that fateful October night.

Our pitching supply was on empty from the first pitch. By the sixth inning we were down five runs.[17]

In the meantime, we did nothing against their starting pitcher, Mike Errigo. He had us completely fooled at the plate and when the final pitch was thrown, the Seawolves stormed the field.

In a fitting end to my season, I was robbed blind in my final at bat. Errigo had errantly thrown a fastball down the heart of the plate which I dutifully dispatched into deep right center. I figured it was a double when out of nowhere centerfielder Brian Witkowski jumped up and plucked the ball out of the air just moments before it made contact with the fence. It was one of the best catches I ever saw. I ran into Witkowski in Hawaii later that summer and he very vividly remembered the catch. He had a little smirk when I brought it up. All I could do was tip my cap.

Once again we had fallen a little short and had to watch an opposing team celebrate. Once again I had to wait another year. This time though I knew I only had one more chance for a championship. I was out of lives.

Stony Brook had beaten us six times in one season. We had failed to score in all 18 postseason innings against them. There was no denying that they deserved to be going to the NCAA Regional. Still, that did not make me feel any better.

When we got back to Binghamton, we had the extremely difficult task of saying goodbye to the seniors. It seemed more real this time. I had been with Ryan James, Zach Groh, and Gio Yannuzzi for three years and they in many ways seemed to be the same age as me. Second, saying goodbye to them also meant I was now "the seniors."

For the time being, I ignored that fact. I was leaving for Hawaii in a week, and all I had on my mind were beaches, palm trees and volcanoes.

Surprisingly, before I left for home Coach Sinicki told me I was going to be getting a few thousand dollars extra added onto my scholarship. They probably had extra money from a guy or two who didn't sign, but I didn't really care. It was a very nice gesture nonetheless, and so I took the money, said thank you, and set my sights on Oahu.

CHAPTER 40

On June 6, 2008 Jeff Dennis was selected in the 39th round by the Oakland Athletics. When we had lost to Stony Brook a few weeks before, I was positive it would be the last time I'd see my best friend for a long time. Going into his junior year, Jeff was already planning to be playing Minor League Baseball in the summer. He had been talking to a lot of scouts throughout the season and was (rightfully) being hyped as a big prospect.

Standing 6-foot-6 from the left side of the mound, flirting with 90 mph, and being an engineering student were all on his side. Being from Binghamton was not. Though Coach Hurba constantly chirped in Jeff's ear about his prospects, all there was to show for it on Draft Day was a 39th round selection. Eventually, Jeff decided to turn down the Athletics' offer and return for his senior year. Ironically, I went from figuring I would never see Jeff again to literally being his neighbor when I moved to his hometown in Syracuse, N.Y., after college. Jeff took a chance by coming back to school. Sometimes risks don't pay off.

Going into junior year I also had plans that did not play out as expected. For me, reality exceeded expectations. Entering the fall I desperately wanted to play in the local New England Collegiate League. When that did not work out, I went for my next best option.

When I woke up on June 9, it occurred to me that by the end of the day I would be in an apartment in Hawaii. The 12-plus hour plane ride seemed to drag on forever, but after flying over pristine blue waters for hundreds of miles we finally hit solid ground.

My time in Hawaii was probably the best two months of my life. I feared that playing baseball there wouldn't nearly be as good as I had imagined it during all of those cold nights during the Binghamton winter. It doubled any of my wildest expectations.

We played a nine-inning game almost every day, but still had tons of free time. I swam with sharks. I hiked through rain forests and jumped off a 60-foot cliff into a lake. I went surfing and swam at the famous Waikiki Beach. I climbed Diamondhead, an old volcano. I saw amazing seaside cliffs on Kauai, and went to a Luau and ate pig cooked in a fire pit. I ate pupu (appetizer) at beach resorts while sipping pina-coladas. I went to Pearl Harbor and saw the U.S.S. Arizona memorial. I snorkeled with man-sized fish and turtles. I partied at the University of Hawaii and ran on Hawaii's famous rainbow track.

All of these things were once-in-a-lifetime opportunities. I had little money, but I was young, single, and in Hawaii for a summer. It could get no better than this.

I expected to have a great time, but I never expected to mature so much as both a hitter and a person. The league was filled with very talented players from all over the country and for the most part operations ran very smoothly. We played most of our games about a half hour away at a park that, 67 years earlier, Japanese planes had flown directly over just minutes before bombing Pearl Harbor.

The field was lined with palm trees and flowers of all colors and forms. It was a great place to play, but unfortunately there were no batting cages. There was absolutely no opportunity for any extra hitting – which proved to be a blessing in disguise.

I started the summer red hot, but in the middle of the season I started to slump badly. Without batting practice I was struggling mightily. As I said before, every slump has a low point than can only be seen from ashore once the slump is over. Mine was definitely an 0-for-5 day with three strikeouts. The last strikeout came on a pitch thrown about 84 mph right over the center of the plate that I completely whiffed on.

All I could do was go home and play the song "You had a bad day" by Daniel Powter. Tom Baileys and I would play this song whenever we had an awful outing. The simple 3-minute, 54-second song never failed to make me feel better.

In the midst of the slump, something clicked. Suddenly hitting became easy. My mindset shifted the way a building's foundation can be altered by an earthquake. Here is my attempted explanation of the unexplainable:

First came my ability to succeed without having to take 100 swings a day. Extra batting practice is important, but having the confidence to know that I could go up to the plate after taking a day off from hitting (or a week off between live at bats) and still rip the ball was vital. Eventually a lot of our games were moved to a new field, one that had a batting cage, so I got to take a few cuts before games. It felt like I was taking steroids.

I loved playing at the new location and being able to take even a few swings before the game. All I began to need was 20 swings at most, and I was locked in and ready to go.

Not only did I love the new field for its batting cages but the scenery was breathtaking. Built inside an old volcanic crater, the field had a postcard-like backdrop with the outfield lined with green mountains which disappeared into rainforest clouds.

The other huge change in my hitting was a mental adjustment that had been 10 years in the making. When I met my roommate, Kurt Steinhauer, all I could think of was how every stereotype I had ever heard about people from Southern California was true. Kurt was a well built, muscular kid with long blond hair and a swagger. He always looked so "chilled out" and loved surfing. And, oh yeah, he could kill a baseball.

Kurt was eventually drafted by the New York Mets in the 27th round in 2009. After getting to know him, which took about 10 minutes, we would have long talks chatting about hitting and the mental approach. I had the unique opportunity to listen to Kurt talk about the science and art of hitting and then see him carry out his strategies in a game. It was like a chess novice watching Bobby Fisher play chess after talking strategy with him before the match.

Kurt was not on Fisher's level, but he really excelled in his mental approach. It all came from the hitter's bible, Ted William's book "The Science of Hitting." Every word in the book brought enlightenment.

I always hear stories about how certain people wouldn't have gotten to the level they achieved but for a certain Mr. X. I honestly feel that I never had my Mr. X at college. I never had that coach who not only believed in me, but who also had the power to truly help me along the way. Coach Folli was close but, as the assistant assistant coach at BU, he was powerless in many aspects. I needed someone to steer me in the right direction and help me get to the right place *mentally and physically*.

On my own it took a lot longer to finally arrive at the level I achieved by May of my senior year. I did really well in college, but I always thought that I was missing my Mr. X. Well as it turned out Ryan Howard, Ted Williams and Kurt were the closest things I had to him.

Ted Williams (and Kurt) broke down hitting to its core. They challenged me to think about my approach and my plan at the plate. My barriers were always mental. Williams wrote about how much *fun* it was to face a pitcher when you have a game plan. It was a mental challenge to store and log all of your at bats and use them to your advantage as the at bat, game and season progressed.

Like the great Ted Williams, I became a guess hitter. By assessing what the pitcher was throwing and how he was getting me and other hitters out, I was amazed at how often I would guess right on the pitch that was coming. *For so many years, people had told me to not think at the plate, but for me thinking was good.* As long as I was thinking strategy and not mechanics, I was golden. I felt like an idiot for having spent so much time and effort trying to *not* think. Now I was spending my effort doing the exact opposite.

From that day on, hitting was much easier. I had always given the pitchers way too much credit, but once I realized that they missed their spots on a consistent basis, had constant sore arms, and had as many insecurities on the mound as I did as a hitter, their mental edge quickly vanished. I started to mash the league's pitching but, more important, hitting became more fun.

I was no longer nervous. If I made an out, I simply stored the information in my head and moved on. Soon I was a confident hitter like I had dreamed I would become. I had always told myself that I was a solid hitter, but until my summer in Hawaii I never truly believed it. By summer's end I knew I had something special in my back pocket for the upcoming season. What opportunities lay ahead, however, still were a mystery known only to those sometimes cruel baseball Gods.

So why did 17 years of hitting all come together during a two week stretch 3,000 miles from home? It can't be ignored that I was now 21 and had three years of college experience. I had learned how to slow the game down, how to deal with failure, and how to adjust to constantly changing conditions. To go along with that, I had created a swing that allowed me to effectively hit both fastballs and breaking balls.

Furthermore, I had learned to succeed without needing 100 swings per day and five at bats per game. Additionally, due to the roller coaster ride during my college seasons, hitting had once again emerged as a fun challenge. I loved competing with the pitcher day in and day out. It made me relaxed, more confident and stronger.

Lastly, I was able to combine my increased physical strength with my improved mental confidence and new game plan. The result was a totally new hitter.

Here is an example of my makeover from the last game of my summer season: I entered the game with a relaxed and positive mindset. After all, I was playing baseball minutes away from the sandy shores of Honolulu. In my first at bat, I ripped a line drive base hit to left field on an outside fastball. The second time, the pitcher started me with a change-up that I took for a ball. He again used a change to go to 1-1. I knew what his fastball looked like from the previous at bat and at 1-1 it was time to sit dead red.

He missed with the predictable fastball to go to 2-1. Before, I would have just looked for any good pitch to hit (most likely a fastball) and hoped it would be a mistake. I would be extra tense for fear of missing my pitch and fretting about the hole I'd be in if I did miss the 2-1 pitch. Now, however, my game plan was radically different. I decided that because he had just missed outside with one fastball and allowed the other fastball to be driven for a hit (in my first at bat), it would be wise to sit on the off-speed pitch. He hung a curveball, and I put it into deep right center for a double. I ended the day 3-for-4.

I returned from Hawaii burnt as a piece of toast, both literally and figuratively. I was exhausted from "relaxing" in paradise. Even in a setting like Hawaii, two months of non-stop baseball is tiresome. I was actually blessed in my three years of summer ball to *never* win a playoff game. We seriously considered missing the playoffs as a blessing because we were all so worn down after the 100+ games we had played in college and summer leagues. At that point we just wanted a few weeks off before school started. My teams' collective playoff record in my three summer seasons' was 0-2, having only made the playoffs once!

As I boarded the plane to head back home I was physically tired, but mentally I was rejuvenated. I couldn't put it into words, but I knew I was leaving Hawaii a different hitter *and* a different person. I knew I had become one of the seniors that had looked so old and mature when I first stepped onto Binghamton's campus. In a few short weeks I would be heading back to Binghamton for my last go-round. It was time to start thinking about life after baseball.

PART 4
SENIOR YEAR

CHAPTER 41

One more trip around the block. One more loop on the carousel. This was my last go-round.

After three years of whirling on the carousel horse, listening to the music blare, the ride was now close to its inevitable conclusion. Similar to the wooden horse bobbing up and down, my career had been like a buoy in a turbulent ocean. Though the seas got rough at times, I always managed to stay afloat.

With the ride coming to its end, I tried to take in all the sights, sounds and smells, but it was to no avail. The world was speeding blurrily passed. All I could really do was make the best of the last rotation. I knew that soon a man would come and force me off the ride, and there was no getting back on.

When I returned to campus in late August for my senior year, I was awestruck by how comfortable and familiar my surroundings felt. It wasn't so long ago I was a freshman just trying to get my bearings. To have become a confident senior was a satisfying feeling. I had friends in all of my classes and, better yet, my best friends were living with me at the baseball house. I had the big, corner room and a guaranteed parking spot. I was 21 and could buy alcohol.

I also had a new responsibility to be the type of person the freshman could look up to. I realized how important it was to remember the feeling of being the "newbie," so I made it a priority to respect the fact that the freshmen were not in the same place as me either mentally or physically. I tried to treat them as if they were senior proven stars. I knew that some of these guys were going to make or break our season (and I was right), so it was important to earn their respect quickly.

I always believed the best managers and coaches were the ones who not only mastered the skills part of the game but also understood athletes and their developmental curve. It is all too easy to forget or ignore the struggles you went through when you were learning and failing. Too many times people ignore the fact that freshmen (or new employees) aren't there yet. There is a lot of room for growth. It goes back to the old saying, "You are only as good as your weakest link." As far as I was concerned, meeting the freshmen was an opportunity to make new friends and good teammates.

I hated when the older guys put up a phony line to separate themselves from the freshmen. When I was in high school, I looked up to the seniors like they were gods. One ended up pitching at Division I Manhattan, another played for Division I Connecticut, and the last played for Division I Holy Cross. I always felt that most of the seniors distanced themselves from the underclassmen and didn't make an effort to become friends with the younger guys. The exception was Tucker Frawley (who went to Holy Cross and now is an assistant coach at Yale).

Tucker was one of the best teammates I ever had, but more important, he treated me like an equal. Based on my experience with Tucker, I made a huge effort to not just talk to the younger guys but to become *friends* with them.

On the field, my fall season was an extension of the end of the summer. I felt like a god armed with a metal bat. Feeling relaxed in the batter's box for the first time in my college career, I absolutely embraced every precious moment there. I was thoroughly enjoying being out on the field and taught myself to focus on the day's events and not worry about what spring time would bring. Like every October though, the snow began to fall on Binghamton and forced us to shut down baseball until the spring. The fall had gone by uneventfully, and I was pleased with what I had shown on the field.

Come winter, I worked hard in school and in the weight room, but also made sure to enjoy my few short months off from baseball. The team had some awesome times together, filled with memories of black light parties, Halloween parties, and weight room sessions. There were many a nights where we "drank the town dry."

If it was scary enough coming back to school for my last year, it was that much more frightening returning for my last semester. After the five-week winter break, it took me a while to get going again. My girlfriend had graduated, and without her around, things initially felt a bit empty. The first two weeks were a drag, but as always, with time I got into a routine of working out, going to class, and living the student life.

Everywhere around us, the economy was having a negative effect. We learned that our hopes for a brand new artificial turf stadium would remain a distant concept. A new stadium had been promised when my class was recruited, but apparently it was still almost two years away from even being started. The economy had tanked and with it went New York's budget surplus and our dream stadium.

The economy was also taking a major toll on my job search. Long before any financial crisis, I had made the decision to spend summers playing baseball as opposed to getting internships. I knew of a few people getting job offers from the companies where they had interned. However by March things had gotten extremely rough. When on March 9th, 2009 the Dow Jones industrial average hit its 12 year low at 6,547, the panic reached all the way into upstate New York State, as the news immediately sent the job market into a downward spiral. It was nerve-racking thinking that in just a few months I would be out of school and possibly unemployed. Baseball quickly became my escape.[18]

My job hunt was a humbling experience. I always thought that my 3.8 GPA, interview skills, and Division I athletic status would automatically get me a job. But during the recession of 2008-2009, I received many rejection notices. It is one of those things that I joked about, but inside it really weighed on me. My goal was to have a job set up by opening day. As Lehman Brothers, Bear Stearns, Washington Mutual, and Merrill Lynch were all collapsing and/or getting acquired during the fall, I became worried that my higher education might land me a job as a driver for Pepsi. (The economy got so bad that Pepsi came to our campus job fair offering truck driver positions.)

Not knowing what the spring (or thereafter) would bring, I treated my last winter vacation as precious time off. I enjoyed lifting with my sister (a pitcher at Emory University) and hitting batting practice off of my dad at Bob Turcio's Batters Box. In previous years I had spent a lot of mental energy wondering if I was wasting time hitting so much 60 days before my first game. However, I had a totally different opinion on hitting during this winter.

For starters, my first game was in mid-February which meant that I needed to get ready earlier than in previous years. More important, however, hitting had become so much more fun in the last year that I was eager to hit at least every other day. My dad pretty much tore his shoulder out throwing me buckets upon buckets of baseballs. In my last batting practice session of the winter, I couldn't help but think that after 18 years and literally tens of thousands of pitches, this was the last time my dad would ever throw me a batting practice pitch. I ripped the ball right back up the middle.

When I arrived at school in late January, I learned one of our captains, Ryan Holley, had become ineligible to play in the spring, his last semester of eligibility. He only took three classes and failed two. Our freshmen loved to joke about how Holley used to give them a hard time about drinking on school nights. Maybe Ryan should have been more focused on his own studies.

It was completely inexcusable for a captain to fail out. Ryan had some issues he was going through, but to let his team down was as big a sin as one can commit against his teammates.

I was taken aback by the news. Then I thought that it might mean a huge opportunity for me. I had slaved away as the backup first basemen my entire junior season and had also played a decent amount there in Hawaii. I was the obvious option to play first now.

Except I wasn't. The coaches decided to replace Holley with outfielder Pete Bregartner and utility man Matt Simone. My coaches were simply not going to give me a break unless they had absolutely no other alternatives.

I could hardly believe the irony. A year ago I was used like a pawn as the backup first baseman. I spent hours working out there with a minimal chance of ever getting any real time. Now I was not even a thought there.

After a week of indoor workouts, I went to coach and inquired about the first base situation. He told me he thought he was doing me a favor by not putting me there. He said it was my senior year and that he wanted to make it as pleasant for me as possible. Apparently, starting every game at first wasn't going to be a pleasant time for me.

He also said he didn't think I wanted to play there. Well, when he told me to be the backup the year before, I did it even though there was little chance of playing time. But now that the starting spot was open, he was concerned about my happiness at first base?

The real kicker was his statement that I had only written down that I wanted to try out for the outfield when we completed the "tryout form" during the first fall meeting. Therefore, he had just assumed that I had no desire to play first base. Perhaps he forgot that he told us to put only *one* position on the form.

Furthermore, he stated that I had told Coach Hurba in the fall that I'd prefer to play the outfield. This was true. But in the fall, Ryan Holley was at first and it was completely pointless to be the backup there at the time! Evidently it didn't occur to my coaches that my desire to play first might change once Ryan was ineligible. It was like a politician spinning a tale to justify his actions.

The truth was that they wanted to keep Pete in the lineup and use me as a DH/pinch-hitter. I don't know why they just didn't tell me this up front. It turned out the entire situation was irrelevant because freshman Dave Ciocchi wound up hitting his way into the lineup and became the starting first basemen and an established star. Still, I felt very cheated that I wasn't given a fair opportunity at first base in the winter.

CHAPTER 42

My last opening day took place right outside of Dallas, Texas. It is a well known cliché that an opening day gives everyone a new start, but it didn't feel that way to me when the first pitch was thrown at Dallas Baptist. It was partly because I knew how rocky the season was going to be on a personal level, and I didn't believe for a second that this was a fresh start. Also, by senior year everything seemed so routine that the game oddly enough seemed like an extension of last year.

In fact, the only real sense that this in fact was Opening Day was the fact that we were playing *outside* and seeing live pitching on a real field for the first time since early October. We were thrown right into the fire, facing a future 49th overall pick in game one, Victor Black. His fastball was easily over 90 mph, but seeing a real pitch outdoors for the first time in months made it seem like 99 mph. I missed the first pitch I swung at by about half a second.

I remember stepping out of the batter's box and seriously thinking I might not touch the ball the entire day. Luckily, the pitch was a slider and I ripped it for a base hit. I never again had to worry about going hitless during a season.

We played competitively all weekend and were thrilled to go 1-2 considering that the year before Dallas Baptist had become the first independent team to get an at-large bid into the NCAA Regional. They lost a lot of thunder from their roster, but they were still a very good team.

The economy continued to tank throughout February of 2009. When Coach Sinicki announced to the team after the last Dallas Baptist game that things had gotten bad, we figured it meant that we weren't getting an extra fleece or T-shirt. Thus, we were shocked when he announced that the University of Vermont, a member of the America East since 1979, was dropping its baseball and softball programs at the end of the season. The baseball team was a significant expense, but instead of doing what Binghamton did, which was slash each team's budget a little, Vermont just eliminated a sport from both the men's and women's sides.[19]

The more research I did on the situation, the worse it seemed. Vermont's head coach, Bill Currier, was going to be jobless in a few months after coaching there for 22 years. (I had played with his son Brad in Bennington, Vermont and it made the situation seem much more personal.) The baseball program had been created in *1888!* Some greedy decisions by Wall Street and Washington had indirectly bankrupted a 100+ year-old program. Worse, all of the players there were without a roster spot for the next season.[20]

I was extremely thankful that our program was staying intact, but I really felt bad for the Vermont community, players, and staff. Baseball isn't much of a revenue sport in the northeast, and to the Vermont officials it was expendable. But the destruction of this historic program made me sick.

My job search was also intensifying and not looking much better than the state of Vermont baseball. Going from a suit and tie in an interview out to the baseball field later in the same day was an odd yet increasingly common transition. Life was extremely busy.

The next weekend was a washout. The Saturday games were immediately canceled, but there was still a chance that we would play in Virginia against Norfolk State on Sunday. Looking at the forecast though, and concluding that the coaches wouldn't want to spend any of our budget driving to Virginia for one day, we decided to chance it and go out partying Friday night. Still, as fun as the night was, I realized the next day how much better the weekend would have been traveling and playing baseball.

I always thought a lot about what I was missing by playing baseball, but that night I *finally* realized how envious all of the other students should have been. A weekend of baseball beat a night of drinking anytime. What we were doing on a weekly basis was a special privilege. The games remaining were far too few and precious.

When I boarded the plane for New Mexico the next weekend, I was already three weeks deep into my last season. It was flying by way too fast. Worse, I was having more fun than ever.

I had never been to the southwest, so I figured that New Mexico was the ideal last state to visit in my baseball journey of new and exciting places. I had played in Connecticut, Massachusetts, New York, Vermont, New Hampshire, Maine, Maryland, Delaware, New Jersey, Ohio, Virginia, North Carolina, South Carolina, Tennessee, Rhode Island, Pennsylvania, Florida, Louisiana, Texas, Kansas, Georgia, Utah, Hawaii, and California. But New Mexico was the last.

Albuquerque was an odd place. The backdrop looked right out of an old western, with brown prairies rolling into a desert sprinkled with large rocks. However, the Applebee's, Holiday Inns, and Ford dealerships peppering the city painted a different picture – one of a sprawling metropolis.

Albuquerque Isotopes Stadium was a modern structure towering above the desert landscape. The facility of 13,279 was home to the AAA affiliate of the Los Angeles Dodgers and would later in the year be seen on ESPN when Manny Ramirez was "rehabbing" from his steroid suspension. The scoreboard put some Major League Jumbotrons to shame.[21]

Without sugar-coating the weekend, we got beat very, very badly. We took a 1-0 lead in the top of the first inning of the first game, but from there it was all downhill. We just couldn't seem to stop their bats all weekend. At times it looked as if they were hitting a ball off a tee. We lost 15-3. We should have been thrilled with the result.

Game two was one for the books. After five innings we were down 11-0. Then things took a turn for the worse, especially when we gave up nine runs in the sixth. My dad wanted to get a bite to eat between the games so he left after seven and a half very long innings. It wasn't until dinner that night that he learned that we gave up 10 more runs in the eighth.

We lost a baseball game 30-2, and we didn't play the New York Yankees. Dane Hamilton went 6-for-7 on his way to the cycle. He added an extra triple and home run in case there was any doubt. We thought he was the greatest hitter since Babe Ruth. Apparently the Major League scouts thought differently. He was drafted by the Padres in the 41st round. Not exactly the lottery pick we had all thought he would be.

Trying to play the second game of the doubleheader after a beating like that was no fun. Coach Sinicki had nothing to say after the loss. What was there to say except maybe we should play a prevent defense in the second half to avoid a couple of touchdowns?

It was one of those weekends where our bad pitching combined with their unbelievably hot hitting led to a clean sweep. We were outscored 65-9. We hit the ball fairly well, but our pitching was simply overmatched. We were convinced New Mexico State would be playing in June in Omaha. It turned out we were something of a curse for them. Before our weekend they were 13-2. After that, they were a very average 24-18. They didn't even make the NCAA tournament. But for that one weekend, they were the best team in the country.

The weekend wouldn't have been complete without some personal drama.

On Saturday night the temperature dipped below 40 degrees. I didn't start game two, so I was huddled in the corner with Henry Dunn. We stayed under a heating pad most of the game. With the score being so lopsided, there was not even a remote thought that I was going to have to pinch-hit.

Our defense was running off the field after the sixth inning when Coach told me I was hitting right now for Baileys. We were down 7-1. Icicles had more mobility than I had at the moment. I was no in state of mind to be hitting, but I scrambled for a bat and ran up to the plate.

Strike one came in at 94. The bat never left my shoulder. Strike two came in at about 93. The bat was still frozen in place. I stepped out of the box and took a swing. I *was* swinging at the next pitch no matter what, so of course the ball traveled about 55 feet before hitting the dirt. I swung and missed the ball by feet. As I jogged down to first base I muttered some not so nice words that Coach Hurba heard. When I got back to the dugout I uncharacteristically took my helmet and slammed it into the bench. I felt like I needed to make the coaches aware of how unfairly they had just treated me.

I guess it worked because the next day Coach Hurba said that in the future he would give me more time to get ready, but that I also needed to be ready to hit whenever a righty came in. When had I heard those words before?

The at bat was meaningless in the scheme of things, but when the year finally ended and I looked up my stats it was stupid at bats like this that had driven my average below the coveted .300 mark.

To make the situation worse, the next day a lefty throwing about 85 mph pitched for the New Mexico State Aggies and I sat. He was average at best, giving up three runs in four innings. I was good enough to pinch-hit against the 94 mph right-hander with a dirty slider, but put a lefty on the mound and I was a lost cause. It made no sense but I was long past fighting it. I wasn't about to let anyone ruin my remaining 45 games.

Still, I left the weekend feeling locked in and very gratified knowing that I was able to hit their pitching without much difficulty. In fact, I may have had one of the best at bats of my life at NMSU.

In my first at bat the pitcher pounded me in with fastballs and forced me to hit a soft ground ball for an easy putout by the first basemen. I wasn't going to let it happen again, so I decided to look hard and in for my next at bat. I stepped off the plate just a bit. The ball was exactly where I had predicted it would be, and I launched the ball deep over the fence, just foul. Out-thinking the pitcher again, I decided it was time to sit soft and away. He hung a curve and I ripped it for an opposite-field single.

It seemed everything I had learned about hitting was revealed in that one at bat: I stayed relaxed and confident, even when I got down in the count. I hit a ball with power. I stayed back on a curveball. I hit the ball with authority to the opposite field. I had an intelligent game plan and out-thought the pitcher.

With the New Mexico Massacre complete, we were 1-6. I don't know if the record had anything to do with it, but back home the vibe around practices was extremely negative. I always played better in a positive atmosphere, but instead of stressing some of the good things we did, it seemed that the coaches focused exclusively on what we were doing wrong.

Obviously a team has to focus some attention on its weaknesses in order to improve, but when the atmosphere is constantly negative it takes a toll. Perhaps I interpreted the tone more negatively than it really was because I was always longing for some positive feedback and did not get a lot of it, but this was how I felt.

For example, when we were hitting on the field, Coach Hurba would more often than not make comments about what we were doing wrong as opposed to what we were doing right. It is a fine line between simply ignoring one's flaws and blindly complimenting one's strengths, but the coaching staff, with the exception of Folli, seemed much more inclined to make negative comments.

I am not pretending I didn't have flaws that needed to be addressed, but I just never felt that making comments that put a player down was constructive. Whether the coaches realized that some of their comments had this effect on me I will never know.

Another good example came during one practice when Coach Hurba strongly implied to the outfielders that we all had weak and inaccurate arms so every throw would henceforth have to go to the cutoff man. This was a coaching decision (and arguably a very smart one), so obviously I would comply. However, the way the words came out sounded demeaning and served as a confidence killer. There were many better ways to get the message across.

I didn't think I had a bad arm. My arm always started weak at the beginning of the year and would slowly build up strength. I would eventually hit a wall where my arm hurt every day, but once I got past that phase, my arm got to the next level. In high school I would long toss all the time to build up strength. At school, we simply did not do long toss enough. Every fall my arm was at its peak because I had six months of throwing behind me. But instead of putting us on an intensive throwing program, we were simply told we had bad arms. (They finally grasped this fact, at least a little bit, because about half way through my final year we started to do a lot more throwing drills, which of course dramatically improved both our accuracy and strength.)

After playing two tough teams, it was a welcome relief to be playing Maryland- Eastern Shore. To put it bluntly, UMES sucked. It would have been three easy wins, but the rain washed the Sunday game away so it was only two easy wins. But then one of the games was actually very competitive, so it became one easy win. I played in the first of the two games and went 0-for-1 with a sacrifice bunt and a walk. I had higher hopes of a "stat padding weekend", but the team did grab two much-needed wins, even if we didn't look very good doing it.

Coach reached his threshold at practice the next day. After we had botched our team defensive drills numerous times, Coach Sinicki rightfully snapped. We really were not playing good baseball, and it was time for a wake-up call.

For the next half hour we ran – back and forth on the warning track 10 times. Then we got absolutely screamed at. It was one of the few times I thought getting yelled at was the right move. We needed to have someone get in our face.

Unfortunately, the running had a side affect for me that did not help me. At some point over the summer in Hawaii, I had strained my upper hamstring and the pain never fully went away. It was healing well, but all of this progress was destroyed within minutes. After every lap I could feel the pain increase just slightly. By the last lap, it was a sharp, cramp-like pain.

Hamstring injuries heal slowly, and I was never able to give it the full time it needed to heal completely. I was lucky that after a 30-minute warmup, it usually loosened up enough to run on it. Most hamstring injuries meant at least six weeks on the bench. I tried to baby it when I could and save my legs for game sprints. After a hard lift or conditioning session, my hamstring felt very stiff and sore and I sometimes thought I was going to have to sit out the day. Thankfully, I never had to. It always felt just good enough to play.

Jim Calderone one time asked me why I was slacking during base running and conditioning drills, and I quietly explained to him my leg situation. I was shocked that more people didn't realize that I had this injury all of my senior year.

I really didn't want the other players, and especially the coaches, to know. They already had enough "excuses" to take me out of a game. Besides, in a game I was able to run 100%. It was just after the game that it started to hurt badly. By the next day it would be just good enough to run on again. The hamstring never gave out on me. I was very lucky.

The injury made practices extremely difficult at times. I did everything in my power to keep the hamstring issue hush-hush. I did my own rehab in my room with ice, massage, and heat. I honestly don't think the coaches ever knew the pain I was in at times. My big fear was that the injury was going to be mistaken for me "dogging it" at practice, but I got the idea that this was never an issue that came up. Again, I was very lucky.

CHAPTER 43

Binghamton became a Division I program in 2001. Since that first day there had been a huge push to make the athletic department a success. Like so many new programs, it was a struggle to get things moving in the right direction. There was a lack of funding which meant a lack of scholarships, facilities, and tradition. Binghamton realized early on, however, how valuable a successful athletic program could be. It put money into the athletic department and began to build it up. Soon seasons like the 2002 baseball record of 10-40 (2-20 in conference) and the 2001-2002 men's basketball record of 9-19 (6-10 in conference) were mostly distant memories.

In 2004 the $33 Million Events Center was constructed.[22] It gave the campus a state of the art basketball facility, indoor track, weight room, and new locker rooms. A few years later, the Bearcat Sports Complex was built to showcase the soccer and lacrosse teams. Watching the athletic department grow was very rewarding.

Due to financial issues and Title IX, Binghamton never had a football team. Although there are only a few home games per year and most mid-major football programs are not very profitable, adding a football team is huge for a university trying to become nationally known. I thought that Binghamton had missed out by not having football. We all knew that without football, baseball got more funding, more time in the weight room and more resources, but we could not ignore what we missed by not having our own team to root for every Saturday.

Without football or hockey, Binghamton depended on basketball to be the profit driver. After years of failing to make the Big Dance, in 2008 Binghamton finally secured an NCAA Tournament berth. After seven years in Division 1, Binghamton showed up in the NCAA brackets for all the world to see.

On opening night of the tournament, everyone came to the RE to watch our team battle the Duke Blue Devils on national TV. Binghamton wound up getting beaten pretty badly, but it was still huge for the school and for the athletic department. Slowly but surely Binghamton was becoming known athletically on a more national level. (Unfortunately, the next season the men's basketball program would make national headlines due to drug and crime related scandals which decimated the roster.)

A lot of people gave the basketball teams a hard time because they received more funding and resources than most other programs. I thought it made sense though that they obtained the funding because they were the ones bringing in the money. The part that confused me was why there wasn't more of a push to make the "non-revenue" sports profitable.

Granted a new stadium would have significantly helped the baseball team's ability to generate revenue, but even without a new facility there were revenue opportunities largely ignored by the athletic department. Most of the sports at BU didn't have banners, sponsors or advertising. Except for basketball, lacrosse, and soccer, there wasn't any effort to operate concessions or sell merchandise.

Even effective marketing though would not have made a dent in the economic crisis we were all facing. The financial situation could be felt throughout the department and the team. Our coaches were rightfully trying to save money in every way possible. This meant, for instance, getting up at 6:30 a.m. on Saturday morning to travel to Lehigh instead of staying there Friday night.

I officially was offered a job a few days before this series, and with that opportunity a lot of pressure I had been carrying all year drifted away. The position was with Wells Fargo Financial in Syracuse, and I took the job right there on the phone. I didn't really want to live in Syracuse, but it was a good opportunity. I would worry about the snow next winter. Now all I had to focus on was playing a game.

I slept during the long bus ride and struggled mightily to awake my body for game one of the Lehigh series. I was embarrassingly bad in pregame – and I was not surprised when my awful batting practice transferred into an awful game.

One bad game was all it took for me to get pulled from the lineup, even though another righty was throwing in game two. I didn't let it affect me any more because I knew it was ridiculous to try and play mistake free.

After being on the brink of losing both games of the doubleheader, we rallied late in game two with back-to-back-to-back home runs by Jim Calderone, Kyle Klee, and Corey Taylor. As Walker McKinven said, "For that one moment, *we were* the best team in the country."

The cold front over Pennsylvania continued the next day. It was sunny, but the field was as brown and dull as I had remembered it. The wind whipped through the dugout and most of the bench players sat outside the dugout in order to soak in any heat the sun was emitting.

After sitting for game one on Sunday, I went to talk with my dad between games. We both kind of just shrugged. Everything had been said many times before, and we both knew that this season was playing out exactly as we had foreseen. At least we were prepared for it this time. He told me how proud he was of me for sticking in there and not complaining or sulking. He told me I would get my chances and to take advantage of them when I did.

I used his advice the next game when, batting in the fifth spot, I went 3-for-4 with two RBIs. Two or three years earlier, I would have never been able to turn the weekend around like that. I was very proud as we pulled out of the campus. I plugged in my audio book, sat back and closed my eyes. I didn't have any school to worry about, I had secured a job, and life seemed all too simple. At least for the bus ride home.

Our last weekend before conference play began was in Connecticut, in the "Northeast Conference vs. America East Conference" showdown.

I had a vision of a weekend where we rolled through our competition, and I hit the tar out off the ball. All week I stayed focused and motivated, keeping my comfort level high. I wanted to be ready for my hometown "fans." Technically the season was only about 25% over, but it felt like the end of my career was starting to come into focus. Perhaps it was the beautiful weather that greeted us at Quinnipiac University in Hamden, Connecticut on Friday afternoon. Maybe it was the surroundings so familiar from years past. I had played on this field many times, but this was the last time – the last weekend after 21 years that I would play in Connecticut.

I started to take the games in on a whole new level. Things that I am sure slipped my mind about games played earlier in my career became lasting images ingrained in my memory. I can recall where I sat in the dugout, what kind of sunflower seeds I was chewing, the cool breeze in the air and my conversation about how the Binghamton Bearcats vs. the Quinnipiac Bobcats had to be some kind of NCAA record for the most letters in the names of two opposing teams.

But even more, I remember the feeling of excitement when I got off the bus and had a game to play. I remember walking to the field thinking about my goals and approach for the day. And I remember more clearly than ever my disappointment when I wasn't starting.

After the game, in which we were on the losing end of a pitcher's duel, I got treated to a fantastic meal at a local restaurant with my family. The "torture" of having to say hello and goodbye within two hours never seemed to wane.

Saturday's games were against Central Connecticut State at the old Minor League ballpark, Beehive Field. The field could have used a facelift or five. The playing field was in decent shape, but it kind of felt like we were playing sometime around the turn of the century. Metal bats seemed a bit out of place. My fan support almost hit double digits though so I had no complaints. My family, some family friends, and even some of my own friends were in attendance. It was really nice of them to come. It meant a lot.

The first game was against a lefty, but because I had been hitting so well the coaching staff decided to put me into the lineup. I was a bit nervous because I so badly wanted to prove to the coaches how ridiculously they had treated the matchup issue. The nervousness faded the second I got to the plate. Just like jumping off a high diving board, hitting a lefty was not nearly as hard or scary as it was sometimes hyped up to be.

I felt completely comfortable. Right there I knew the whole righty/lefty thing was a big joke.

I went down 0-2 on the count in my first at bat, and all I could think of was swing! Do not take strike three looking! The next pitch was on the black but I was still able to connect solidly and smash the ball into the hole between first and second. As the ball squirted through the infield it looked like an automatic base hit, but the second baseman dove, knocked it down, and threw me out at first by a split second.

I would have traded two hits off of a righty for that one hit any day of the week, but the kid made a great play on me, and that was baseball.

I walked the next time up, before popping out to right on my last at bat. It was an 0-for-2 game, but I felt really good and thought I had proven to my coaches that facing a lefty was nothing extraordinary. I knew that this late in my career nothing was going to change their minds, so I was mostly proving to *myself* that I was capable of hitting *any* college pitcher.

It seemed like every week I was growing leaps and bounds as a hitter, and it was exciting. Ever since my final weeks in Hawaii, hitting made a lot more sense. It became less of an effort and more of a simple fluid motion. I felt like a 95-year-old man who despite his age still loves to learn. He wants to gain as much knowledge as possible while he is still alive. I was close to the end of my career, but was thoroughly enjoying learning more about baseball each day.

One of the biggest improvements I noticed was how much slower the game seemed to be. I always used to reject the argument advocating the importance of experience, but after hundreds of college at bats I was able to come to the same conclusion – experience counts.

Some people are "geniuses" at a young age and ready to flourish immediately. But there is another class of skilled workmen, the "late bloomers" – people like me who take a bit longer to mature and grow. The thing about this latter group, however, is that they need a supporting cast to allow them to reach their potential. Who knows how many "late bloomers" never develop fully because someone cut them off too early? People too often assume that if ability isn't shown right away then it will not come at all. I think my coaches didn't see what they wanted early on and assumed it was not there. By my senior year I was proving them wrong.

The first game vs. Central Connecticut eventually got a bit out of hand so pinch-hitters were put in, and I lost a few at bats/hits. We put up 11 runs after I left the game on the way to 20-1 win.

What a funny game baseball is. We went from winning 20-1 in game one to losing 4-3 on a walk-off error by our shortstop in game two. Experiencing such polar results in the same day made you scratch your head in confusion. To add to the oddity of the weekend, as beautiful as Saturday was to be outside playing baseball, Sunday's game against Sacred Heart was a washout. One more lost game I could never get back.

The rainout made me remember a time when I was 13 and decided to go to a friend's barbecue instead of to my Babe Ruth League game, where I was the superstar. We lost by one run and my dad, who was the coach of the team, was furious with me. It wasn't until this rained-out Sunday that I fully understood why he had been so disappointed. I had let my team down by not going to the game, but it was much more than that.

We all have a finite amount of games in a career. Our time is limited. I was blessed with an ability to play baseball, and being able to play the game was a privilege. I owed it to my team to be there, but *I also owed it myself*. After working so hard and putting so much on the line, it wasn't okay to skip a game for a party.

At age 22, I would have given up 10 parties for just one baseball game. I hated losing any game now, whether due to rain, parties, or mudslides. The drive back in the damp bus was a depressing one. Thankfully, we had a mid week game against Marist to look forward to.

I always felt bad when my dad or mom missed work and drove hours, hoping I was going to be in the lineup. Even though I told my dad all week I didn't think I was going to play at Marist, he insisted on making the trip. I hated feeling bad because I knew if I was in his shoes I would have left a day's worth of pay on the table any day to see my son play baseball, but I still couldn't help thinking about him traveling two-plus hours to watch me sit.

Amazingly, by the time my dad made it to the field I was already 1-for-1. It was another hit that a year before I never would have gotten. I was down the entire at bat and looked hopeless. I fought to even the count by fouling off three or four pitches. Finally, the pitcher missed up and in with a fastball, and I ripped an easy line drive single.

I didn't get another hit but it was almost a moot point. I had excellent at bats all day and did everything within my power to help the team win. Our team looked surprisingly fluid out on the field. It was a sure "good win" until Marist decided to mount a last stand and hit a walk-off homer off our usually very solid closer, Greg Lane. It dropped our season record to 7-10.

As the years went by, Coach Sinicki got much better at controlling his anger. However, after their best hitter put the ball over the fence for the win, Coach was not happy. He took a chair and flung it. Then we were told to board the bus and to not talk to our parents. That was frustrating; I really would have loved to say hello to my dad. The team boarded the bus to head back to Binghamton. There, to Coach's credit, he did apologize to us about the whole chair incident. The negative energy spreading throughout the bus was put to a stop right then and there. Swiftly, the entire team shifted their focus to the very important upcoming weekend series vs. Hartford.

CHAPTER 44

It was time for conference play. I was confident we were going to make the playoffs, so the regular season almost seemed like just one of several steps to reaching a Regional. The season would come down to two playoff games in late May, just as it did every year.

We couldn't start the playoffs though until we started our conference schedule, and we couldn't start that until the rain went away. In years past, a rainout during conference play wasn't a huge deal. We had three days to get the four games in and, if need be, we could play on Monday. The poor economy had changed all of that.

The first major change was altering the format of the conference weekends. Friday games were moved to Saturday. Now we would play four games in two days. The Monday makeup game was eliminated – and so was the minimum number of conference games required for playoff eligibility, as well as the conference playoff banquet.

All of this meant that any rainout would wash away two conference games without any hope of making them up.

The new scheduling policies produced a huge shift in strategy. For starters, there was a lot more pressure to have your pitching staff go deep because your bullpen didn't have as much rest. Also, preparing for the weekends was different because now we either left a day later for an away series or we had an extra day of practice for a home series.

It made those two weekend days of intense baseball a blur. You could literally move from one end of the standings to the other.

The format was set up so that the first game of the series would go seven innings. The second would be nine. If the first game ever went into extra innings, the nine-inning game would become a seven. We only received a 30-minute break between games.

The format was doubly hard on Sunday, because we were usually exhausted for the fourth game. What other sport but baseball was played on the field of competition for 15 hours over the course of two days? College baseball certainly was different.

The new conference format started with a home series against Hartford in early April. Of course Saturday was rained out and so the series was immediately reduced to two games.

The hitters were especially anxious to play. We had just been given brand new Demarini Voodoo Black bats, and we were eager to try them out in a game. The way it worked was that the big time schools got the new bats first and, as production geared up, schools like ours finally had access to the newer models. The pop in the new bats was uncanny, and we were dying to try them in a game.

Sunday wasn't perfect but it was just good enough to play baseball. Thus, after 17 straight games on the road, April 4 was the first day of 2009 that an official pitch was thrown at Varsity field. It felt good.

Considering that we "lost" two games the day before due to rain, we knew that an actual loss on Sunday would almost be like losing three games on the weekend. More likely than not, the other top teams would win at least three games from the hapless Hartford Hawks and so our margin of error was very slim. Trailing 4-0 going into the sixth inning of game one, we were shaking our heads in amazement.

Thankfully, we would not have to suffer the same 0-4 start as the season before. We put together a five-run rally in the sixth, including a base hit I ripped up the middle to drive in the tying run, and we won the game. I added another hit in the second game on our way to a sweep. The world was restored to order.

Our team was on a roll, and I was riding along for the good time. Every time I went to the plate I felt like I was going to hit the ball hard. It was a great feeling, and one that only took me 1,000 days to achieve.

I was feeling at peace after the Hartford series. Things were good. I had a job waiting for me when school ended, it was getting warmer day by day and my swing was feeling right. Then we played a midweek game vs. Cornell and everything changed. First went the nice weather. It was so brutally cold outside that the combination of bitter winds and snow flakes nearly caused a cancellation. I was the designated hitter, which meant sitting in the unheated dugout all game.

But it wasn't the cold weather that led to my 0-for-4 day. Most of that was my own fault. I simply tried to be too perfect. My aggressiveness left, and with it went my quick decision-making ability. I almost bailed myself out of a bad day but the Cornell left fielder made a diving play on a loopy fly ball down the line. It would have been a cheap hit, but I would have certainly taken it. It was the closet I came to a cheap hit all season.

I knew that bad days happen, so I had to figure out a way get back to what I was doing right. I had to *quickly* forget about the loss to Cornell.

Due to the excessive rain, our coaches were able to schedule an extra game vs. Canisius the next day. Even with the additional contest, we were still well below the average number of games played for a Division I team. Though we ended up losing and I didn't play, it was good to be at a ball game. It helped me forget the 0-for-4 game and move on.

If we thought that Cornell was cold, the games at Albany the following weekend were absolutely frigid. I didn't hit a ball more than 100 feet in batting practice. It was like being back in the dead ball era. The old balls we were using for batting practice seemed to weigh five pounds.

The wind and the freezing temperatures kept my body rigid for our Saturday doubleheader. Every time a ball would smack into the raw, taut leather of a player's glove, you would hear a small shriek of pain. Their coach tried to get the games postponed due to coldness. Our coach was having no part of it.

We ended up taking three of four games from Albany. Better yet, no one died of hypothermia. I ended up getting on base a ton but had a limited amount of hits when two identical groundballs past the second baseman on consecutive days were both ruled errors. Both times I stared at the scoreboard and became frustrated that some 18 year old intern had just decided how my weekend would fare. There is something to the fact that certain years are "luckier" than others, and I had the overriding sense that this wasn't a year in which the batting average cards were being dealt my way. Nonetheless, with a few weeks of baseball left in my career, I was much more concerned about how I was playing with the cards that I held in my hand rather than the things *I could not control.*

Despite the unseasonably cold temperatures, the Binghamton train kept rolling. I played in three full games at Albany and got the 10 at bats I desperately desired in order to stay hot at the plate. I only had one at bat in our mid week game vs. Siena, a pinch-hit double, but it was obvious that both the team and I were locked in. We were ready for Stony Brook, which was coming to town for my last regular season games against them in my Binghamton career.

CHAPTER 45

By mid April, the school's appearance finally started to improve. The trees and flowers were blooming and the pretty girls who had been hibernating all winter came out to tan. Even the precarious winter obstacles, like the deathpath were slightly more manageable.

The infamous "death path" was a shortcut from our dorms on the hilltop down to the main part of campus. It was created by the wave of students who traveled up and down it each day on their way to and from class. For whatever reason, the school refused to build stairs connecting the two, so we unintentionally created a makeshift path on a 35-degree angle. On icy days you could spend hours watching people fall on their butts and slide all the way down the hill. *Everyone* fell victim to the hill, even the people who swore that they never made the plunge.

By mid-April, the snow had melted and the path had thawed. Except for an occasional mudslide and periodic flooding, the path was fairly easy to navigate.

The baseball field was starting to look like a well-groomed park. Hours of watering the infield, tarping the field and dragging and raking the surface seemed to be working. When Stony Brook finally arrived, it was treated to an emerald ballpark.

"From goat to hero" in a matter of moments is just one more cliché that must have been created by a baseball expert. There are very few sports like baseball where the opportunity for redemption is a daily possibility – make that an instantaneous possibility. Strikeouts, errors, or mistakes can all quickly be forgotten in just a moment's time. There are countless times when a player has gone 0-for-5 before hitting a walk off home run in extra innings.

Sometimes you simply need the opportunity to be a hero. Sometimes all you need is for a game to go to extra innings to go from "zero to hero." This I learned on a gorgeous Saturday afternoon when we found ourselves in an absolute dogfight with Stony Brook. There was no love lost between these two teams. Going into the last inning, we were down 7-3 and all but dead. I was 0-for-3 and on the verge of watching the rest of the weekend from the sidelines. If five of the first six guys up that inning didn't get on base, I would have had zero chance of getting a huge hit. But we did get those guys on, and when I stepped to the plate for my fourth at bat, the tying run was 90 feet away.

Their closer, Jeremy Nowak, had dominated me a year prior, but this time he made a mistake and left a fastball over the heart of the plate. Even at the college level most mistake fastballs are crushed. I roped a liner to right field, and just like that the game was tied. Jeff Abrams ended the game two batters later. It was an amazing win for our team and totally changed the weekend. From goat to hero, just like that.

I didn't play in game two, but after being a key contributor in game one, I was more than content. A few hours before coming up with the big hit, I wasn't even sure if I was going to be able to play. For whatever reason, at practice the night before my ailing hamstring worsened. The pain usually subsided as the practice went on, but on this night the pain kept getting more intense. When I got back to my room, I felt the hamstring lock up. I couldn't walk, and the pain got really bad. I seriously thought that my college career might be over. I couldn't imagine how I was going to be able to sprint to first base the next day.

An act of God, ice, and Advil loosened up my leg just enough to play on Saturday. I sat on the bench during game two in absolute relief as I watched another dramatic game in which we went into the sixth inning down 1-0. Dating back to our last game of the previous season, SBU pitcher Mike Errigo had kept us scoreless for 14 straight innings. No one thought it was funny that I was keeping a "silent" tally in the dugout.

We finally broke through in the sixth and ended up winning another dramatic come from behind, walk-off victory with the help of a Corey Taylor single.

Game three was *another* nail-biter in which we once again came up with the winning run in walk-off fashion. We won 8-7 and all of our runs came in the last three innings. None of us could believe that there was still a nine-inning game left to play.

In a weekend full of opportunities, the final game was no different. Opportunities often come when you are least expecting them.

If center fielder Henry Dunn was healthy, I would have sat in game four. But he had a hamstring injury (worse than mine), and the coaches were almost forced to play me. Other options were unavailable. Tom Baileys was home sick in bed. Jeff Skelhorne-Gross was sick as well. So I found myself in the game against a lefty.

I was 1-for-2 when I got up in the fifth inning against left hander Marc Brown. The first pitch was a slider that I fouled straight back. I was right on him. For some reason, he came back with another slider and this time I put the ball 20 feet over the right field fence. As I circled the bases, two thoughts simultaneously popped into my head. One was how many lost "home runs" never happened on days that I wasn't playing against lefties. The second was what thoughts were going on inside my coaches' minds.

My guess: Hurba tried to play it off as a fluke; Sinicki was probably glad I hit a home run but didn't think it proved anything. And Folli was probably smiling inside, proud as heck.

When I reached the dugout, Hurba was standing there with nothing to say. I really think he was in total shock. I nodded and walked right by him.

My dad told me after the game that Ryan James' dad, who was in town to see the parents and watch our game (even though his son had graduated), yelled in a loud, sarcastic tone about how I supposedly couldn't hit lefties.

Now I don't believe I should have faced every lefty and never should been taken out of a game, but it was so clear how ridiculous their lefty/righty matchups were. It felt great to stick it to them on that sunny Sunday afternoon.

In a twist of fate though, we lost the heartbreaker this time. Stony Brook was down 5-0 going into the top of seventh inning when our bullpen had a total meltdown, and this time SB beat us by one run in the last inning. All four games had been decided by one run, all in the last inning.

Even though our bullpen folded, we were still thrilled about winning three of four. The series was proof of how important good bullpens are, and how college bullpens, even at places like Texas and LSU, were generally weaker than starting pitching. Bullpen arms were simply easier to hit, and if a team could get to the pen early and often, it almost always resulted in more runs scored by the end of the weekend. Coach Hurba constantly preached to us about getting the opposing pitcher's pitch counts up. Come playoff time, we would truly see that once we got to America East bullpens, we always had a chance to win.

CHAPTER 46

There is an old cliché, this one definitely a baseball one, that during a season you see more of your team than your family. We were constantly together. It was great for team bonding, but it was not so great when a virus funneled through.

In a matter of weeks, half of our team was sick. Guys were throwing up left and right, and it didn't look like the Bearcat Flu was going away any time soon. I was lucky not to get sick, but everyone agreed that I already used up my sickness quota for the year. During the winter I came down with the flu for two weeks during which I lost 25 pounds. Those were two agonizing weeks.

Because so many guys were sick, Coach let them stay home during our road trip to Army. Some of our pitchers who weren't going to throw that day, especially our weekend starters, also stayed home. We traveled with half a team. I just assumed I was going to be playing because I didn't think we had even nine position players.

West Point is an unbelievable campus and a breathtaking experience. The campus was filled with magnificent stone buildings that resembled castles. The cadets all were in full uniform, quickly hustling around campus. In the middle of this pristine campus sat a baseball field.

Baseball at Army is serious business. Their players must complete a full regimen at the Academy *and* play baseball every day. It is an extremely tough commitment, but Army always fields a very competitive team. I was recruited to play there, but I wasn't ready to spend four years after school in Iraq.

We hit batting practice first in order to give the Army players more time to get to the field. *Only* their starting lineup was excused from classes in order to get to the game on time. Everyone else had to get there after their classes ended.

My dad and Kathy came to the game. When I looked at the lineup card I was crushed. I was the *only* position player not in the game. I couldn't even look over at my dad because I was either going to break down crying or start yelling.

It turned out that John Miele, our walk-on outfielder, had asked coach to give him a game in left field. Coach had granted him this wish. John was one of the best guys on the team and a true team player, but it was total crap that my spot was taken because he needed a game in the outfield. Where was my one start out there? To think of the hours I spent practicing in the outfield still makes me sick to this day. I loved playing out there, but to spend so much time practicing when I realistically knew I wasn't going to be placed out there killed me.

I was not mad at John, who had done what no other kid at Binghamton had ever done before him: walk onto the Division I baseball team. He did everything he was asked and became a great teammate (and friend), so I was glad to see him out there – just not instead of me. Out of all the times I thought I was wronged at Binghamton, this was close to the top.

I watched in disgust from the bullpen. There were so few players that I had to guard the bullpen for our pitchers. I didn't mind helping out with some grunt work, but I was in such a sour mood I just wanted to go home. I expected to be hitting doubles in the gap and here I was guarding the damn bullpen catcher from stray foul balls.

As the game went I started to calm down. John Miele struck out twice and I didn't think too much of it. He had worked hard and deserved to get a full game in. But as the game crept on and the score remained close, Coach Sinicki must have decided that he thought he could steal this game. I was in the bullpen in the bottom of the sixth warming up one of our pitchers. I was literally 50 feet from where Sinicki was standing. He had all inning to tell me that he was thinking about having me hit for John.

When I got the word that I was hitting, John was already on his way to the batter's box. I did my best to run to the dugout and take a few swings, but it was a lost cause. Only after taking strike one, a curveball, did I even realize I was at the plate. On the next pitch I decided to take a chance and told myself if it was a fastball close to the plate I was hacking. With a runner on third and less than two outs this was not the time to be down in the count 0-2.

I wound up getting a pretty hittable fastball but had zero torque and softly grounded out to first. Looking back I can laugh, but I had rage in my eyes as I jogged back to the dugout. I can only imagine what my dad was thinking.

We ended up losing 5-2 to a very good Army team. Army was so good in fact that they were only three outs away from beating Texas in a Regional when Texas rallied to win 14-10 on a walk-off grand slam by Preston Clark. But that was still a month into the future. Teams like Army and Binghamton were fighting and clawing in April just to make a Regional.[23] I left Army a "Bitter Bearcat."

Unlike the working world, I loved Mondays. It was an easy day of school, and I had no practice. I was able to come home early and nap. I was deep into my cat nap this particular Monday when I heard a pounding on my door. "The police are outside!"

I sprinted down to the parking lot. There, literally inches from my car, lay a billboard that had blown over in the wind. The billboard had actually scraped some paint off the car. A few inches to the left, and the car would have been totaled. It was the talk around the RE for days.

School was also filled with excitement. Things were starting to wrap up, and the seniors could feel that the dreaded real world was approaching. I knew it was close because I had just completed the huge Management 411 Case Competition. It was the final project in the cumulative final business class. It wrapped up four years worth of learning. The class was considered the last stone in the path to a business degree, and walking out of the presentation I could hardly believe that the class was all but over.

My sister was on the exact opposite end of the path. She was still a freshman, just trying to get acclimated to life outside of home. She was thousands of miles way in Atlanta, trying to adjust to college life. She had a "ferocious" softball coach who seemed to be draining the fun out of softball one pitch at a time for her.

As she was just trying to find her comfort zone in an entirely new setting, I was trying to deal with the fact that my time in the comfort zone was almost over. I could see that my sister was beginning to head down the path that Michael Quinn took, and the path that I almost walked down. I could hear the anguish in her tone when softball was brought up, and it greatly saddened me. The pain I felt during the low days of my college career, when things were going so miserably wrong, still felt very real to me. I still remembered the night I talked to Michael Quinn, long after he "quit", when I realized that baseball was no longer fun to play. I didn't know you can get the feeling back.

The journey that it took to dig out of that hole and rekindle the dormant flame was not easy. I tried to tell my sister what I had learned, but it was a fruitless effort. She too would have to go through her own growing pains and when *her* time was right, she too would rediscover the love of the game. I had always kept a journal at school as an outlet, but it was after talking to my upset sister on the phone one cold February night that I decided that I was going to share my story in the hope that it helped even one person learn how to "go with the pitch".

CHAPTER 47

Just like the previous two seasons, we played New Jersey Tech during our weekend off from conference play. I disliked playing a team like NJIT because the best case scenario was doing exactly what we were expected to do: Win all four games and mash the ball. Anything less than that was a failure.

Thankfully, we came out quickly and buried NJIT before it had a chance to fight back. My hot hitting continued as I blasted another home run to deep right center. It rattled through a big oak tree and settled well over 400 feet from home plate. I came within inches of a second home run, but the ball tailed just outside of the foul pole.

Game two was an even worse massacre as we put up 25 runs against the helpless junior varsity pitching. It was a complete mismatch.

NJIT became Division I in 2006. It is a great thing to move up in the college rankings, but I saw way too many schools label themselves as Division I but do nothing to back it up. Such schools bring down Division I baseball and Division I sports in general.

NJIT played at a very nice stadium, the Newark Bears Stadium, but it was a surface feature that covered up a lack of funding and interest in the program. It was obvious that NJIT was not fully funded. Baseball is allowed a total of 11.7 scholarships, divided as the head coach sees fit. I didn't understand how teams like NJIT, Fairleigh Dickinson, Maryland Eastern Shore, or Coppin State (which went from 4-52 in 2008 to

0-29 in 2009) could annually be bottom-dwellers without the NCAA complaining about it.

I assumed that opponents were either thrilled to steal wins from them (like us) or that they were so superior (like Miami or USC) they couldn't care less that in 2008 North Carolina Central went 0-22. I thought it was a sin to allow these teams to continue to flounder.[24]

Teams should be required to fund a certain number of scholarships and maintain a minimum athletic budget to continue their programs. As for stadium facilities, NJIT was the exception. Most weak baseball teams had horrific baseball stadiums.

The NCAA should mandate that for a team to become Division I and *remain* Division I, the school has to make a long term financial commitment. That means making a commitment to give out more than, say, two or three scholarships and to build an adequate stadium within 10 years. But no such rules exist, and year in and year out schools are allowed to put on their recruiting pamphlet that they are of Division I caliber, when in reality they are only pseudo Division I programs.

Early on Sunday we had to make the drive from Binghamton to Newark, N.J. to finish our sweep of the NJIT Highlanders. We easily won game one, though I did nothing noteworthy at the plate. It was by far the hottest day of the year, and pitcher Walker McKinven and I joked how we finally thought we might be done playing in the cold weather. (We weren't).

I loved playing in the heat, but after being in 40 degree weather a week earlier, 90 degrees seemed excruciatingly hot. It drained the team's energy levels quicker than any of us had expected. Between games, I visited with my family and told them they should leave because there was no way I was playing both games. I was fairly disgusted with myself, but at least we were winning and were now a respectable 19-15.

The coaches surprised me, however, with another chance in the last game, and I took full advantage of it. Tom Baileys was struggling at the plate, and Henry Dunn was still recovering from a hamstring injury. This left me in the DH slot.

As my approach matured, the first at bat of a game was always important to me. It allowed me to assess how I was feeling and what pitches I thought I was seeing the best. It also allowed me to see their starting pitcher's repertoire. For this reason, I often took the first pitch. I started to notice how many players got a hit on their first swing of their first at bat and was shocked at how low the number was. The percentage of hits was even lower when comparing hits to swings at the first pitch seen in the first at bat. Using my first at bat as a learning tool allowed me to understand what I had in store for the day. The only time I generally broke this rule was during a pinch-hit appearance, where my approach was swing hard and swing often.

Being able not only to learn about a pitcher, but also being able to start the game with a hit was a double treat. It's like acing the first test of the year. You learn a great deal about how you will fare in the class, and get a huge leg up with the first A. Dominating the first exam removed a lot of pressure for the rest of the semester, and also gave me the confidence I could get an A in the class. Likewise, a base hit in my first at bat not only ensured the day wouldn't be a total disaster, but gave me the belief that the day could be a special one.

My first at bat that Sunday was a perfect example. After taking the first strike, I battled hard and got the count to 3-2. I had seen his curveball three times already, so when I saw it coming again, there were no surprises. I disposed of the ball deep into left center field. As I stood on second base, I thought this could be one of those great games.

When I returned to the dugout after scoring, I had to take a minute and sit down. I was not used to sprinting home in the extreme heat and could not believe how much trouble my body was having (I was not alone) adjusting from the extreme cold to the extreme heat in a matter of days. I chugged an entire bottle of Gatorade and felt the energy return. I still had at least two more at bats to make this good game a great game.

My second at bat was a replica of my first one. I once again battled to 3-2 before hitting another hanging curveball for a double. I had simply remembered from my last at bat what the pitcher threw at 3-2 (a curveball). Knowing that he wasn't a sophisticated pitcher, I predicted he would repeat his sequence. As I slid into second base, my dad was more convinced than ever that I looked faster than my 7.2 60-ard time. On a warm "summer" day, my legs felt healthy and I was able to move pretty quickly, especially when a double was on the line.

We ended up winning the series four games to none as I finished the last game 2-for-3. Things felt great. It didn't seem like anything could stop me.... However, over the course of the next 14 days and six games, I batted only three times. That's what stopped me. Where had I seen this story before?

First we had a midweek game against Marist. I sat. Kyle Klee, our starting third basemen, was sick so coach moved him to DH. Once again I felt like an idiot preparing for a game all week that I never got into.

We left for UMBC on May 1. This was my last month of baseball. I was enjoying the game more than ever, and it was sad to think about it ending in a matter of *weeks*. I woke up late some nights scared and in a deep sweat just dreaming about being much older and not being able to take batting practice off my dad. I was petrified that when I left the game, everything I had learned was going to vanish within a few years. My life as I knew it was about to end, and it was the single most frightening thing I had faced in my young adult life.

My friends all had the same insecurities. And I was one of the "lucky" ones who had a job. I used to get annoyed when someone said I was lucky that I got a scholarship to college or that I was fortunate enough to land a job. Hours upon hours of practice and preparation, dozens of rejection letters, and heartbreak after heartbreak preceded my scholarship offer from Binghamton and my offer of employment from Wells Fargo Financial. Luck was founded on hard work.

My Dad and Kathy came down to Maryland in hopes of a great weekend of baseball. My mom would have been there as well, but she could not make this weekend. I had played great against UMBC the two previous seasons, and I was confident I was going to repeat those performances this final time around the block.

When I stepped into the batter's box for the first time *in a week*, however, the pitcher looked as if he was a mile away. That was not a good thing. My brain was miscalculating velocities, distances, and curvatures. We only played two games (Sunday was rained out), and I only played in one of those two. By the time I reset my scope to its proper caliber, my game was over.

We had a nice dinner in the inner harbor of Baltimore. Dad, Kathy and I just talked. There wasn't any yelling or crying about my poor game. In the old days I would have been a wreck, and my dad would have been infuriated with my 0-for-3 day. But now at 22 that process seemed juvenile and unproductive. We discussed what went wrong in the game and how to try to fix it. Then the game was put on the backburner and king sized crab cakes became the main focus. After dinner I couldn't help but think of why my dad ever thought that the confrontational/yelling approach was the most beneficial way for me to improve.

Anyone who knew me should have realized that what I needed was patience, support, faith and a good discussion about baseball over crab legs. I am built on responding to positive energy and without baseball I don't know how well I would have figured this out about myself. I had never responded well to yelling and screaming. Baseball, and for that matter life, was and is supposed to be fun. Talking and thinking things out slowly became a much more effective approach for getting through to me. I have always learned more from reading a book than from a coach yelling at me. As I matured on the field, I gained the ability to acknowledge my mistakes and to identify the things I could control and change.

I don't know if my attitude changed because I matured a bit or because I saw the light at the end of the tunnel. Perspective is everything, and both my age and point in life added to my overall enjoyment of playing baseball. I was finally able to compete on the field and then leave the game behind me, still remaining a confident man.

It took a lot of effort and time to disassociate success as a hitter from my worth as an individual. Granted, my situation, in which every at bat potentially determined whether I would continue to play that weekend, did carry a lot of pressure. However, it was a *huge* relief when I was finally able to be at peace with myself both as a baseball player and person no matter what happened on the field. It had all begun at Vermont a year earlier, and now I had proof that my new attitude was real and was working.

CHAPTER 48

I stared at the computer screen for 10 minutes, unable to move. My emotions were running wild. Over the last four years many of my homework assignments, quizzes, and tests had transitioned from paper and pen to computer. It seemed fitting that my last test ever was on a lap top. In a way it reflected the speed of change over just four short years. As Bob Dylan said "The times they are a-Changin."

I continued to stare at the screen, unwilling to click "submit." Once I hit the button I knew it was all over. I was damn proud of my School of Management 3.83 GPA, and now I was only one click away from seeing all of the hard work pay off. I would have sat there another hour if the timer wasn't running out and if I didn't have to run to baseball practice.

Click. I was done with college. Four years of pouring over textbooks (or in some cases the Cliff Notes), four years of studying and stressing over grades, homework and tests.

I had come to school clueless and was leaving with real knowledge. I had worked my butt off for my School of Management grades. I stared at the computer screen as the "log out" button appeared. I had been so preoccupied with baseball coming to an end that I didn't take much notice that school was ending as well. The memories of four years blended together as I placed my books in my backpack for the last time. Strangely I could not recall a single homework assignment. Already I was forgetting memories of school.

I shook my professor's hand and walked out the classroom door. I would never be an undergrad again. It really was a relief to have succeeded academically and to have achieved my goal, but the fact that there was no class "tomorrow" was a startling thought. At least I still had baseball.

Traveling to Maine felt strange without any academic concerns. Baseball still had four weeks and 14 games remaining. It was our last regular-season road trip of the season. What a relief it was to sit back and enjoy the ride.

Saturday, May 9, was a dark and dreary day, full of looming and ominous clouds. The games normally would have started at noon, but Maine forced us to start later in order for fireworks to be set off in honor of Senior Day.

Game one took a long, long time. Maine's offense was relentless, scoring 11 runs to our 2. Starter Jeff Dennis was totally off his game and was forced out in the second inning. Watching Jeff's reaction to his debacle was actually a bit gratifying. As one of his good friends, it was nice to see that Jeff had matured a lot over the last four years as well. Instead of ranting and raving like he would have in years past, Jeff simply put ice on his arm and watched the rest of the game. I knew how disappointed he was, but I was really happy to see how well he dealt with the adversity.

He also started a new tradition at the school that day, the anti-game ball. Jeff found the most scraped up, dirty ball and awarded himself the anti-game ball. From then on the worst player in each game was given an anti-game ball.

Because of the late start and long game, the day was behind schedule. Thus, when rain started pouring in the seventh inning of game two, we could do nothing but laugh sarcastically. Everyone saw it coming four hours before. All the forecasts had predicted rain late in the day. Instead of being in our warm hotel rooms, we were now shivering in the wet and cold dugout.

We were trailing 2-0 in the 7th inning of game two when the skies opened. As the score stood, we were lined up for the loss. Maine had screwed us over by starting the games late. As the game was called, we heard the fireworks streaking through the gloomy sky. I say "heard" because the combination of dusk and heavy rain made the fireworks look like sparklers that had fizzled out. Everyone was running for their cars. It was a complete disaster.

After a nasty rain storm there is usually a period of sunny skies and calm winds. Sunday morning was the exact opposite. It was cloudy, cold, and filled with more nasty winds. Game three was one of the most painful games to watch all year. And though the weather didn't help, it had very little to do with the outcome.

Centerfielder Henry Dunn was a spark for our team, and we were definitely better off when he was in the lineup. When he went down with his hamstring injury, someone else needed to step up. The coaches asked me to be that needed offensive presence. I would like to think that I did my job very well.

However, when Dunn came back into the lineup in early May, he displaced me. My "services" were no longer needed.

This was my predicament as I sat both games on Saturday and the first game on Sunday. I was ripping the ball in batting practice, but there simply wasn't a spot for me, according to our coaches.

What made game three especially hard to swallow, however, was how long the coaches were willing to stick with "their guys". Pete Bregartner was in the midst of a dreadful slump, and to watch him go 0-for-5 with three strikeouts while I sat killed me. Worse, the coaches toyed with me by telling me to get ready every time Pete got up.

This happened three times. I would get loose, get my helmet on, get into the on deck circle and then the coach would let Pete hit. After the third time, I took off my helmet and tossed it under the bench. I was done. I took a seat and watched the rest of the game as a fan.

Luckily we won the game in 11 innings, but it was truly painful to watch. I really thought I could help my team win, and it was hard to have everyone on the bench keep telling me to be ready and that I should be up there. "Tell the coach," I said, "not me."

After a brief break time between games, the coaches let me know that I was in the lineup in game four. I glided up to the plate for my first at bat in eight days. I had only been up three times in the last 11 days, so I wasn't about to let an at bat go by without enjoying it. I was thrilled that my parents were getting to see me hit after driving eight hours and watching three games.

I hope they didn't blink. I had a feeling that this was one of the final at bats they'd ever see because the next weekend they would be in Virginia for my brother's law school graduation.

I worked the count to 2-2. I knew I wasn't supposed to be guessing on a pitch after two strikes, but I knew the pitcher was coming with a change-up and when he left it up in the zone, I belted it. The ball took off for deep right field but caught a wind current that forced the ball back to earth a few feet away from the fence for a line out. I shook my head and jogged back to the dugout.

What happened next still infuriates me. After all the times I felt I got "over looked", this next at bat tops the list. We were in the middle of an intense battle with Maine, and if we won the game we would be the first team since Delaware in 1996 to win three America East regular season championships in a row. The game had intensity similar to that of a playoff game.

I led off the fifth inning with an opposite-field base hit. I got to first base, undid my batting gloves as was standard tradition and listened as first base coach Folli reviewed the situation. As I was nodding in response, I caught sight of a green uniform running toward me. It was John Miele.

There was a bizarre moment where we both stood on first base. I refused to move. I looked at Coach Folli and gave the facial expression of "what the heck is he doing here?" Coach looked at John like "what the heck are you doing here?" John looked back at me like "I have no clue what I am doing here."

We were *winning* the game 1-0, and I was more than capable of running. My legs felt great that day. Sending in a pinch runner in that situation was simply insulting. I have no other words to describe it.

In shock that I was being taken out with three innings still left to go (after not playing for three games), I regrettably told John where he could go stick it, as I jogged off the field. I was so shocked, way more than pissed, that for some reason I decided to yell at poor John. I apologized right after the game.

I got off the field and hopped down the dugout steps. Like that my weekend was done, 1-for-2. As the inning went on, I started to calm down a bit, but if one situation underscored my Binghamton career this was it.

As unfair as the move was, I decided to focus my attention on making sure that John Miele scored. And when he did cross home plate, I felt satisfied that I was the one who started the huge rally that ultimately led to victory. I was happy until I saw Pete Bregartner pinch-hit for John Miele in that same inning. I have come close to exploding on a baseball field only a few times, but I never came closer than that day to making a scene in front of my coaches. I have said it many times, but it needs repeating, that Pete was an excellent hitter and a good friend, but it was the fact that he was in such a bad slump that made the move so inexplicably bad. My dad was as furious as I was when he saw Pete go to the plate. He had to get up and leave. It was the only time he ever did that. There was only so much he could take.

The blood boiled in my veins as I watched Bregartner fly out to left field. I wasn't mad at Pete, who was just doing what he was told. I was livid at being taken out of a game after two really good at bats and then having to watch a kid who was 1-for-10 hit in my place. All I wanted to do was yell at the top of my lungs "Go to hell" – or something far harsher. Instead, I bit my lip and watched from the bench as we clinched our third consecutive regular season title. The days of being a selfish child were over. I tossed my batting gloves in the air and joined my teammates in front of our dugout for the celebration. This was not a moment to miss out on.

By the time I talked with my dad and boarded the bus, I had put the events of the day behind me. The bus ride was supposed to be an easy all-nighter back to Binghamton but our alternator broke and we were forced to stay in some random hotel in southern Maine as a new bus was dispatched from central New York to pick us up in the morning. It was a circus, but everyone was in a good mood about our championship. The next day we finally made it home. Just a simple 16-hour ride down Memory Lane.

After our "ride from hell" I spent the following week watching TV, lifting, hitting, and trying like heck to spend the last of my dining hall money. I knew it couldn't last forever, but those few days were a dream. We all scrounged to get the most food possible for the cheapest price possible. Sometimes we got lucky, and our favorite lunch lady would give us the meal at a discounted price. When times got tough, though, it was pasta, bread, and "disappearing burritos."

We had a trick where we would put food, say a burrito, in a cup and pretend it was tea. Thirty four cents was a lot cheaper than three dollars. We all felt a little bad about this shady maneuver, but the "disappearing burrito" never failed to save us a lot of money!

My track record against Vermont was somewhere between abysmal and nonexistent. My freshman year I was 1-for-9 against them. My sophomore year I sat all three regular season games. My junior year I was 0-for-2 in the regular season and sat both games in the playoffs. I was ready for a different outcome this time.

Vermont needed a minor miracle to sneak into the playoffs. We were already the number one seed, and we weren't taking UVM lightly. These games were our preparation for the playoffs. Vermont needed to win a minimum of two games, but realistically needed three.

There is an old sports cliché that goes "It's never over until the fat lady sings." Well the fattest lady was singing at the top of her lungs for Vermont. She was one note from the song being over. We had won game one 3-2, and it seemed throughout the game that no matter what we did to lose, Vermont was not meant to win. For every mistake that we made, they made an even worse one.

Vermont was dead. We had beaten them on a walk-off hit in game one and had crushed their spirits in the process. We were winning 8-1 in game two going into the top of the ninth. There was one out and no one on base. Vermont was two outs away from oblivion as the university had already announced the elimination of baseball. It was an eerie feeling in our dugout knowing this. Many of our starters had been pulled, and the bench was joking around.

How many bad innings start with an error or a walk? How many disastrous innings start off with both an error *and* a walk? Here is the play-by-play for that half-inning. We went through three pitchers over the course of the inning. Keep in mind that two outs *anywhere* after Micowski strikes out to lead off the inning, and it is the end of the Vermont program *forever*.

1. Micowski struck out looking. **1 out.**
2. Moylan reached on a throwing error by 3b.
3. Duffy walked.
4. Milo singled through the left side.
5. Kelly singled to left field.
6. Paquette walked.
7. McCarthy singled to center field.
8. Soltis struck out looking. **2 outs.**
9. Jackson singled to center field.
10. Micowski walked.
11. Duffy homered.
12. Milo struck out looking. **3 outs.**

10 runs, 6 hits, 1 error,

When Duffy hit the three-run blast into the trees in left field, there was true disbelief. Vermont had just scored 10 runs with the barrel of a gun jammed down its throat. It was the most remarkable comeback I had ever seen – well, except for when Albany beat us in the playoffs two years earlier. Vermont was making a historic film about its last season, and we were the climax.

We were still shell-shocked when we came to the field on Sunday. We lost the two games by a combined score of 30-13. We were outplayed in every facet of the game. Vermont's stunning comeback put it in the playoffs and knocked Maine out.

My pitiful record against Vermont was fully intact after three games. I was 1-for-6. That made me 2-for-17 in 16 games against Vermont. Apparently, what I needed was an average righty to break out.

By the time my second at bat came up in the final game, we were down 12-5. I got a fastball right over the plate and hit one of the hardest line drives of my life directly at the first baseman. I was sure it was a line out, but I hit the ball so hard that first baseman Ethan Paquette was late getting his glove up. The ball nicked the top of the leather and bounced into the outfield for an RBI single.

Some luck had come my way. As I got to first base I was sure to thank Ethan. I had played with him in Vermont two summers earlier, and we both joked about the hit.

In my next at bat I was a tick late, but got enough ball to hit a solid liner to shortstop. He leaped and was just late getting his glove high enough. It bounced away for another hit. Two hard-hit balls that could have gone for outs. Sometimes it was nice to get a break out there.

I walked in my last at bat ever at Varsity field.

So much had happened on that field in the last four years. There were great successes and disappointing failures. I experienced enormous smiles and painful tears, blissful happiness and complete bitterness. They were all left in the batter's box when I peacefully trotted down to first base after my last walk.

A batter's box is freshly lined before every game, but by the ninth inning all that remains are some blurred white patches. Every game requires new boxes, a new and clean start. I had stood in that coveted area for thousands of at bats. As I glided toward first, I knew that I would never return to that particular box again. The shivers ran down my spine.

I stood on first base thinking about years past. Sure I would be remembered for a few years, but essentially at the end of my four-year journey, the only physical evidence of my career would be a few lines in a buried stat book. It would be up to my memory and writings to keep these games alive. What seemed so important at the time of those exhilarating and tense moments at the plate was now a small notation in the Binghamton record books. It was right then that I realized that this trip through college was about *me*, for I was the only one who would truly remember my time there.

I knew as the years went by, my at bats would be forgotten one by one, first by casual fans, then by other players' parents, then by teammates and coaches, then by my family and finally by me. I hated that I was going to forget the details of big home runs and pinch-hit doubles.

I also knew how much of my college years I was going to forget. No matter how much description I included in my journal, most of college simply wasn't journal-worthy. The day-to-day life was what made college – the times hanging out with friends or playing catch in the outfield. The hours spent relaxing in our locker room talking non-sense or a casual night out for a few drinks. These were the true memories of my college experience. Unfortunately though, it is not humanly possible to catalogue these memories.

So what was this journey all about?

I suppose it was about everything not mentioned in this book. It was about living life, learning, growing, and enjoying myself. It was about the road to the end of the rainbow, not the pot of gold. It was about the friends I made, the lessons I learned and, most importantly, the times I enjoyed. It was about the walks from class to practice. It was about the time the guys spent in the RE recollecting the scattered memories of the previous night. It was eating as team in the dining hall.

It was about everything mentioned in this book. It was about setting goals and accomplishing them. It was about becoming a great baseball player and winning games. It was about focusing on getting a base hit as if it was the only thing that mattered in life. It was about winning a damn championship.

The 24-square foot box next to home plate was where I grew up and became a man. As I looked at the plate from my position at first base that day, it looked a lot farther away than ever before. It looked unreachable from my new perspective.

Later, as I crossed the plate on CJ Lukaszewski's single, it was as if solid stone settled over my footprints. Whatever memories were created at home plate in all those wonderful years were permanently etched in that dirt.

Countless batters will enter and leave that batter's box but for one moment in time I was the king of that plot of land. The batter's box taught me so much about baseball, life and manhood. You can't see my markings there anymore, but I assure you they are very much there, as are the cleat marks of everyone who came before me. I really do feel that all of us as alumni now carry some of the dirt with us every day of our lives. The game will always be with us.

Now there are days when work is rough and I long for that familiar 4-by-6 plot of land. After spending my youth in that box, I knew that in a few weeks I would be cast away, never able to return again. My time was almost up.

In a fitting farewell to Varsity Field, the game was called early due to rain. We walked away from the weekend totally spent.

CHAPTER 49

As I was working on staying back on curveballs and struggling to take an outside fastball to left field against Vermont, my classmates were nearby graduating from college. The main graduation ceremony was held at the same time as our games, so I never got to walk with my class on graduation day. I never got a cap and gown.

The funny part is that I didn't really care about missing graduation. I would have rather been on a baseball field than at a ceremony any day of the year. I knew what I had accomplished in the classroom and that was enough for me. My parents were at my brother's law school graduation in Virginia, so I didn't even have to feel bad about not walking for them.

It was fitting that my last sacrifice of school activities and academics for baseball was my graduation. We had all given up so much for baseball. Now we were three wins away from the NCAA tournament. Three wins away from *everything* being worth it.

My diploma arrived in the mail a few weeks later and that was the first confirmation that I had actually graduated. I stared at the diploma for five minutes. Four years for a sheet of paper. Magma Cum Laude. Four years well worth it. I wouldn't have traded it for the world.

On Saturday night after the Vermont series, most of the guys had a celebratory toast or two, or probably more like ten. As I was walking downtown with a few friends, we came across a garage gate lying broken on the sidewalk. In a comedy of errors, I picked up the gate to throw it over the fence at the exact time that a patrol car was driving by. The timing could not have been worse.

The police officer accused me and my friends of breaking the gate and took all of our names. We were scared beyond belief that this ridiculous incident was going to keep us off the playoff roster.

The rest of the night we were all in an awful mood. Every day until the conference tournament, we expected a call from Coach. We wouldn't have gotten into trouble, but by the time everything got sorted out, the playoffs might have already been over.

Thankfully, we never heard another word about the incident. It did make me think, though, about all the "incidents" that college athletes find themselves in. Sometimes it is the athletes' fault. They are stupid, reckless and/or drunk and get themselves into deep trouble. I imagine, however, that there are plenty of cases just like mine where an athlete is simply in the wrong place at the wrong time.

Athletes walk around with a bull's eye on their backs. We were strictly forbidden to ever go to a bar or party wearing anything associated with Binghamton baseball. Some people just disliked athletes, perhaps out of jealousy, spite, or resentment. Maybe they got cut from a tryout; maybe they were mad that we get so much funding; or maybe they simply wished they were on the team. Regardless, we always had to be very aware of our situation and to avoid fights at *all* costs. If we ever got arrested, we were indefinitely suspended until the case got settled. In New York that could mean months.

The incident that night was by far the closest I ever came to getting into any trouble at BU. Still, it did make me think that many good kids probably ended up in bad situations and were made scapegoats. I am sure that athletes at bigger schools and in bigger programs had to be even more careful than us. It isn't a question of fairness. It is simply a reality that athletes are held to higher standards given their greater visibility.

It was a sin that our Division I field didn't have lights, but because it didn't, we were forced by conference rules to hit the road the previous two years to try to win a tournament in someone else's backyard. It was a clear disadvantage. This year we prayed we could stay home.

We couldn't host the tournament at NYSEG stadium either because the Binghamton Mets were home for the weekend. The only option with lights that remained was nearby Union-Endicott, a high school! After much deliberation, the field was accepted by the league officials. It meant we could sleep in our own beds all weekend long. Once you go on the road, you realize the advantage a team has playing at home.

Obviously it was nice to have the home crowd, but to have our own place to sleep, eat, and lift along with the ability to maintain a relatively normal schedule in our own surroundings was a huge help for the conference tournament. It should not be understated.

CHAPTER 50

I knew 362 days before game one of the playoffs that our entire season was going to come down to two games in late May. This was my last chance to get to a Regional, and the fact that one costly mistake could spoil everything was a frightening one.

I also knew I was definitely not playing game one and this changed my outlook coming into the playoffs. With our total breakdown against Vermont at the end of the regular season, we not only let the Catamounts slip into the playoffs but also set up a rematch against them in the first round. Vermont's two top starters were lefties, so I knew where I was going to be seated. With Henry Dunn back and healthy as well, I feared that after being in the lineup for the majority of the year, I was going back to my reserve role. I wanted to play and help my team win, but I wasn't in the plans for the playoffs. My coaches never once talked to me before the game. Because I had kept my mouth shut for four years, they must have just assumed that I would be fine being on the bench after leaving my sweat and blood on the field for three months.

The few days leading up to game one barely exist in my mind. I don't have one single memory from the conclusion of Sunday's loss until game day on Thursday. It was a surreal week. The "normal" seniors were all in town still partying it up during "Senior Week," and here I was trying focus on playoff games that I suspected I wasn't even going to play in. I still had to prepare on the off chance that I did get a shot, so I resisted partying.

It was the tradition of the upperclassmen every May to enjoy "bar crawl," a fancy name for a day when everyone got drunk by strolling from bar to bar. On an unusually sunny and warm May afternoon, a huge party was suddenly brewing in our parking lot. The scene reminded me of the last episode of *Seinfeld*, where past characters all came back for one last reunion. Four years worth of friends and acquaintances came up to me like this was my final episode of college.

It was the last time I ever saw a lot of my good school friends. That is the way it worked. There was no big final goodbye. It was usually an "I will see you later" after which I did not ever see them again. A lot of friends simply left for home after graduation, and I never got to say a final goodbye. It was almost better that way. Grandiose goodbyes only seemed appropriate for my best of friends. As far as I was concerned, those real goodbyes could wait a week or two, until after we had made a Regional.

Vermont had all of the momentum going into the playoff series. The Catamounts had literally wiped their feet with us on their way to the playoffs. As badly as we had played though, it now meant nothing. The score was reset to 0-0.

With little else going on in the greater Binghamton area, the story of our regular season success made big new. People all over town showed a lot of interest, and we were flooded by local media following us around. Fans not related to any of the players came out in large numbers to watch us play Thursday evening. A lot of baseball alum had come back as well. Once you are part of a program, you are always part of the program. We were trying to win for the players of the past who never got to a Regional as much as we wanted it for ourselves.

After a three day honeymoon of waking up after 11 a.m., eating on Binghamton's dime, lifting, going to practice, eating again on Binghamton's dime, and then playing video games, Thursday finally came. The game wasn't until 7 p.m., so we had all day to lounge around. The coaches took us out for pasta at lunch to help break up the day. Finally, after hours of anticipation we headed to our locker room to get dressed for batting practice.

Because there was no place to hit at the high school, we hit on campus and then drove to the high school. It was a bit inefficient, but it allowed us to hit in peace without any distractions.

After hitting, we headed back to the locker room to get into uniform. During the week leading up to the game, I had imagined a scene out a movie where all of the players sat quietly in their lockers, shaking their feet up and down just slightly, showing their nervous anticipation. The coach would storm into the room and command our attention. "Forget about the crowds, the size of the school, their fancy uniforms and remember what got you here. Focus on the fundamentals that we have gone over time and time again. And most importantly, don't get up caught up in winning or losing this game. If you put your effort and concentration into playing to your potential, to being the best you can be, I don't care what the scoreboard says at the end of the game, in my book you are going to be winners, OK?!" But this speech from "Hoosiers" never happened.

I had imagined the team captain standing up in front off all his peers and inspiring the team to glory. "You all know what you have to do. Remember, no one, and I mean no one, comes into our house and pushes us around. This is your game now gentleman, and for you seniors (one of) your last one(s) so make it count, because you'll remember it for the rest of your lives. Lets get 'em!" This speech from "Rudy" never happened either.

When coach finally did come into the room, I was ready for the speech! "Great moments are born with great opportunity. And that is what you have here tonight boys. That's what you've earned here tonight. One game. If we played 'em ten times they might win nine. But not this game. Not tonight. Tonight we stay with them and we shut them down because we can. Tonight we are the greatest team in the world!"

This speech from "Miracle" never took place in our locker room either. In fact there was no speech. No one even looked nervous. The guys were joking around and telling stories of previous nights out. We all got dressed and when coach came in all he said was, "OK guys, let's head over to the field."

It was a good enough motivational speech for me. I pumped my fist in the air and ran out of the locker room.

We took the 10-minute ride to the field with Eminem blaring at mach 3 level. When we strolled into the parking lot, I couldn't help but feel that this was a meaningless summer game. I could envision a couple of my summer teammates driving an old '02 Town and Country to a high school field.

I knew that none of these details mattered. All that mattered was getting out to an early lead and burying Vermont. I considered our early 4-0 lead a worthy start, and so I started to relax on the bench just a bit. I could do nothing to contain my nervousness but cheer and chew sunflower seeds.

This game was everything college baseball should be. It was loud, exciting, and, soon enough, it was filled with offense. Well, it was everything it should be excluding me actually playing.

Our go-to ace Murphy Smith was mowing down the Catamounts through six innings. He looked like the type of pitcher who would in a few weeks get drafted in the 13th round by the Oakland Athletics organization. Having a top number one pitcher was a crucial component for making a successful playoff run. It gave our team a solid pitcher who we knew would give us a chance to win game one. The confidence Murphy gave to the other players was invaluable. From the Little League level to the Major League level, having an ace is key.

We would come to find, however, that it doesn't take a lot for a rally to get started, even with your number one guy on the mound. A single and an error are about all you need for the entire bridge to collapse. By the time the rubble had settled, Vermont had scored seven unanswered runs. Going into the bottom of the eighth inning, we were down three.

If I was playing, my nervousness would have been masked by my adrenaline, but being forced to watch was killing me. I loved playing in big games. All I could do from the bench was cheer for one big play to change the game. And cheer I did.

In any playoff series there are always a few game-changing plays. However, people often forget the play directly preceding the actual game/series-changing moment. People forget the basketball player who made his two free throws the possession before his teammate hit a game-winning buzzer-beater shot. People forget the running back who stretches the third-down run for a first down early in a drive that results in a game-changing touchdown. And people forget the big base hit or walk that sets up a game-changing rally.

CJ Lukaszewski walked to the plate in the bottom of the eighth with one out and no one on base. If he doesn't get on base there is a very good chance that we lose the game.

But he did get on base, and three more singles followed CJ's opposite field line drive. Before Vermont had a chance to blink we had scored six runs.

We had risen from the grave. After three years of finding ways to lose, it was good to see us make a comeback. We had dodged a bullet.

CJ's hit was so overlooked when we reflected on the series that it made me think about all the unsung heroes in crucial games. Everyone remembers Kirk Gibson limping up to home plate in game one of the 1988 World Series. The Dodgers, trailing 1-0, were down to their last out when Gibson hit his moon shot off Dennis Eckersley. No one brings up Mike Davis, however. He was the one who worked a two-out walk to get on base for Gibson. If Davis strikes out, Gibson never hits his home run. (According to Baseballreference.com, the Dodgers had only had a 9% chance of winning the game when Mike Davis walked to the plate.)[25]

We ended up winning the game 10-7 and were now just *one* game away from being in the driver's seat and an almost guaranteed spot in the NCAA tournament. Three years in a row we had gotten to this point. The previous two times, we came up one run short. I prayed to the baseball gods that this cruel fate would not repeat itself a final time.

The next day literally crawled by. Our game wasn't scheduled until 7 p.m., so we had all day to do nothing. I was getting very good at this. Our coaches tried to break up the day again by having a team meal at Tony's Restaurant.

After everything I had been through, I wanted to be on the field that night. Not only had I sacrificed so much, but I had been hitting so well whenever I got a chance that I truly thought I belonged in the lineup. The coaches, however, decided to go with Pete Bregartner.

It was truly a dagger. I knew I was going to miss playing baseball, but during my final moment of weakness stemming from this benching, I was ready to die as a baseball player. Even with my transformation, the constant let downs were becoming almost unbearable. Every year I improved as a player, so it made the rejection that much harder to deal with.

To me, there was just one more thing to do before walking away; win a championship. I was in a constant struggle the last month of my career between saying goodbye to the game I had grown up with and the exertion I spent pouring my heart and soul into a game that was (seemingly) giving me nothing back. This is the feeling I would guess Minor Leaguers feel after six years in the minors without ever getting past the AA level. It is not a hatred of the game of baseball as much as it is a hatred of the business of baseball.

I did not want to end my career on a high school field that did not even have a full scoreboard. I wanted to end it in a Regional, so I cheered until my throat grew sore. It was tough to watch that game, especially with my mom, dad, Bob, Kathy, and my sister in the stands. I knew I was better than I was being treated, and it took everything I had left within me to stay positive. I was close to empty.

CHAPTER 51

We started out game 2 abysmally. Albany was walking all over us. The low point came when Corey Taylor misplayed a fly ball in left field that allowed an extra run to score. Corey was by far our best hitter, but it did sting continuously to see an outfield group, one I apparently wasn't good enough to join, allow balls to literally fall at their feet. After three and half innings we were down 7-1. Our coach brought us into a huddle.

"I have good news and bad news. The bad news is we can't play any worse. The good news is that we still have six innings to fix it." This was the speech I had been waiting for.

The team responded. The scoreboard for Binghamton over the next four innings read four runs, three runs, one run, and two runs. Going into the ninth inning, we were ahead 11-7. A gutty pitching performance by freshman Mike Augliera had saved our season and had given the offense a chance to catch up. Now we were three outs away from being in the driver's seat.

I pinch-hit in the eighth inning – my only at bat of the tournament. I was rusty and uncomfortable in the box, and before I even got settled in, the count was 2-2. The pitcher threw me a dirty slider and I swung right through it. It was a great two-strike pitch.

I was thrilled beyond belief about the team being 2-0, but after that at bat I knew I would not get another chance. All I could do was support my team.

With a groundout to Kyle Klee at third base one inning later, we were finally in the position that had eluded us for the last two seasons. We were in the championship game and, though no other team wanted to admit it, this tournament was all but over. Albany or Vermont now had to win in the morning and then beat us twice.

There is an old saying that goes, "I have waited years for this to happen; what's another five minutes?" I came to understand it on championship day.

Superstitions have been part of baseball since its inception. I didn't care for them because I felt they were a simple way to explain a complex outcome. However, my words fell on deaf ears when our team decided we couldn't change *anything* from the previous two days. Thus, we had to eat pasta and meatballs at the same restaurant for the third day in a row. The entire team yelled at me when I changed my order to sausages. I guess they didn't want to take any chances.

The plan was to get to our locker room early and relax. We didn't want to feel rushed getting to the field. We took our time with batting practice. Game time was slotted for 8 p.m. We expected the entire town to be in attendance. As we pulled up to the field, we eagerly checked the scoreboard to see who was winning the Albany-Vermont game.

Their game had started at 4 o'clock, so that meant the teams had been at the field since at least 2 p.m.. They probably took batting practice around noon. If that wasn't enough of a disadvantage, both teams were forced to use *every* pitcher they had in an elimination game that resulted in 19 runs. It only got tougher for them as the night continued.

In the ninth inning, lightning flashed. We were ordered into the high school gym to wait for the storm to pass. (I wish these were all metaphors, but these rain clouds were real.) It looked as if our championship would have to wait a few extra minutes, then an extra hour, and then several extra hours. We waited and waited, growing more impatient with every passing minute. The lightning just wouldn't stop and the game could not restart until 30 minutes after the last bolt. It was going to be a long night.

When you put 25 baseball players in a room with nothing to do, it is amazing the games and activities they can create. We played a game that involved rolling multiple balls near the groin region and an X-rated version of *Simon Says*. After getting particularly bored, one of our freshmen decided to "floppy cock" the team. This highly difficult maneuver consisted of player X pulling down his pants and, with a humping motion, flopping his privates up and down. The pain must have been excruciating but the laughs were well worth it.

This player was in mid flop when from the other side of the gym walked in our assistant athletic director, Jim Norris. The way the curtain was set up, this player couldn't see Norris until it was too late. For a split second before player X was tackled and covered with a gym mat, he was fully exposed. He had just given our assistant athletic director a full frontage. We found this hilarious and the perfect tool to keep us relaxed.

After a long delay the Vermont-Albany game finally ended in a Vermont defeat. Vermont fought mightily, in more ways than one, but the Vermont program was officially finished after 100+ years of success.

Poor Albany had about 30 minutes to relax. We were fully rested and had a lot of pitching left. Our senior stud Jeff Dennis was ready to go.

Albany got a nice breather when lightning struck again before the first inning was over. Back into the gym we went for another hour and 53 minutes.

We had aspirations of winning the tournament early in the evening so we could host a huge party at our place with all of the parents. That idea was destroyed when the game didn't resume until around midnight.

We were going to do anything to play this game because we were fully rested, and if we waited until tomorrow, Albany would get most of its pitching back.

Finally at 11:44 p.m. the game resumed. The only spectators remaining were the parents and the very, very loyal fans, aka the girlfriends.

From the bench I watched the Great Danes warming up a lefty freshman. I figured I wasn't in the lineup, but my main thought was that there was *no way* this kid was beating us. I was right, as before the game even really got going we had already pounced to an early 3-0 lead.

It was obvious that Albany was on empty. It was written on the players' faces.

I had the unfortunate luck to have watched game seven of the 2004 American League Championship Series when the Boston Red Sox destroyed the New York Yankees. After 3½ innings, the Red Sox were up 8-1. I was in the upper deck, but could see even from my bird's eye view that the Yankees looked defeated. Teams had come back from seven runs down with 18 outs remaining many times. It just didn't seem that this would be one of those nights. The Yankees looked dead. This was the same feeling I got staring across the field at the Albany Great Danes.

The fourth inning all but put them out of their misery. The pressure was already on their rattled freshman pitcher when Corey Taylor hit a line drive home run. It was the dagger into the heart. As Corey touched home plate for our ninth run, the long-sought berth in the NCAA Regional was within reach. Three more runs in the fifth made it 12-0. Jeff Dennis pitched an absolute gem for us and shut down any remaining hope for Albany.

We were all getting ready to celebrate when in the seventh inning, at 1:45 a.m., the game came to a screeching halt.

At first I thought I was seeing things. I saw a sprinkler shoot water and soak the Albany catcher in the bullpen. I thought it was a mirage. When the rest of the outfield sprinklers began operating, I knew I wasn't seeing things. The outfield was being drenched. No one knew how to turn the sprinklers off as we had to wait an agonizing 32 minutes for the sprinklers to finish watering the field.

Albany (players and parents included) had been at the field for 12 hours, through over 15 innings and several weather interruptions. They had seen a total of 32 runs score over the course of the "day." It was now 2 a.m. and they were watching sprinklers douse an already-wet field while being down in the game 12-1. They were tired, cranky and defeated. The metaphor of the water washing away their season could not be ignored, at least by me.

Over in our dugout, Coach Sinicki had waited over a decade for this moment. The seniors had pushed through sweat, blood, and disappointment for four years to get here. The team was a few outs away from glory, and here we were waiting for the sprinklers to stop. "So this is why championship games shouldn't be played at high school fields," I thought to myself.

Finally, the game resumed. The game flew forward and we carried a 16-5 lead into the ninth.

I was going wild in the dugout. I didn't care how tired I was or about being on the bench. This was the moment I had been imagining for years. This made all of the pain well worth it.

Coach Sinicki had come so close and lost so many heartbreakers that he was an absolute lunatic in the dugout. Every time we cheered, he yelled at us for cheering too loudly. However, every time we looked down to tie our shoes he yelled at us for losing focus on the game. I never got yelled at so much *on the bench* in my life.

Redshirt freshman Walker McKinven was on the mound for us. He recorded the first two outs with little effort and now we were just one out away.

We huddled right outside the dugout, ready to run to the mound for the dog pile that had eluded me all of these years. Closer Greg Lane was throwing in the bullpen just in case.

Albany wasn't magically going to score 10 runs. In a normal game maybe it was attainable, but not at 3 a.m., not after all Albany had just gone through. As Greg Lane came running down to join us outside the dugout, Coach Sinicki exploded. It was like after so many years of losing he wasn't used to winning. "Get back to the bullpen. This game isn't over. And you guys get back in the damn dugout." It was a real buzz kill, but to be fair I understood how badly he wanted this, and I am sure he was trying to deal with all of emotions circulating in his body as well.

As the final pitch was nearing, my teammates pushed me to the front of the "huddle" near the dugout exit. It was a small gesture by them (mostly the freshman and sophomores), but it meant the world to me. To know that the other players respected me enough to let me go first meant a lot. I know they didn't really understand all the turmoil I had been through during the four years, but they still showed a lot of respect when they let me be the leader to the dog pile. It truly touched my heart.

That moment waiting in the dugout was one of the most special moments of my life. It confirmed that all of my effort through all the peaks and valleys had helped the team reach its goals. We had done it! I slowly let the tears drip out in pure happiness. I believe there are about 10 times in a person's life when they feel true happiness. Births, weddings, and graduations all make the list, but championships must be placed there as well.

As good as it felt to be a champion, what was equally important was knowing I had earned my teammates' respect. They knew I should have been out there. I really think they understood, to some extent, how badly I was getting played. It seemed like every year the freshmen would ask why I wasn't in the lineup every day. "You hit the ball hard every time you get up," they would say. "Tell coach," I would respond, and walk away. Not for one day did I trick myself into thinking I should never sit, but suddenly I felt that my contribution to the program had been a success, and I was a big part of something that Binghamton had never before achieved. By the end of that season, the Bearcats were 17-8 in games I started and 13-14 in the remaining games.

As Jeff Abrams put his glove down to scoop up the softly hit final ground ball of the championship game, I was already feet from the first base line. Looking back, it was a stupid maneuver because if Abrams ever botched that groundball I would have been stranded in the middle of the field.

Thankfully, Abrams fielded the ball cleanly and tossed it to Calderone at second base for the final out. A 5-hour, 21-minute game was over. We were America East champions!

Walker McKinven was the first one to toss his glove in the air. I was on him like a cheetah pouncing on a helpless deer. We both went down hard as the guys piled on top of us. It only lasted a few moments, but as the weight pressed against me from the top, I couldn't help but think that for this one moment there was completeness. It was pure happiness.

Dog piles can only last a moment. But what a moment it was. Charging full speed into a pile of men cheering like little kids is only allowed for an elite few who are lucky enough at some point in their lives to win a championship. I could forever say I was among them.

After a magical minute we gathered ourselves and started to shake hands. All the while, Albany players had been watching from their dugout. I didn't feel bad at all. I had been there too many times to feel sorry. If anything, I felt a little bad for the Albany seniors who were done for good. In truth, I was really too happy to feel any compassion.

After a very brief ceremony, we took the trophy and ran into the outfield, where all of the seniors got to hold it. We doused Coach Sinicki with a water jug as cheers erupted.

I saw my family after the game. We didn't say much but there was no need to. The looks said it all. We were going to a Regional. My season and career weren't over just yet.

Winning a championship is hard. When you win consistently, it is easy to assume success. I imagine you can get spoiled pretty quickly. It is only when you lose, and lose hard, that you truly appreciate the enormous challenge of trying to win a championship. The veterans got this. They experienced the crushing losses and the disappointing seasons year after year. It was the rookies, the freshmen, whom I feared didn't know how lucky they were. Winning was all they knew.

When we arrived at the Events Center it was close to 4 a.m.. We were determined to celebrate *that* night, but there was one small problem — we were locked out of our locker room. Our keys had been deactivated for the night, and we had to wait over a half hour for Coach Sinicki to make it back to campus. By the time we got back to the RE it was 5 o'clock in the morning.

Time was not a factor as the beer flowed hard for the next few hours. It was around 8:30 AM when I finally got to bed. The sun was shining through my window. It was a beautiful Sunday morning in Binghamton.

I woke up a few hours later to get breakfast with my dad before he headed home. We talked about the night before and the journey of the season and came to a mutual conclusion that at the end of the day, no one would remember what player X did. No, they would remember 2009 as a whole, the year the Bearcats finally won.

That night we were honored at the Binghamton Mets game. It was a small gesture, but it showed that the community actually cared about us. For a brief week we had real fans – fans who weren't also girlfriends or family. The market was there for exciting college baseball if resources were available to motivate the fan base.

CHAPTER 52

At 12:30 p.m. on Monday we piled into the Events Center TAU room, our version of a banquet hall. We had just finished practice and were dressed in our official black travel pants and black BU t-shirts. We watched the large screen set up at the front of the room as ESPN began its broadcast of "The Road to Omaha: Selection Show Special."

Ever since the last out in the wee hours of Sunday morning, we had been speculating about where the selection panel would send us. It felt like high school again where everyone floated rumors about who was taking who to the prom. The various websites mentioned our destination as anywhere from California to Texas to Mississippi.

After minutes of unbearable waiting, our name finally came up. We were matched up against 17th ranked East Carolina in the Greenville, North Carolina, Regional.

It wasn't the Cal State Fullerton Regional or the University of Texas Regional, but complaining about which Regional we were sent to was like a lotto winner complaining that he or she only won the $5 million jackpot as opposed to the $10 million one.

South Carolina, ranked 26th nationally was the No. 2 seed, George Mason, ranked 29th, was the No. 3 seed, and Binghamton, unranked was the No. 4 seed. I had so much energy and excitement in my system that I headed straight for the weight room after the selection show.

By the end of the day I knew everything there was to know about East Carolina. The Pirates joined Conference USA in 2001 and won their first C-USA title in 2002.[26] Their team batting average was well over .300 in 2009 and their 42-17 record was good enough to be ranked No. 17 in the country.[27] They had lost their conference tournament and had been selected as an at-large bid. South Carolina was resentful that East Carolina was selected to host the regional.

We had a light workout on Tuesday, but I spent most of the day hanging around the RE packing – not just for the weekend, but for good. As I put away winter clothes and tidied up my room, I came across objects that I thought had been lost in previous years. I found old tests from freshmen year. Why did I still have these things? It surely wasn't fun taking them, and for the most part I forgot everything on them. Why did it feel so calming to look over my old exams? What about reviewing them gave me a feeling of comfort?

Along the road I had picked up little objects to go with my memories: A home run ball from my freshman year, a Bearcat megaphone given out at a soccer game my sophomore year, a gift bag from an ex-girlfriend during my junior year, a bottle of half-used medicine from my senior year. Alone they were just objects, but together they reflected my journey through college. They marked my highs and lows. Most of the objects I threw into the trash. I had no more need for them. It was soon time to move on. But right now, the Regionals loomed ahead!

CHAPTER 53

The engine grew louder as the cabin began to vibrate. The wheels started churning faster. Suddenly the blacktop became smaller and smaller. Our plane had lifted off the ground.

This is was my last baseball trip, and it was to be a memorable one. I could barely contain my excitement on the crowded plane with my teammates. I didn't have the words to thank them for helping win the conference championship. I would have loved to have been a bigger part of the conference tournament, but it didn't matter how we won, just that we did.

When the plane touched down I was amazed at how hot North Carolina was. Late May in upstate New York was warm, but Carolina was in full summer mode. This was the weather that had eluded me for four years, the type of weather that baseball was made to be played in.

Greenville could have been named Purple-and-Yellowville. The entire town was painted with ECU team colors. Banners, signs, and flags filled every street corner and restaurant booth. A lot of other schools were mad that ECU got the bid to host a Regional, but the fans here were dead set on proving the naysayers wrong.

Things were clearly different at a Regional. First off, we got $35 per day for food. I don't know if we were getting ripped off before or if we were getting rewarded now, but I didn't care. I gladly accepted the extra cash from coach.

The little perks didn't stop there. The hotel lobby had a table with a "Welcome Binghamton Bearcats" sign. If that wasn't cool enough, next to the sign was a table piled high with chips, gum, sunflower seeds, and candy bars – a baseball player's dream.

I am sure most teams walked by the table, grabbed a candy bar or two, and went to their rooms, but we weren't most teams. We were first-timers. Twenty-five guys swarmed the table, scooping up sunflower seeds bags like they were the only supply left in the entire state. It was mildly embarrassing, but none of us cared. We all just wanted to make sure we each got our necessary four bags of sunflower seeds, two Snickers bars, 10 pieces of gum, and two beverages...for the night.

Things got even better. Jim Calderone, the conference tournament MVP, and I had an entire suite for ourselves. After years of as many as four players to a room, it was a fitting way to go out. There is no better way to exit than to exit in style.

The NCAA gave us t-shirts, a memento coin, and all the food and drinks we needed. Wilson kicked in a pair of new batting gloves. I appreciated the gift, but it was kind of like your boss giving you a raise a week before retirement. It was more of a nice gesture than a practical gift for me. At best I had five at bats left in my life. But again, I was going out in style.

I already knew the countdown was officially on. I really didn't need a six-foot timer on the stadium scoreboard ticking down the time as well. Each team got 75 minutes to practice on the field the day before the games. The second you put the front of your turf shoes onto the field, the timer started. Every passing second of happiness on the field was recorded and then subtracted.

Clark-Leclair Stadium was a beautiful new stadium, built on the model of brilliant stadiums being constructed around the country. It had a new field turf, a large scoreboard, luxury boxes, and plenty of box seating. The field cost about $11 million to complete and was designed to seat about 3,000 crazy Pirate fans. Not listed as part of the stadium's capacity was the Jungle.

The perimeter of the outfield was reserved for the most rowdy and unforgiving fans. The Jungle quickly gained a reputation as extremely hostile to opposing teams. Our outfielders found out first-hand the true power of the Jungle. What a great baseball atmosphere!

But everything was still quiet when we stepped onto the field for our short practice. We had only 75 minutes, so you could understand why coach wasn't thrilled that we had to waste the start of practice having our photo taken by our Associate Director of Athletics for Communications, John Hartrick.

Binghamton athletic department employees whom none of us had seen all season, suddenly were big supporters of the baseball team. I don't know if they actually had a job to do in North Carolina or if the NCAA funded their expenses, but all off a sudden we had a full support staff. I admit I didn't see a lot of the behind the scenes work, and I am sure a lot of these people played an important role in making our season a success, but it still felt odd to see all of these new people traveling with us.

We had our strength and condition coach and our trainer, the associate director of athletics for communications, two senior associate directors of athletics, the associate director of internal operations, three assistant coaches, and of course our head coach. Now a lot of these guys did deserve to be there. I was thrilled that guys like Dave Simek, our amazing play-by-play guy and Bearcats Lifer whose son Matt two years earlier ended his extraordinary career in our cataclysmic loss to Albany, were able to attend. Likewise, Brian McGovern, our strength and conditioning coach who lived and breathed (and talked) baseball all day was deservedly able to make the trip.

Anyway, Mr. Hartrick was responsible for all press relations and had "asked" our coach to take a quick picture on the field. He had a little trouble getting the camera to work, and Coach Sinicki made a comment that we only had 73 minutes left. Mr. Hartrick laughed, but it was *not* a joke. It was a very subtle moment, but it proved to me that our administration didn't fully understand our coach's intensity on the field. He was a different man when things got rolling in the dugout.

Coach had promised us the day before that he wasn't going to get aggravated even once at the Regional. I think it was in large part because, quite simply, we had made it here and nobody could ever take it away from us. Also, I think that he was on extra special behavior with so many administrators around. He had shown all of these administrators how well he did, and inappropriate behavior in the dugout would tarnish his dream season.

After 73 actual minutes of practice, we boarded the bus back to the hotel to get ready for the Regional Banquet that evening.

The ECU banquet hall was located in the Murphy Center which overlooked the 43,000 seat Dowdy-Ficklen football stadium. There are much bigger stadiums, but this one was large enough to convey that this school had a big-time athletic program. It also made me realize how nice it must be to have a legitimate football team supporting some of your other programs. ECU's athletic department did not look poor.

The banquet hall overlooked the end zone and provided an unbelievable view of the football field. I thought about how in a few short months a whole new set of freshmen football players would be playing in front of a sold out crowd there. That is the thing about the NCAA baseball tournament: By the time it ends, the football season is only two months away. The transition from one year to the next is even further blurred when you consider that intense football practices begin in early August. One year flows right into the next.

The banquet was a barbecue style meal that I absolutely devoured. All four teams were there, and it was cool to think of all of the talent in that one room. The beautiful thing about baseball is that, unlike football and basketball, for the most part it is hard to determine just by looks who the top baseball players are. A visitor unaware of the Regional could have easily assumed that we there for a chess tournament.

The banquet went very well even though the speaker thought that George Mason's coach had won the America East Coach of the Year and then proceeded to call our coach Tim *Sawiki*. Further, Binghamton was listed as the America West representative. Oh well, just getting here was a big step for our school, though it did piss me off a little that we weren't getting the respect we deserved. Respect would have to come over the next few days on the playing field.

Game day was filled with anticipation. We had the night slot, so the day was spent eating and watching Sportscenter. I am sure this is exactly what a professional often does on the road to relax before a big game. We arrived at the field extra early to watch the end of the George Mason-South Carolina game. South Carolina was rolling along until the clouds started rolling in. Just like the week before, lightning struck and the game was delayed. Again, it was raining on our parade.

We were forced back onto our bus to wait for the storm to pass. We started to get seriously concerned that our "hammer" crowd was not going to stick around for the game. Hammer was just one of many words our team used in conjunction with about six different terms. Baseball teams develop their own lingo as the season goes on, and hammer became one of our most popular words. Hammer really meant anything large and powerful. That ranged from a hammer curveball (a tight, late breaking ball) to a hammer crowd (a large, loud crowd).

After a lengthy delay, the game finally ended, and we were hurried onto the field to get loose. The home crowd was already filing in. I wasn't starting, but at this point of the season I was just happy to still be in a baseball uniform. We took batting practice, infield and outfield, and were all ready to play ball. I looked into the crowd and saw waves of purple and yellow. I felt like a gladiator staring up into the roaring crowd of the Coliseum. I was quickly snapped out of my imaginary world by a flash of lightning.

This time the lightning, soon to be followed by rain, was here to stay. At 10:30 p.m. the game was cancelled.

This meant we would now play at 10 o'clock the next morning and then again in the afternoon. John Miele and I just stared at each other and laughed. We had sarcastically hugged and congratulated each other the week before when we thought we were finally done enduring two nine-inning games on the same day. Now we still had one more long, long day of baseball to go. I was just happy to have at least another day of baseball.

A few of the guys weren't having any laughs, though. A select few were randomly chosen to be drug tested by the NCAA, and a three-hour nightmare ensued until every testee was able to give the tester a proper urine sample. Thank goodness I was one of the lucky ones not selected.

When we got to the field at 8 a.m., I was downright tired. I didn't want to think about it, but there was a good chance that this would be my last day as a baseball player.

The crowd was good, but certainly not the "hammer" crowd we had envisioned. The crowd seemed plenty big, though, when it exploded with a roar after Murphy Smith's *first* pitch was launched over the fence for a home run.

I hoped things would not quickly spiral out of control. Just getting to a Regional was a dream, but we wanted to compete. Things were close to getting out of control going into the fifth inning. We were down 11-2 and in danger of getting embarrassed when we finally started to turn things around. Playing a nationally-ranked team in a threatening environment was intimidating. Like anything new, it was scary and took time to get going.

From the fifth inning on, however, we outscored the Pirates 5-0. James Giulietti came out of the pen and threw a brilliant 4 2/3 innings of shutout baseball. All of a sudden these gods came to the plate looking very mortal – more like college hitters with flaws rather than the Major Leaguers we had been comparing them to. We lost 11-7, but definitely earned the respect of the fans.

Respect aside, I was now one loss away from the end. I should have been more emotional, but I was just going with the flow. We took our stuff and moved across to the other dugout, the home team dugout.

We sat patiently as George Mason prepared. I don't know if it was the big crowd we had just played in front of or the hype that playing ECU created, but for whatever reason GMU didn't look special to any of us. They didn't have the big name, and playing in front of a quarter-full stadium almost made it feel like a regular-season game. We were pumped up to play, but felt no intimidation. Not for one second did George Mason scare us.

They really should have. Six players got drafted from that nationally-ranked team, which had compiled a record-breaking 42-14 season. They were damn good. But for whatever reason on this random day in this random game known as baseball, we were a lot better.[28]

Whether it was out of respect or strategy, Coach finally put me in against George Mason. All I wanted was one hit. Just one hit at a Regional. Just one more hit in front of my family. Just one more.

I was rusty, having gotten only one at bat in the last two weeks. I looked awful in my first at bat, striking out on a change-up way out of the zone. My hitting instincts were not yet back.

I didn't have time to sulk or whine. I had to stay focused. This was a battle of two top mid-major teams living out their dream seasons. Only one could continue this dream.

Luckily, everything was working for us. Our bats provided run support and Jeff Dennis was pitching his heart out in what would be the last game he ever pitched. Going into the top of the sixth we were winning 4-2. You couldn't ask for anything more out of a pitcher, and when he walked off the field after the fifth, he simply took a seat and went to ice his arm. He justifiably believed he would be pitching again in a few weeks as a professional.

But he never did. He got the very short end of the stick. It is ironic that out all of the guys in my class, Jeff Dennis is really the one who should have transferred. It is ironic because he got treated far better than any of us. The rest of original 2009 class got beaten down but at the end of the day it was Jeff Dennis who got the worst of it. He just didn't realize it until after he graduated. It was such an uphill battle to get drafted from Binghamton that I truly believe he would have fared better at another school. Although the rest of us lost out on some at bats, Jeff lost out on a chance to be a big-time draft pick. As a 6'6" lefty with good stuff and speed and the heart of a lion, he should have fared better. He deserved better.

Jeff and I weren't among the extremely select few All-Americans who succeeded effortlessly and naturally at the college level. Most of us had to struggle and grind.

Every year I read these great stories of college athletes who had super-successful seasons. Every blog had the top 100 list of some category X. But the fact was that 99.9% of the athletes never made any national stories. Most had to simply fight and battle every day just to be their own success story. Guys like Jeff Dennis and I seemed to be the norm. There were so many good players who just didn't seem to get that lucky break, have the unwavering support of his coach, or receive the rewards that reflected their excellent performance.

There are a million explanations as to why, but the reality is that it is just the way it is.

Jeff Dennis came into college tall and skinny with a fastball floating around 82 mph. By his junior year, he was a well-built, tall, athletic pitcher – the perfect example of how much of a difference three years of maturing could make. After a highly hyped junior season, Jeff was disappointed to only be drafted in the 39th round. He deserved better considering he had a 3.97 ERA with 62 strikeouts in just 81 2/3 innings. It wasn't just his impressive stat line that commanded attention. It was also his towering frame, his arm, his proven intelligence, and his potential to hit 90 mph consistently. But the 39th round pick by the Oakland Athletics was not enough for him to leave school, so he came back for his senior year.

I was thrilled because it meant having my best friend back. However, I really wanted him to succeed and see him play professionally.

Jeff's senior year started out rough and though he showed signs of brilliance, he at times struggled mightily. Rumors spread that he was uncoachable and that he had lost his flexibility in the weight room over the winter. Despite these rumors and early struggles, he had righted the ship in his last two starts, throwing 12 innings and giving up only one earned run while striking out 12 in the America East Tournament and the NCAA Regional. It should have been worthy of a look from the scouts, but no one seemed to notice.

June 7 and June 8 went by and Jeff's name was never called in the draft. He had been blown a lot of smoke over the last two years regarding his draft status, and I know that he felt burned when nothing came of it. Jeff never got that one break he needed. He never had the coach who would fine-tune his mechanics and help develop his inner game. He never had the necessary connections with scouts. He never had that one perfect start that would have caused huge headlines.

Jeff felt crushed when he was not drafted after his senior year, and he hung up his cleats. To see such potential never get a chance to pitch a professional inning was a sin.

But all of this was still in the future when he came out after five quality innings against George Mason. I said, "Great game, Great Bearcat career" and gave him a handshake.

I led off the sixth inning. After falling behind 0-1 on a change-up, I decided to sit fastball. The next pitch was a fastball, but it was in on the black and a definite take. I was still a bit rusty, however, and when I saw a fastball I swung. I shouldn't have, as I hit a weak pop up to the pitcher's mound.

I couldn't believe I had swung at that pitch, but it was so purely based on my limited number of swings that in a very strange way I was at peace with the mistake. I knew that in another at bat I would have taken that pitch. The only problem was that I didn't know if that one more at bat would ever come.

As the rest of the sixth inning played out, however, I was pretty sure I would have one more crack up there. My wishes were confirmed in the seventh. Being up 7-2, we had all of the momentum and George Mason looked beaten. I knew we were going to hold this lead; I just wanted a hit to make my mark.

I was 95% sure this would be my last at bat of the game. I can only imagine how hard my parents were rooting for me. If a hit meant a lot to me, I was sure it meant double that to them.

I took a deep breath before entering the box like I had done so many times before. I dug my cleats into my normal spot; my left foot scraping the white paint off the back part of the batter's box, my front foot lined up with the back of the plate.

Slowly I loaded my hands.

The pitch was a fastball over the outside corner. For one split second, leather connected perfectly with metal. A loud pinging noise erupted from my Voodoo as the ball reversed direction and headed right back to its point of origin at the pitcher's mound. The ball got there in a flash that by the time the pitcher's glove got to the level of the ball, it was 10 feet past him. The baseball landed softly in the gentle grass in front of the centerfielder. I hit the corner of first base and took a hard turn toward second, just as I had been trained to do for 15 years.

It was the last hit of my career and by far the most special. The feeling of satisfaction I felt when my cleat smacked into the first base bag is engrained in my mind for all of time.

As it turned out I had one more at bat but it resulted in an uneventful RBI walk. Still, it meant that I was 1-for-3 with a single and RBI. Better yet, we had easily defeated GMU 11-7. In the scope of things, it was a huge upset.

The win was our 30th of the season, a record for the program. It was fitting that the record-breaking win was of this magnitude. It also marked the sixth straight season we had increased our total wins.[29] No other team in the nation had completed such a feat.

Still, I thought about all of the games that were rained out and wondered how many wins this team really could have gotten. We didn't play three games vs. Norfolk State, whose final record was 22-23. We lost one rainout with University of Maryland-Eastern Shore (14-42), a game vs. Sacred Heart (29-27), two games vs. Hartford (15-32) and two vs. University of Maryland-Baltimore County (9-36) – nine games against teams with a combined record of 89-160. I figured we would have won at least six of those games.

Regardless, it truly was a dream season. We won our third consecutive America East Regular Season championship. We won the America East Conference Tournament. We got to the program's first Regional. We earned the program's first victory at a Regional. We won a school record 30 games. We had the America East Coach of the Year. We were ranked 12 out of the 69 Northeastern teams. We had a player drafted in the 13th round. Not a bad season.

As we watched GMU cast their heads down, it occurred to me that I had lived to fight another day. It was a magical feeling walking out of the stadium into the throng of family, friends, and fans. Everyone was cheering and celebrating. The parents were throwing out congratulations like it was a wedding celebration. It was genuine joy in its purest form.

We were the first America East team to win a Regional game since Maine in 2005. We had just defeated a team with a .788 winning percentage. The game was so emotional that a lot of the parents just lost it. This game was the crescendo for the seniors and their parents. To me, it represented 15 years worth of practices, games, and memories. All of the pain and sweat climaxed in this victory. It represented the best parts of college, the best parts of competition, the best parts of hard work, and the best parts of sport. It made worthwhile everything that the players and parents had invested into this program and into this game. This was our payoff, a decade plus in the making.

It wasn't the *biggest* win of my life, though it was close, but it was by far my favorite win. After 15 years of baseball, that is saying something. We had bought one more day. Our pitching was depleted, and it would take a small miracle to dethrone East Carolina. We would then have to beat South Carolina at night...It was going to be my last day of baseball.

CHAPTER 54

Even if I had tried, it would have been impossible as a 12-year-old to even think about my last day of baseball. How could something end after 15 years? How do you react to something like that?

It is hard enough to see the light at the end of the tunnel when looking a few months ahead. At ages 7, 13, 15, or even 18 it seemed baseball would never end. How could this be the day of my last game? I had so much youth left in me. I didn't know what to make of my emotions as I slipped into a quiet sleep. So many games, so many memories, so little time left.

I woke up groggy. I went to breakfast and forced down some food. I put on my uniform. I boarded the bus. Everything seemed normal. I had done this routine for four years and 204 games. Number 205 would be my last.

Even to the last day, politics and business factored into the team makeup. Being a senior in my last game ever and having played well the day before, I thought that I should have been given the nod over Pete Bregartner. It wasn't meant to be and so I was forced to sit and watch my last game from the best view anywhere off the field, the dugout.

I tried to enjoy the ballgame, but the innings just kept flying by. We had a depleted pitching staff but our pitchers were giving us enough to allow our hitting to keep us in the game. Going into the top of the fifth we were winning 4-3, and there was no reason to think we couldn't give ECU a run for its money.

Defense had killed us all year. It had allowed rally after rally to occur when we should have been out of an inning. Our shortstop, Jeff Abrams, seemed to be at the epicenter of a lot of our struggles. I loved Jeff, but it bothered me that somehow he had just fallen into the starting shortstop position for a Division I college team. After freshman infielder Lane Warner was cut midseason due to poor grades and an even worse work ethic, we were left with one backup infielder, a freshman that the coaches had no plans to ever use. To no one's surprise, he was cut at the end of the season. I think we all got the hint of his pending termination when due to "budget issues" he stayed home on a weekend trip while strength and conditioning Coach Brian McGovern went on the trip in the "empty seat" instead.

Ironically, the last mistake that killed us was not even ruled an error. A tailor-made ground ball to Abrams was bobbled and only the second out of the inning was recorded. You can't assume the double play, so no error was charged.

But four *extra* runs scored after that play to give the Pirates eight runs in the inning. Instead of being tied 7-7, we were down 11-7.

The eight-spot was devastating. East Carolina slowly chewed away at the back of our bullpen and by the time the ninth inning came around we were down 14-9.

After our at bats in the eighth inning, I ran down the left field line with the other subs as we did after every inning to stay loose. I just stood there for a second and looked at the stadium. My career started out as a 4-year-old in my front yard. If I hit a tennis ball 60 feet over the stone wall it was home run. It was quite the feat for me when I put one out of the park. Now here I was as a young adult at a NCAA Regional. How far I had come.

I thought I was done for good. Coach hadn't mentioned a word about getting one more at bat so I figured that was that. I looked up into the crowd and jogged back to the dugout.

Coach told me I was *leading off* the ninth inning as our team was running into the dugout for our last licks. It was fitting that even to the last at bat I was still being treated this way. I was in such a panic to get into the batter's box with all my equipment properly fastened that I had no time or energy to think about anything else.

Their starting pitcher, Brad Mincey, was still in the game. I had watched him for eight innings and really thought I had the upper hand. He was exhausted, but was not getting taken out for anything. ECU needed to save the rest of its pitching for South Carolina, so Mincey's right arm was being sacrificed for the good of the program. He ended up throwing 142 pitches, a staggering number for one outing.

The first pitch came in hard. Strike one. I stepped out of the box, breathing for the first time since my name was called on to hit. Okay, I thought, get something to hit early in this count. He's just throwing whatever he has left. He isn't being fancy, so just look hard. All of my hours preparing for at bats like this one made my mental game second nature.

Ball one, fastball away. Ball two, fastball away. He was staying outside to most lefties so I definitely wanted to look away. I knew he had a slider and decided that at 2-1 it was a perfect pitch so sit on. The cues were now firing off in my brain. Years of studying the mental side of baseball had become deeply ingrained.

I couldn't have guessed any better. As the slider curved towards my body, I took my final swing. I smoked the pitch. It was an outside slider that a quarter-inch up on the barrel may have resulted in a home run. The ball was struck with such authority that the entire play happened in a flash. The shortstop moved to his left, scooped up the short hop, and fired the ball across the diamond for the out. My foot touched first base a fraction of a second too late. I always thought it was cool that I was still running to first base for a split second even after I was out. Even though I was done, I still had a few tiny steps to go to cross the finish line.

My cleat smacked the base as I ran past it into shallow right field. I had crushed my last ball.

I didn't want to turn around. I didn't want to go back to the dugout, to the end of my playing days. I just wanted to stand in the outfield and freeze the moment. I couldn't believe I was done. I never thought the last out would arrive.

I turned and jogged ever so slowly off the field. I looked up into the bleachers and took one last mental photograph for old time's sake.

As I passed Coach Sinicki in the third-base coaching box, he whispered, "Nice job." It was if he had been rooting for me the entire time but some puppet master controlling all of his strings was playing out a different story. Maybe it was just a "nice job" to say congratulations on a great career. But maybe it was more. Maybe it meant "nice job," I am not surprised you hit that ball hard after *everything* we put you through. Maybe it was "nice job," I am sorry for how we treated you at times.

I watched from the steps as Matt Simone grounded out to third base. Just like that it was over.

I stood there for a second and stared at the field. I couldn't believe that 18 years of baseball were over. My eyes started to tear up just a bit, a precursor of things to come. I took off my hat and pushed back my hair. OK, I thought. It is over. It is time.

We shook hands with the ECU players and went down the left field line to talk. We got some end of the year speech, but I didn't listen to a word. I was lost in thought. All I heard was the back end of a speech by Coach Folli, who told the younger guys to thank the seniors and pay their respects for what they accomplished. I was completely composed until I got back to the dugout.

I just wanted to sit on the bench for a moment alone and gaze at the field. I knew deep down I had a lot more to give to the game, but I also knew that in a lot of ways I was ready for something new and different. I was done with the rolling highs and lows of the seasons. I was ready to move passed being treated unfairly and investing so much time in something that too often didn't reciprocate the favor. At some point it comes time to try other things in life, even though I knew that life outside of baseball often throws you a tough curve. I just needed five minutes alone before my new life started.

One of my favorite scenes in any movie is from "Field of Dreams" when Moonlight "Doc" Graham crosses over the magical line in order to save Ray Kinsella's daughter. As he steps off the field he transforms from a young rookie back into his older self. Ray realizes that the Doc can never get his youth back and says regretfully, "Oh my God. You can't go back." The days of running down fly balls in the outfield were over. Now he was just Doc.

    This scene is not intended to be depressing, however. On the contrary, it is a scene of pride, joy and love. As I sat on the dugout bench I thought of Doc's response and suddenly I felt okay. "It's all right." It was such a simple yet perfect response. The Doc had gotten his one at bat in the "big leagues." He had lived out his dream. He was able to accept that his time was now over. It was all right.

    It was all right that I was done. Of course the Doc and I both would have liked more time, but we had our moments. We got to feel it with our own skin. It was all right that I could never be a baseball player again, that I could never hit a game-winning double again. It was all right that I could never wear a uniform again. It was all right that my mom wouldn't be there after the game to take my mind of a bad game or that my dad wouldn't be there forever to throw me batting practice. I knew that I had my time. I knew I needed serious time off from baseball, but that one day I would return to coach and bring everything I had learned back to the game.

    As I thought of the final scene of the movie where Ray plays catch with his dad, tears started to accumulate in my eyes. I looked down at my cleats, then my pants, then my jersey, and then finally my wrist guard. I wanted one last image of being in uniform.

    In the movie, the great Shoeless Joe Jackson blurts out to Moonlight Graham as he is walking away from the field for the last time, "Hey Rookie! You were good." It was by the far the greatest compliment one peer could give to another. The Doc's idol had shown him the ultimate respect by telling him that he belonged, that he was special, that he would be missed.

    As one by one my teammates came to give me a hug, I lost my composure. The flood gates opened and the tears came streaming out. My peers saying "thank you" was as good as Shoeless Joe telling the Doc he was good. It was the ultimate compliment.[30]

    I appreciated every single player and coach saying goodbye. As I was hugging the other seniors, a sense of disbelief washed over me.

Something I had carried with me my *entire* life was over. The tears kept rolling down my face.

I sat there on the bench, not wanting to take off my jersey or cleats. It was a moment I will never forget...but then it was time to go. We needed to clear out the dugout for the next game.

I laughed to myself as we were getting kicked out of the dugout. There would always a "next game". There would always be the "next young prospect." The faces and names were going to change but that was about it. Baseball would live on forever.

I got my stuff together, tipped my hat to the non-existent crowd and walked off the field into the group of parents. I am not sure what my parents were thinking as I fell into their arms. Happiness? Sadness? Pride? Anger? Satisfaction? Delight? Gratification? Sorrow? I would say probably all of them, all at the same time.

I really did have a great career, and I was so glad my entire family was there to celebrate it with me, even if just for five minutes. I know my mom loved watching me play and that my dad knew I still had a lot left to offer the game, but this moment was not about that. It was about handshakes, hugs and pats on the back. I hugged my mom one more time as I tried to hold it together. Sheepishly, I managed to crawl onto the bus with some fluids still left in me.

I sat in silence on the way back, with almost two decades of memories flooding through my brain. Championships, home runs and comebacks. Slumps, errors and defeats. I had grown up as a baseball player. Now what was I?

That is a question that is not answered in a day or even a month. I think it takes years to find a new comfort zone. The next part of my journey was/is trying to rediscover who I am. It took a long time after I stopped playing to accept how many games, weekends and seasons I had all but forgotten about. How could moments that seemed so important and vital now not even exist in my mind? Weekends where I put everything on the line are little more than a blip now. It took me a great while to come to peace with this and to understand that life is about living in the moment. At 15, my AAU travel ball tournament was my life. That was what was important. At

22, it was the NCAA Regional, and at 24 there are new moments to live for.

Still, on the bus ride back to the hotel I refused to forget about some of the bad things I was leaving behind in North Carolina. The crappy winter workouts dating back to my Little League days that I absolutely despised. The painful slumps that never seemed to end. The days when I was tired and didn't feel like working out but forced myself through it. There was a lot of bad, but that also was part of my journey.

It's funny, but what I miss more than anything is taking batting practice with my dad. I am fine with not playing games. I miss the competition but I get that in different forms now. I miss my teammates, but I have other friends now. I miss the feeling of connecting on a fat pitch, but I have other means of fulfillment now. I don't tear up when I think of those things. I can't help but feel emotional though every time I think of the countless hours of batting practice my dad threw to me.

My dad was my baseball inspiration. Many of his teachings I didn't even understand until my last year of playing. So much of the preparation I had undergone didn't fully make sense until my senior year. Finally, though, I was able to prepare and then just go out there, relax and *enjoy* the games. It's what my dad was trying to teach me for years: To work hard and enjoy the *process*.

There were more than a few days in my life when I simply did not want to go hit or lift. Similarly, there were plenty of days when my dad had more productive things to do than spend over an hour throwing to me or driving me to baseball practice. Still, day in and day out, we went to the field and invested our time and energy into my play.

I am forever grateful for his dedication and attention. He showed me what it's like to be a man and how to be a father. I hope he understands how grateful I am for every pitch he ever threw to me, even when they started coming in a bit slower and a bit more off the plate. I enjoyed every swing I took. I know I will look back a long time from now on the memory of my father and think of him throwing batting practice on an open field, with my dog Obie hanging out in the shade. These were happy days.

When I got back into my hotel room I shut the bathroom door and am not ashamed to admit that I collapsed on the floor and again started to tear up, if ever just slightly. It wasn't even the fact that baseball was over, but it was more that I knew my life was about to dramatically change and it scared the crap out of me. I just needed to get it out of my system. Every baseball player must go through this at one point, and there is no avoiding it.

An inning is only six outs long. A game is only nine innings long. A season is only 60 games long. And a career is limited as well. Baseball is a game with no clock, but it is a very finite sport. There is only a small window of time one has to play this great game, and it is time to cherish. Then the window closes forever.

I came out of the bathroom feeling a lot better. Jim and I decided to do a photo shoot of me taking off my uniform one last time, and though it was a silly thing to do, it made me feel better. That night I got to talk to my mom on the phone and, after that, I went out with my sister and dad for ice cream. We just talked about my career. It was a heck of a career. I had so much to be proud of. I had put up great numbers, made countless all star teams, and got the scholarship I so badly wanted. But even more than that, I had become the man I wanted to be.

Thank you, Baseball. It was a pleasure.

East Carolina went on to beat South Carolina that evening to face off with the Gamecocks in a winner-take-all championship game on Sunday. As the East Carolina website described the ending of the game: "With his team trailing 9-6 in the bottom of the ninth, Devin Harris hit a three-run home run to tie the contest before also delivering the game-winning single in the bottom of the 10th, lifting top-seeded East Carolina to a 10-9 victory over No. 2 seed South Carolina in the Greenville Regional Championship Game Monday evening. A crowd of 5,047 witnessed the contest at Lewis Field inside Clark-LeClair Stadium, representing the fourth-largest single-game attendance in facility and program history."[31]

What a game it must have been. It was extremely cool to watch East Carolina battle North Carolina on ESPN the next weekend. Though

UNC disposed of the Pirates with little effort, it showed how far we had come in the season.

We flew back to Binghamton and I immediately had to get all of my things in order. The RE was being retired, and we had to get everything out of the place. But first we had one last party. We laughed and hugged, drank beers and said our goodbyes. The next day I had to drive to Syracuse to find an apartment. Work started in a month.

AFTERWARD:

Saying goodbye to baseball was an awkward thing. Only a select few ever get more than a firm handshake and a pat on the back. Most just get a slip of paper or a phone call. The prolonged ceremony for an aging future Hall of Famer is the exception. Most people kind of just leave one day and move on with their lives. Things function seamlessly. Life goes on, as they say.

I started work a few weeks after the season ended, and to say it was strange was an understatement. I was living in a foreign world. Before I knew it, the fall had come and just 60 miles from my apartment, fall baseball was in full swing on campus. Practice as usual. Long and at times tedious practices, but at the end of the day 25 young men were getting the opportunity to play baseball at the highest amateur level. Classes were gearing up, and the first wave of tests was coming. Everything was the same. The only things that changed were the new faces that replaced the recently graduated seniors. Since the beginning of the "American Dream," college baseball has been the same. It is the people in the jerseys who change.

With us seniors now gone, a new crop of freshman were making their presence known. We were now a memory, just some photos, stat lines, pictures and banners. This never felt more real until the moment I saw the 2010 schedule on the athletic website. Our season now was simply a great memory, recorded in history.

I watched a big football game that fall after college was over in which Southern Cal played Ohio State in front of 100,000 fans. The players were treated like Gods, rightfully so, but I had to wonder if these players ever thought about life after football. I am sure they thought much the same as I did: This will never end.

Thank God I had prepared for life after baseball, so when that last pitch did get thrown I had a plan for moving forward. Four years go by quickly. This too I learned at college.

Life right after college for anyone is a very weird and awkward time. Being an ex-athlete only made it seem even stranger to me. I had to get used to waking up every morning before 7:30, getting dressed in a shirt and tie, and going to work until 6 p.m. It wasn't a worse life – just a completely different one.

I used to get my competition by stepping into the batter's box. Now I get it from running marathons. I used to develop friends from baseball teams. Now my friends come from the workplace and the gym. I used to have baseball to keep me focused on a daily basis. Now I use newer goals of a full business career instead.

Baseball is still a huge part of my life. I always thought that once I was done playing I would be able to walk away from the game completely. I was very wrong. I still watch hours of Yankee footage, pore over Fantasy stats, and read countless baseball blogs. I am a fan now, and it is a totally new perspective. Life has a totally new perspective.

Nonetheless, I knew that I was going to need a break from playing baseball upon graduating. Still, I cannot wait for the day to come when every bone in my body shakes because I need a baseball fix. I cannot wait until the day where I *need* to get involved again with the game and run down to the local community center and volunteer to coach. That day might not come for another a year, another five years or perhaps even another ten years, but I am eagerly looking forward to the next time I step onto a baseball field as a member of the game.

College ends. It is a fact. The people you see at some local bar drinking alone on a Saturday night are probably the ones who could never accept that some things end, whether it is high school, college, or a relationship. I have my entire life in front of me now, and I am enthusiastic to see where I am headed. I do not sulk when I think about my playing days being over. I had the time of my life playing baseball, and I don't ever regret giving up what I did to play.

But now it is time to look forward. No doubt baseball will forever be in my heart, and now I know why fathers are so eager to start coaching. The desire to get back into the game remains in one's blood long after you stop playing. When the right time comes, I too will return to the game.

I still sometimes look in the mirror and take a few shadow swings. I even instinctually make a few small arm circles with my left arm, as if to keep it loose. Only after a few cycles do I realize that I don't need my arm anymore to be able throw a 250-foot strike to home plate. Once in a while late at night, my dreams take over and I forget that I am retired. Then the alarm sounds that I have to get up for work.

And every now and then while watching a ball game, I analyze a pitch and mentally think of the best way to approach that situation. I have to catch myself when I start visualizing my swing on an outside fastball.

But all of these images quickly fade and I always snap back into reality. It is tough to start a new life all on my own. In a lot of ways it is like starting out all over again. I am worse off than a freshman. At least freshmen come in having played baseball in high school. I literally am starting at block one, working my way up the business career ladder one rung at a time.

I am on an entirely new route, but the goals are the same: Fight the competition, work harder than anyone, believe in myself, and at the end of the day find a way to come out on top. Most important, though – enjoy the process!

I will forever cherish my time at Binghamton. In a flash I logged four fantastic years. Still, I refuse to completely block out the bad times. The lows were real. The hammer days of classes, practices, lifts, and homework were daily occurrences. Walking to class in the dark with the snow and hail bouncing off my face is a memory stitched into my subconscious. The stress I felt about an assignment, a baseball game, or a girl still feels real. The horrible group meetings, the 0-for-4 days, and the times I had to sit on the bench when I knew I should be playing all happened. They all hurt and they defined my college experience as much as the highs. But at the end of the day, the positives so outweighed the negatives that for some reason I can only recollect the most fond of memories. Time really is a strange thing.

I went out as a champion. It was a dream season. I got to a point where I always knew I could as a baseball player, and though I *know* I could have played professionally for at least a year, I am thrilled at how my career ended. In many ways I reached the top of the mountain.

Perhaps my experience at Binghamton was meant to be. Maybe the journey I took was supposed to teach me important life lessons about business, politics, and growing up. It's possible that I needed to experience growing pains at college in order to mature into the man I will become. I know for a fact that I would not have loved baseball as much as I do now without this experience. I am not as sure, however, if I would have ever learned to adjust and adapt in life as well as I do now without this experience.

I remember so vividly when my dad, Kathy and Jaclyn dropped me off that first day of college. I was filled with a feeling of sadness, loneliness, and the lack of belief that the day had come. I also remember Kathy saying that when I left college, I would be a totally different person.

I can never know what would have happened if I had gone to a different school. I don't know where my life would be if I hadn't run the 60-yard dash five extra times in Florida and gotten invited to the showcase where Binghamton first saw me play. But I did end up at BU, and I did have the experience of a lifetime, and so I leave it at that.

I know a lot of people are (and were and will be) in a similar situation at college, and I hope that my story can at least give them some comfort knowing that they are far from being alone.

We all feel doubt and confusion. At one time or another, we think about the future and get scared. We all get lonely in our most dark and vulnerable times, even if we do it behind closed doors. We all put our hearts out on the field. And we all eventually have to stop playing baseball and start a new life. It's the truly lucky one who gets to grow up and make a family of his own so that one day he can go to a college baseball game and watch his kid play baseball as if he can't ever imagine a final game. I hope my kids are half as lucky as I have been to have an experience like mine at Binghamton.

I did everything in my power to freeze time while in Binghamton, New York, but inevitably the clock ran out. Nevertheless, I am forever grateful for the friends I met at BU and the times there that I shared with them. I know I can never go back to my college days again, but the memories and lessons I accumulated there will last me a lifetime. Now it is my responsibility to share this knowledge with anyone who is willing to listen.

This was my story. This was my experience. This is what I learned from "Going with the Pitch".

ACKNOWLEDGMENTS

I am deeply indebted to my teammates who were with me everyday throughout this journey. You became my best friends and without all of you I could not have survived my time at Binghamton. This book is for you.

To my mother, Marilyn, and Bob Costanzo for your continued support throughout my baseball career. A day has not gone by without me truly appreciating everything you both have done for me. This book is for you.

To my step-mom Kathy. The care and interest you took in my experience at Binghamton is truly remarkable and I am extremely thankful for everything you have invested in me, even when you watched my games from the car because it was too cold outside.

I also must thank my father, Paul. You were with me on this journey long before I started college. From my first days of Little League when we used to bring the dog, Obie, to the park, to my travel ball/AAU baseball days, to my collegiate days you were *always* there for me when I needed it. Also, thank you for all your hard work on this book. You were with me every step of the way as this manuscript was transformed from scattered journal entries into an organized book. This book is for you.

To my editor, Frank Roessner, thank you for being part of this project. To Chris Sidarweck for helping me design the front and back cover, as well as helping me design and run GoingwiththePitch.com.

To Binghamton University, for allowing me to use their photos and records. This book is for you.

And finally, to all of my readers. Thank you for taking part in this unbelievable experience with me. At the end of the day, this book is for you.

REFERENCES

1. http://www.bubearcats.com/sports/base/coaches.html
2. http://www.gobulldogs.com/sports/m-basebl/spec-rel/011900aab.html
3. https://www.nmnathletics.com/ViewArticle.dbml?SPSID=97884&SPID=12013&DB_OEM_ID=20500&ATCLID=1465132&Q_SEASON=2008
4. http://www.yankeessuck.com/YankessSuckArchives/2004/04/wanted_yankee_killers.html
5. http://www.hurricanekatrinarelief.com/faqs.html#What%20date%20did%20Hurricane%20Katrina%20hit%20New%20Orleans
6. NCAA Working Group to Study the 20/8-Hour Rule, www.ncaa.org/wps/wcm/connect/.../Presentation.pps?...AJPERES
7. http://nycbl.blogspot.com/2007_05_01_archive.html
8. http://www.pepperdinesports.com/SportArchives.dbml
9. http://www.goshockers.com/ViewArticle.dbml?SPSID=61172&SPID=2844&DB_OEM_ID=7500&ATCLID=648628&Q_SEASON=2006
10. http://www.ncaabbs.com/printthread.php?tid=338162
11. http://newyork.yankees.mlb.com/nyy/ballpark/audi_yankees_club.jsp
12. http://www.goshockers.com/ViewArticle.dbml?DB_OEM_ID=7500&ATCLID=1478582
13. http://www.d1baseball.com/
14. http://www.baseball-almanac.com/teamstats/schedule.php?y=2003&t=FLO

15 http://www.baseball-almanac.com/teamstats/schedule.php?y=1969&t=NYN
16 http://www.goseawolves.org/sports/m-basebl/archive/ston-m-basebl-sched-2007.html
17 Joe Torre "The Yankee Years"
18 http://www.huffingtonpost.com/2009/12/18/economic-crisis-timeline-_n_397360.html
19 http://en.wikipedia.org/wiki/America_East_Conference#Membership_timeline
20 http://www.burlingtonfreepress.com/article/20090813/OPINION/908130006
21 http://web.minorleaguebaseball.com/ballpark/page.jsp?ymd=20081103&content_id=476889&vkey=ballpark_t342&fext=.jsp&sid=t342
22 http://www.pressconnects.com/article/20100807/NEWS01/8070323/Thomas-Libous-quest-Restore-GOP-power-in-the-Senate
23 http://www.dailytexanonline.com/sports/baseball-walk-off-heroics-push-texas-past-army-1.1757913
24 http://www.warrennolan.com/baseball/2008/rpi
25 http://www.baseball-reference.com/boxes/LAN/LAN198810150.shtml
26 http://www.ecupirates.com/trads/ecu-trads-highlights.html
27 http://www.ecupirates.com/trads/ecu-trads-highlights.html
28 http://gomason.cstv.com/sports/m-basebl/sched/gema-m-basebl-sched.html
29 http://www.bubearcats.com/sports/base/ncaa09-mason.html
30 http://www.script-o-rama.com/movie_scripts/f/field-of-dreams-script-transcript.html
31 http://www.ecupirates.com/sports/m-basebl/recaps/060109aad.html

***All other game notes and accounts, statistics, and biographies were used from Bubearcats.com and/or AmericaEast.com

Cover Photo courtesy of Binghamton University

APPENDIX

Appendix I- Career Stats

Year	AB	Games	Runs	Hits	2B	3B	HR	RBI	BB	SO	SB	AVG
2006	111	40	14	26	2	0	1	12	10	28	1	.234
2007	58	24	10	18	7	0	1	8	5	11	2	.310
2008	107	40	15	23	7	1	2	17	6	20	0	.215
2009	84	35	13	23	5	2	2	11	12	13	2	.274
Total	360	139	52	90	21	3	6	48	33	72	5	.250

Appendix II- Binghamton Season Results

Year	Final Record	Conference Record	Result
2006	27-23	12-11	5th place
2007	28-19	17-5	America East Regular Season Champion
2008	29-27	15-8	America East Regular Season Champion
2009	30-22	13-7	America East Regular Season Champion. America East Conference Champion- East Carolina Regional
Total	114-91	57-31	N/A

Appendix III- Binghamton University Information

Undergraduate Enrollment: 11,475
Out-of-State Enrollment: 11%
Average High School GPA: 3.6
International: 10.13%
In-state Tuition: $4,970
Out-of-State Tuition: $13,380
Founded: 1946

Made in the USA
Lexington, KY
27 June 2011